ABOUT THE AUTHORS

Charlie Bird is one of Ireland's best-known and beloved broadcasters and journalists, with a stellar career spanning almost forty years. In 2021, he was diagnosed with motor neurone disease, and he has since worked tirelessly for charities across Ireland to increase awareness about this illness, while raising millions of euros for organisations such as Pieta and the Irish Motor Neurone Disease Association.

Ray Burke is from Galway and he is a graduate of University College Galway. He was News Editor of the *Irish Press* and Chief News Editor of RTÉ News. He is the author of critically-acclaimed books on the *Irish Press* and on James Joyce. Since retiring from RTÉ News he has written for the Century Ireland website and for the *Irish Times* and the *Connacht Tribune*.

TIME AND TIDE

TIME AND TIDE

Charlie Bird

With Ray Burke

HarperCollins*Ireland*

HarperCollins*Ireland*
2nd Floor Macken House
39-40 Mayor Street Upper
Dublin D01 C9W8
Ireland

A division of
HarperCollins*Publishers* Ltd
1 London Bridge Street
London SE1 9GF

The edition published by HarperCollins*Ireland* 2023

1

First published by HarperCollins*Ireland* 2022

To all those who extended the hand of friendship
and supported Climb With Charlie.

CONTENTS

1. SCOOP

Nobody could have known that it would be my last journalism scoop.

The sensational story of the attempt by a criminal gang to extort millions of pounds from the Irish government had remained hidden for more than four decades. Only a small and declining number of surviving former government ministers, senior civil servants and Gardaí knew the details and none of them had ever spoken publicly about it.

It was a genuine scoop, and one of the most incredible stories that I would tell in my forty-year career in journalism – a career that coincided more or less with the span of years that this story had remained secret.

I came across the story in early 2021 when a former RTÉ Newsroom colleague, the long-time leading Security Correspondent Tom McCaughren, suggested that I talk to a retired former Garda superintendent for a series of podcasts I was doing for the website and magazine, Senior*Times*. Another former RTÉ colleague, Mike Murphy, had invited me to do the podcasts and several had already been broadcast before I followed up Tom's suggestion.

The man who Tom put me in touch with was the retired former head of the Garda Fraud Squad, Detective Super-intendent Willie McGee. My only knowledge of Superintendent McGee was that, as head of the Garda Fraud Squad in the late 1990s, he had sent one of his detectives to warn my colleague George Lee and myself that there was a strong possibility that our telephones were being tapped because of the stories we were doing for RTÉ News on National Irish Bank's tax-evading overseas accounts and overcharging of its customers. We took the warning seriously. Strange things had been happening on our work phones. It was suggested that they were being tapped by former British soldiers who might have been working for NIB. We purchased pay-as-you-go mobiles that we used for the rest of the time we covered that story.

I had rarely covered Garda or crime stories and I was not a follower of Gaelic games, so I had never heard of the nickname by which Superintendent McGee was univer-sally known.

I learned from friends that for the previous fifty-four years the retired superintendent had been known through-out the Garda force and among GAA followers all over the country as 'Four-goal McGee'. This was because he had scored all four goals when Mayo beat Kerry by 4–9 to 0–7 in the All-Ireland under-21 final replay in Duggan Park, Ballinasloe, County Galway, in 1967. He went on to play senior inter-county football for Mayo for the next nine years, and to represent Connacht as a goal-scoring full-forward.

Despite my being one of the few men of my age in Ireland who had never heard of 'Four-goal McGee', he

2

invited me to meet him at his home in Leixlip, County Kildare. He was only two years older than me and had never lost the soft west of Ireland accent of his native place, Newport in County Mayo, although he had lived and worked in and around Dublin for more than fifty years.

The story he told me was astonishing. He had worked on the ransom case from beginning to end. His memory of the entire episode was encyclopaedic and he showed me copies of the *Irish Times* newspapers in which the gang exchanged coded messages over several months with the Department of Agriculture, which responded under Garda guidance. I quickly realized that this story could not be told in one 50-minute podcast. I decided that I would need two or maybe three podcasts to tell it.

Willie McGee told me that the saga began when a letter addressed to the Minister for Agriculture, Jim Gibbons TD, arrived at the offices of the Department of Agriculture on Kildare Street on Wednesday, 29 August 1979. This was just two days after the IRA had massacred eighteen British soldiers at Warrenpoint, County Down, and had killed Lord Louis Mountbatten and an 83-year-old woman, Lady Doreen Brabourne, and two teenage boys at Mullaghmore, County Sligo. It was also just a few weeks before the historic visit to Ireland of Pope John Paul II, and the beginnings of Charlie Haughey's heave against Taoiseach Jack Lynch.

The letter received by the Department of Agriculture said: 'To get straight to the point, this is a demand for £5million. The reason for you paying us £5million is very simple. If you do this, we shall not introduce to this country one of the most deadly and costliest diseases that could afflict any country, in particular an agricultural country, namely foot and mouth disease.' It went on to demand a reply from the minister by the following Saturday morning via a special notice in the social and personal columns of the *Irish Times*. In the absence of a response, it threatened: 'We will immediately take steps to introduce the disease. We shall, as soon as cattle begin to go down, send copies of this letter to all national newspapers.'

Foot and mouth disease was a lethal infectious disease that had previously threatened Ireland's seven million national cattle herd in 1967, when farms were quarantined, sporting fixtures were cancelled and emigrants were asked not to return home for Christmas. As a rookie Garda at that time, Willie McGee had been deployed on the border at Scotstown, County Monaghan, to stop unauthorised people crossing into the Republic. The £5million ransom would be equivalent to about €30million today – more than the amount sought by the cybercriminal hackers behind the ransomware attack on the Health Service Executive's computer network in 2021.

By 1979, McGee was a detective based in Pearse Street station in central Dublin. He was assigned to place the special notice in the *Irish Times* and he became one of the Garda team that worked to trace the gang. A special telephone line was installed in the office of the Department's secretary general and the gang continued to issue demands and fresh instructions over the following seven months, including a demand for a diplomatic passport and a doubling of the ransom to £10million in multiple currencies.

The drama didn't end until the second Saturday of March 1980, when, after a bizarre day of cat-and-mouse manoeuvres involving six unmarked Garda cars over several counties in south-east Leinster and Munster, the Gardaí held their nerve and the gang lost theirs. No ransom was paid, and no arrests were made. The gang was never heard from again. Willie McGee and his colleagues strongly suspected that the gang was led by a practising barrister and comprised some former members of Saor Éire, a Republican splinter group, but the Gardaí lacked the evidence to prosecute under the legislation in place at the time.

I told the story in three 50-minute podcasts. It was called *Ransom '79* and I introduced the series as 'one of the most amazing stories I have ever stumbled on in my whole career' and as a story 'that would not fit in the pages of a John le Carré novel'. As well as Willie McGee, I also interviewed the now-retired private secretary to the Minister for Agriculture, Kevin Cassidy. He was astounded when I contacted him. He said he had never spoken of the episode to anyone other than his father. Two former prominent Agriculture correspondents, Joe O'Brien and Paddy Smith, also contributed to the podcasts. Neither of them had ever heard a whisper about the ransom demand, but they explained how a foot and mouth plague would have had catastrophic consequences for the Irish economy and agriculture sector. The armed undercover Garda who had driven the unmarked car with the fake ransom on Saturday, 8 March also spoke to me, anonymously, in Episode 3. He too had never spoken publicly about the case before.

The first podcast was made available on Saturday, 5 June 2021. The *Irish Times*, by prior arrangement, devoted a full page to my exclusive story on that Saturday. The article was written by Colm Keena, the Legal Affairs Correspondent, and it was accompanied by a photograph of Willie McGee and me with the 1979 and 1980 editions of the newspaper that carried the cryptic special notices he had inserted.

The third *Ransom '79* podcast had not yet been broadcast and it was while I was recording that episode, at the beginning of June, that I began to become conscious of slight changes in my voice. For the first time in my life I was having trouble enunciating and swallowing. I knew from the playbacks that my voice did not sound the same as on the first two podcasts nor as it had sounded during more than thirty years of broadcasting almost every day on RTÉ radio and television.

I had had minor health scares in recent years, but each one had turned out to be a false alarm. These definite changes in my voice alarmed and distressed me as soon as I noticed them. My voice was my currency. It was distinctive and instantly recognizable. It was central to how I earned my living and to how I connected with the people I wanted to interview. It was one of the main reasons that my entire career had been spent as a broadcast journalist, rather than as a print journalist, even though I had had approaches from newspapers. I loved talking to people – it was one of the perks of my job.

Looking back now, I realize that the first alarming signal of my health problem had occurred just over two months earlier, on St Patrick's Day, when my wife Claire and I were walking with our dog, Tiger, on Sliabh Carraig near our home in Ashford, County Wicklow. We were right at the top of the mountain after which our home is named. There was not another sinner in sight when we sat down to eat a sandwich and to give Tiger a treat. I suddenly developed an awful coughing fit, completely unlike any cough I had ever experienced previously. I was frightened and for a few minutes I thought I was going to choke to death. I remember thinking that a rescue helicopter would have trouble finding us in time to save me on that remote mountaintop.

I got my breath back after a few very frightening minutes and we returned home to make dinner, but I had another violent coughing fit while eating a peanut before our meal. I remember thinking that this was not just a coughing fit brought on by a peanut stuck in my throat. I was very bothered because I thought that I was as fit as a fiddle physically. I had always looked after my health. I walked up to 10 miles most days and I swam in the sea frequently. I had had my first sea swim of the year on the previous day and was delighted that I had done it before St Patrick's Day. My last health check-up had been just before Christmas. I got the all-clear and had told my friends afterwards that I was confident that I had at least another five good years ahead of me.

I could not hide my worries from Claire. We had been together for sixteen years and we thought that our relationship was made in heaven. We met when we were both working for RTÉ, where Claire still works as a Promotions Producer/Director for RTÉ Television. We had been admiring each other from a distance on the RTÉ campus for a year before I got her telephone number through a Newsroom friend, Edel McAllister. Although my day job often involved throwing brash questions at distinguished people and doing what is known in the trade as a 'piece to camera' that would be seen on TV news by maybe 500,000 people, I am innately very shy, and I had to pluck up the courage to ring the number and say: 'Hello, I'm Charlie Bird, would you like to go on a date with me?'

Claire said 'Yes' and our relationship blossomed. We hit it off immediately. We both drove Saab cars of the same colour and we both loved outdoor activities. We found true happiness together, despite a nearly twenty-year age difference. In our 17 years together we have never had a major row or gone to bed not talking to each other. She calls me 'Bird' and I call her by her surname, 'Mould'. We had been seeing each other for a couple of years when I asked her to move in with me in 2010. We married in 2016. The front of the wedding invitation we sent to friends said: *Bird and Mould are getting married*. After a civil ceremony in Dublin on a beautiful May Saturday, we had our wedding photos taken at the Patrick Kavanagh statue beside the Grand Canal. 'Love birds in the sun' was the punning caption on one of the Sunday newspapers the next day.

It was Claire who bore the brunt of my health worries as spring turned to summer in 2021. She was shocked when the tree surgeon who used to trim the tops of our trees with a chainsaw, Bill from Wicklow, called in to her one day to say that he had noticed a slurring in my speech and he feared that I might be about to suffer a stroke.

I seemed to notice new and ominous symptoms every week. I began to surf and 'doom-scroll' Google. I was very troubled to see suggestions of motor neurone disease (MND). This was the disease that less than a decade previously had killed my dear RTÉ friend and colleague Colm Murray, one of the loveliest and most popular broadcasters ever to grace Irish TV screens. I used to visit Colm and his wife, Anne, at their home in Clontarf with my best pal Joe O'Brien and our boss, Ed Mulhall. I was always distressed by how quickly the disease was draining away his life.

I began to bombard my GP to get me an urgent appointment with a specialist. I knew that MND could be one of the most difficult conditions to diagnose. I was never fully reassured, despite being told constantly by Claire and my daughters, Orla and Neasa, and by my GP and a specialist, that whatever I had, it was not motor neurone disease.

I sent the *Ransom '79* podcasts to a few friends before broadcast and I asked them if they noticed anything about my voice. It was the first time I had asked anyone outside my immediate family if they had noticed any changes in my voice. They all said that my voice had changed and was noticeably different. I was slurring my words slightly. My worries intensified, even though some of them suggested that the changes in my voice may have been due to a bad reaction to the COVID-19 vaccine, or to some other mystery virus.

Joe Duffy invited me onto his RTÉ Radio 1 *Liveline* programme to discuss *Ransom '79* and I was exhausted after I spent 45 minutes on air with him on Tuesday, 8 June. Within minutes of the programme finishing, a journalist from one of the tabloid newspapers rang me. He said that he had just listened to me on the radio and had noticed that my voice seemed to be off. He sensed that he might have a story for his newspaper, and he was not wrong. I was more than a bit thrown by his question, but I told him that my voice was fine and that I only had a bit of a cold.

I had told Joe Duffy before going on air that I was having difficulty with my voice, but we both wanted to discuss the story and we went ahead with the interview. Joe said that he too had thought that the story would fit into John le Carré's oeuvre. I told him on air what I hadn't said in any of the podcasts – that I knew the name of the barrister that the Gardaí believed was a member of the gang. I told him that one of my daughters and one of my sons-in-law were barristers and that the Law Library was 'agog' with speculation about the rogue barrister's identity. I told Joe that the barrister was now dead, but that I would not name him publicly because the Gardaí had never got the conclusive proof that would have enabled them to mount a prosecution.

I was pleased with the interview, although I did find it tiring and I was conscious that my voice did not sound perfect. The interview injected new life into the *Ransom '79* story and I was trying to decide how to develop it further. I wanted to be able to concentrate on my work, not my health worries.

Two days after my *Liveline* appearance I drove to Galway for the long-postponed get-together with a group of former west of Ireland RTÉ colleagues that I had christened the WestAwake Gang. My pal Joe O'Brien, from Carlow, was an honorary member of the gang because he had wooed his future wife in Galway when she lived and worked there. Joe and I booked into our regular Galway base, the Ardilaun Hotel on Taylor's Hill. Michael Lally, who was himself in the middle of a serious health setback, Jim Fahy and Ray Burke joined us outside the hotel and we walked to the Salthill promenade, via Rosary Lane, Oaklands and the Salthill Catholic Church. Sean O'Rourke and Tommie Gorman joined us on the Prom opposite Seapoint Ballroom.

It was the first time any of us had seen each other since before the Covid lockdowns had begun the previous March. We talked non-stop as we walked along the Prom, the Grattan Road and 'the Swamp' (South Park). We were having a couple of outdoor, socially distanced drinks beside the Eglinton Canal on Raven Terrace when a woman who was not much younger than our average age approached me and began to tell me how her late father used to always to talk about my appearances on the TV news.

We had a good laugh when she moved off because she herself was not young and because she said it was her late father, not even herself, who knew me from the TV news. Our merriment was slightly uneasy because some of the lads had been worried that the sight of seven well-known RTÉ faces socializing in Galway while many Covid restrictions were still in place might cause more bad publicity for RTÉ. This was just seven months after embarrassing photographs of a few well-known RTÉ presenters sharing impromptu hugs with a retiring and popular TV Building receptionist had been splashed on the front pages of national newspapers under the headline 'Distancing with the Stars'.

We laughed nonetheless because one of our gang dismissed the others' fears of being stalked by paparazzi by pointing out that most of the people who would see us in Galway would likely be under 35 years of age, which meant they wouldn't have ever seen an RTÉ News bulletin in their lives and would never recognize any of the former newsmen.

As residents of the Ardilaun Hotel, Joe and I were able to host a meal there for our friends that evening. With more than half-a-dozen strong personalities at two adjacent tables, it was hard to get a word in edgeways but, in truth, I was less and less able to try. I was feeling upset because I was struggling to swallow my food and my voice was not strong or clear enough to carry across the two tables. I shocked my friends by suddenly excusing myself and saying goodnight. I did not want to spoil what had been a very enjoyable get-together by voicing my health worries or by struggling noticeably with my food. I went to my room, very worried and uncertain about what was happening to my body.

The next day I tried to fly to Inis Oírr, the smallest of the three Aran Islands at the mouth of Galway Bay, to see my friends Peadar and Brid Póil, but the weather was too bad and the plane turned back after a few minutes in the air. I returned to Wicklow, where my fears escalated. I was on my own for a few days while Claire took her mother and her sister to Clifden for a short break. On the first night that Claire was away, I was lying in bed when my arms and legs began to twitch. I became very stressed because I knew in my heart from what I had read via Google that something serious was wrong with my body.

I rang Claire and told her what was happening and, for the first time, I uttered the nightmare words 'motor neurone disease' out loud to myself.

Claire and my daughters kept pleading with me to avoid Doctor Google, but I became fixated with it. By now I was getting little or no sleep at night and I was beginning to avoid chatting with my neighbours when I went for my daily walks with Tiger, while Claire worked from home because of the Covid restrictions.

Joe Duffy rang me again after I got back from Galway. I told him that I was now really worried about my voice. He offered to help me to get an appointment with a consultant and he even offered to drive me to and from any appointments. He took to ringing me every week, offering constant support and help to Claire and myself over the following months. We really appreciated it as we knew we were going to need the support.

In mid-June I had my first long session with a specialist neurologist in Dublin. I told my friends that he had already ruled out Parkinson's disease and felt that I was not presenting with MND. I had about ten further blood tests and a few more scans. The specialist said that he thought that whatever I had was treatable and he promised that he would leave no stone unturned to find out what was ailing me. He said that he, not Doctor Google, was now in charge. I felt much happier that I was going to get to the bottom of my issues.

On Saturday, 18 June the *Irish Times* carried a big advertisement for the *Ransom '79* podcast. It was headlined 'Charlie Bird at his very best', but I was feeling very far from my very best because of my worsening health fears. Further brain scans and dozens of blood tests continued to reveal nothing sinister, but I was sent to a speech and language therapist, Dr. Ciarán Kenny, who lectured in Trinity College Dublin and who worked in a number of hospitals. I met him one Saturday morning in a consulting room near St. Vincent's Private Hospital. After a series of tests, he concluded that my speech problem was neurological in source. It wasn't the news I wanted to hear but I felt that, at last, someone was pointing me in a specific direction.

I returned to the neurologist who was looking after me and he ordered a whole new round of blood tests and brain scans, including an EMG, which is a nerve conduction test that is designed to assess the function of the nerves and muscles. The results, once again, showed nothing negative. He said that he was 90 per cent certain that I didn't have MND, or Parkinson's disease or multiple sclerosis.

It was mid-summer and I still had no concrete answers, but I was convinced that I had MND. My voice and my ability to swallow were worsening. My nights were mostly sleepless. Most of my muscles continued to display twitching. The investigations continued. Before the end of June I had two more major, intrusive tests. But after 90 minutes of nerve conduction tests and needles into my muscles, the results were very positive. I had two more brain scans the following week.

All of my tests and scans were completed by the end of the first week in July. Claire and I took Tiger for a short break in Allihies in West Cork. In our B&B one night,

Claire noticed that the muscles in my arms were twitching. By now I was totally stressed. I just wanted an answer.

My first meeting in person in just under a year with my close pals, known collectively as Kehoe's Gang, was on the Saturday before my next appointment with the specialist. We had been able to communicate only by phone or text, or via Zoom a couple of times, since the Covid restrictions had been reintroduced in July 2020.

What I had christened the Kehoe's Gang was me and three close friends who had been meeting regularly in that pub, off Grafton Street, for the past several years. We used to meet, usually every two months or so and usually in the snug, for a couple of drinks before moving next-door to The Gotham Café for a meal and more chat, laughs and drinks. The gang comprised: Joe O'Brien, who had been my closest friend ever since we had started work sitting beside each other in the RTÉ Newsroom in the early 1980s and who has spoken to me on the phone almost every day since we both retired on the same day in 2012; Dympna Moroney, who was the editor of the *Six One News* or the *Nine O'Clock News* during much of my time as Chief News Reporter and Chief News Correspondent and who had produced our award-winning news reports on road deaths in 2006, as well as some of my other special features; and Ray Burke, who was a News Editor and later the Chief News Editor of RTÉ News during the second half of my career there.

Saturday, 10 July 2021 was a beautiful summer's day. We sat on one of Kehoe's pub benches on Duke Lane, the narrow little laneway that runs between South Anne Street and Duke Street. Claire stayed with us for a while before venturing off to the shops. Eric Luke, who had shared countless doorsteps and press conferences with me when he was a staff photographer on the *Irish Press* and later on the *Irish Times*, stopped for a chat. Three relatives of victims of the 1981 Stardust nightclub fire spotted me and we shared warm words and hugs. June, Louise and Selina McDermott lost three siblings – George, Marcella and William – in the tragedy. Their grace and good humour nearly made me forget my worries, but I did ask them to say a few prayers for me.

Next to Claire and my daughters Nessa and Orla, my Kehoe's Gang pals had become my inner cabinet as my health worries increased. They told me after that Saturday meeting that they had noticed that I had got thin and that my voice was not normal. The dreaded words 'motor neurone' were mentioned. I had admitted quietly to them that, apart from my voice issues, Claire and I had noticed at least one other worrying symptom, a near-constant twitching in my arm muscles.

Despite my worries, and theirs, it was a wonderful afternoon of laughter and reminiscing. When I got home, I sent the three of them a text message saying that, although I had no idea what I was facing, the afternoon with them had filled me with joy and courage, which was exactly what I needed.

On Monday, my meeting with the specialist was very positive. After three brain scans, a battery of nerve conduction texts and ten blood tests, he told me that he had found nothing nasty. He told me that he was still 'confused' and 'puzzled' over my voice issues, but that I should go away and 'destress'. He said that the tests had not shown any sign of motor neurone disease, therefore he was '90 per cent certain' that I did not have it. In order to be one hundred per cent certain, he would do the nerve conduction tests again in six months' time. He was very positive overall and suggested that many of my problems in recent weeks had been caused by stress. He told me to go and live my life to the full. Naturally, I was somewhat relieved, but I was not at all convinced that I was out of the woods.

Claire and I were planning to spend a week on the Burren and on Inis Oírr in late August, but I made a sudden, solo visit to the island at the beginning of the month. I stayed with my friends of more than fifty years, Peadar and Bríd Póil. They agreed that my voice had changed, but Bríd, whose mother had died of MND, assured me that my symptoms were not like her mother's.

On my return to Wicklow, I was very saddened to hear that a dear old friend and colleague, Katie Kahn-Carl, had died in St Vincent's University Hospital, Dublin, after an illness. Katie had been Foreign Editor for RTÉ News for many years before her retirement in 1999 and we had worked very closely together on most of my foreign assignments. We also shared the same GP in south Dublin and I often met her at his surgery after we had both retired from RTÉ.

Katie's relations and some of our former RTÉ colleagues asked me to deliver the eulogy at her private funeral on 11 August. I was honoured and privileged to do so, even though I could not hide that I was struggling with the reality that my voice was weakening. How could I refuse when I recalled how Katie had never complained about her own extraordinarily tragic early life, but had always exuded constant good cheer and bonhomie in the RTÉ Newsroom every single day? She was born in Paris in 1934, but had to flee with her mother to Africa as a young child after her father and several of his close relatives were sent to concentration camps, where they were murdered by the Nazis. She was educated by Loreto nuns in Africa and won a scholarship to University College Dublin in the early 1950s to study French and German. Her linguistic abilities won her a job with the nascent Telefís Éireann in 1961 and she was appointed Foreign Editor in 1991.

Her *Irish Times* obituary quoted me accurately. I said that Katie was 'a mammy to generations of RTÉ reporters who travelled all over the world'. I said that nobody ever had a bad word to say about her, not just in RTÉ but also in the European Broadcasting Union, the BBC and ITV, and that wherever you went, everyone knew Katie.

After her Requiem mass – Katie had converted to Catholicism after coming to Ireland – in the Church of St Laurence O'Toole in Kilmacud, I joined some of our former colleagues in the Mill House pub in Stillorgan for a meal and some drinks. But, just as in Galway two months earlier, I was having trouble swallowing food and my weakened voice prevented me from talking much. As had happened in Galway, I left the gathering early. I was unable to enjoy, or even tolerate, the bonhomie and clatter of my friends in the public house.

Claire and I spent four beautiful days on the Burren followed by a day and night with Peadar and Bríd on Inis Oírr, but the entire visit was overshadowed by my growing worries about my health. Nonetheless when we returned to Wicklow, I climbed the miners' trail near Glendalough with Sean O'Rourke. We walked for four hours and twenty minutes. I felt I still had plenty of physical energy, despite my anxiety about voice and throat problems.

Claire and I were in the habit of going to our local pub in Ashford, the Chester Beatty Inn, after she had finished her week's work on Friday evening. The pub was always nearly empty at that time. One evening in August, as we sat chatting over a drink, I completely lost control of my emotions. I started to cry. I told Claire that I knew I was dying. She tried to reassure me, but the months of stress were taking their toll.

A month or so later I was in the pub on my own, drinking my favourite tipple, a pint of Guinness, when I broke down again. Some people saw my distress. The pub owner, Padraig Humby, who is a really lovely man, asked me a few days later if I was OK. I told him of my medical woes and I really shocked him when I said that I thought I was dying. I just couldn't shake off the feeling that I was going to die.

In early September I was back with my consultant, accompanied this time by Claire. He again sought to reassure me that I did not have MND. He told me: 'Charlie, you are not going to die from motor neurone. Yes, you will die, as will we all, but you won't die from MND.' Due to my scepticism and my obvious stress, he recommended that I should arrange to see a psychologist and also that I get a second opinion from a speech and language therapist.

The psychologist listened to my account of my previous six months. His report to my consultant, my GP and me said: 'Upon review of Mr. Bird's mental health, it is apparent that he experienced severe shock and horror at the onset of his recent physical health concerns. He developed a significant fear that he might encounter a prolonged deterioration of health, which he worried might be fatal. A range of psychosocial and personality factors contributed to this traumatic stress response. As a result, Mr Bird struggled over several months with clinically significant symptoms of post-traumatic stress disorder (PTSD). Such stress and anxiety may have also exacerbated some of his primary physical health symptoms.'

Yet another medical professional was telling me that I was stressing too much about the idea of MND and, irony of ironies, that I was suffering *post*-traumatic stress disorder. I was confused and annoyed at being told that I was suffering only from stress. I had reported from war zones and from multiple natural disasters – I knew what stress was. If I was displaying stress, it was because I felt that I was not being listened to properly.

I was prescribed a short dose of anti-anxiety tablets. They provided some relief, but they did not improve my voice or prevent another awful coughing fit. I feared that I could end up with a croaky voice, but I thought that would be far better than the alternative I had been living with in my head for the previous four months.

I decided that I was no longer going to hide the fading of my voice. The deterioration in my speech was now so bad that I was avoiding my neighbours and I was feeling awful about that. I had also started to decline invitations to be interviewed on radio shows about *Ransom '79*, COVID-19 or the forthcoming anniversary of the kidnapping of supermarket executive Don Tidey. That was a story I had covered in 1983, when a young soldier, Private Patrick Kelly, and a young Garda, Gary Sheehan, had been killed by the IRA during the rescue operation. My 72nd birthday on 9 September 2021, some 38 years after the kidnap and killings, prompted me to begin to consider saying something public about my voice.

I had a happy get-together with the Kehoe's Gang on Friday, 17 September. A few days later, on impulse and with a heightened sense of foreboding, I had a photograph of the four of us that was taken in the Gotham Café on that Friday evening developed and enlarged. I bought three 10 x 8 inch wooden frames and posted the framed photographs to the home addresses of my three Kehoe's Gang friends. I was in such a state over my health worries that I feared that it might be one of our last get-togethers.

By the end of the following week I had decided to go public about my voice problem, via social media. On 24 September I posted the following on Twitter: *Declined two radio interviews today on Don Tidey kidnap and shoot-out which I reported on at the time. Why – over the past four months I've had major issues with my speech. Despite series of tests still don't know what is going on. Thanks to my pals for their support. Stay safe.*

Within hours the post had garnered 3,500 'Likes' and retweets. More than 200 people sent me direct messages. I was blown away by the support on Twitter and by the amazing text messages I received from former RTÉ colleagues and other journalists. I was no longer hiding.

One week later I returned to Twitter as follows: *Last week I posted a message about my speech issues. I have*

been overwhelmed by the positive response from all over
the country. I can't respond to everyone but I want to
thank people from the bottom of my heart. I'm fortunate
as others are facing more serious issues. Stay safe.

Over the following week my speech worsened considerably. I became very scared and uncertain. The language therapist, Dr Ciarán Kenny, recommended that I seek a second opinion from a colleague of his, Margaret Walshe, an Associate Professor in speech and language therapy at Trinity College Dublin, who had consulting rooms near St Vincent's Hospital. Another nerve test was scheduled, this time to include my tongue. I was back in uncharted territory.

Wednesday, 13 October was the day of the next scheduled test. I sent an early WhatsApp message to my friends saying that my voice was continuing to fail quite dramatically and that I was facing another crucial nerve and tongue test that afternoon. I knew that this was D-Day. I believed that these tests would decide which road I was going down.

The detailed nerve test took two-and-a-half hours. It showed that there was a definite neurological issue with my tongue, but provided no definitive answer as to what was causing it. A more detailed report was to be sent to my consultant. I was still in limbo, with no definite answers either way.

When her report arrived, Margaret Walsh's prognosis was definite and unforgettable: it was possible that I had 'a unilateral upper motor neurone dysarthria'. It was the first time that the words 'motor neurone' had been used officially. She recommended that I have another EMG nerve study done as soon as possible in St Vincent's Hospital. This was carried out in early October.

I was walking my usual daily routine at a place called The Murrough, near Wicklow Town, heading towards Killoughter and Greystones, at 11.00 a.m. when my consultant neurologist rang me with the result of the EMG. The news was devastating. The new EMG test had shown some disturbing features – 'markers' for motor neurone disease. I rang Claire immediately. I cried. I could barely hold back my tears when, later, I told my daughters and close friends. We now had a definitive answer, and it was everything that I had feared.

The consultant said he was referring me to Professor Orla Hardiman, the country's leading MND expert. I spoke to her twice on the telephone that day and she fixed an appointment for the following week, when she would have reviewed my files. There was now little doubt but that I was entering the same place that the dear, departed Colm Murray had occupied. I told my family and friends that I would try to be brave.

I arranged to meet the Kehoe's Gang on the following Saturday week, 23 October. On Wednesday of that week, 20 October, I told the gang that my big appointment was on the following morning and that no matter what I was told, or whatever journey I was facing, Saturday with them was a day that I did not want to miss.

I was drowning in fears and uncertainty, but my friends were a life raft. I was clinging to them and praying for rescue.

2. HARDIMAN

Professor Orla Hardiman is Ireland's best-known consultant neurologist. She is one of only two full-time Professors of Neurology in the country, working in Beaumont Hospital, Dublin, and as head of the neurology unit at Trinity College Dublin.

I knew her name only too well because she had overseen the diagnosis and treatment of my dear colleague Colm Murray when he was afflicted with MND in March 2010. I had visited Colm at his home in Clontarf many times before he died a little over three years later. Each visit was more harrowing than the last one as his condition deteriorated. My heart used to go out to him and to Anne, his lovely wife, who was looking after him with such dignity and courage.

My appointment with Dr Hardiman came seven months and four days after my frightening St Patrick's Day coughing fit on the Wicklow mountains – more than 200 days of spring, summer and autumn 2021 overshadowed by increasing symptoms and escalating fears. Claire and I drove to our 11.00 a.m. appointment at Beaumont Hospital on Thursday, 21 October with mounting dread.

Professor Hardiman confirmed the news that I had been expecting and fearing for months. She told me that I had motor neurone disease. She said that I would lose my voice and my ability to swallow and that I would have respiratory problems. She said that I would need a feeding tube and that I ought to have it inserted immediately. Among other questions, I asked Professor Hardiman how long did she think I would live? She said that she could not answer as the disease affected different patients in different ways. People with my form of the illness lived, on average, for two to three years after diagnosis. She was the first medical consultant to call MND 'the one-thousand-day disease', but she told me that its trajectory differed from person to person and that, for example, she was treating one man who had been living with the condition for more than twenty years.

In a strange way, I briefly felt a small bit of relief. After months of mounting and unbearable uncertainty, there would be no more guessing or wondering. Now we had the cold, stark facts.

Towards the end of the consultation, Professor Hardiman wrote a note. She said that there was no need for us to read it, but just to get it countersigned by our GP and send it off to the HSE. She explained that this form would entitle me to a medical card so that I could get the very expensive tablets that would help to slow down the advance of MND.

Claire and I ignored her advice about the note. We looked at it as soon as we returned to our car. I was in such a state that I cannot recall the precise words, but there in black and white I read that 'this patient' has been diagnosed with 'a terminal illness'. We left Beaumont in a state of total panic and despair. We had started to cry as soon as we left Professor Hardiman's office. We cried throughout the entire journey home, along the busy M50 and the N11 to Ashford.

Everything had changed in less than half-an-hour in the professor's office. I had gone to my appointment as a 72-year-old broadcast journalist with ominous voice problems and other worrying ailments. I was hoping for a miracle explanation that would allow me to resume my career. I emerged with a death sentence. Professor Hardiman had confirmed that I had an incurable, progressive, degenerative disease that promised ever-worsening debilitation and imminent death.

In our bubble of shock and grief, Claire and I paid no attention to the motorists speeding along the N11 motorway beside and behind us. If I strayed out of my lane of traffic or broke the speed limit or drove through a red light, I could have killed or injured other motorists and their passengers, but my own life was over in any event. Normal rules no longer applied to me. I understood clearly Dr Samuel Johnson's remark of nearly 250 years earlier: 'Depend upon it, Sir, when a man knows he is to be hanged in a fortnight, it concentrates his mind wonderfully.' But the remark had lost all its humour for me.

The only topic that Claire and I discussed on our journey home was when and how I would break the news to Orla and Neasa. My voice and my diction had deteriorated badly over the previous six months, although they were nothing like as bad as they would be in another two months, but I cannot remember a single other remark that

Claire or I made on that hour-long drive to Ashford. We just cried and cried all the way home.

For most of my adult life I had been healthy and happy, comfortable in the spotlight, but now I wanted only to hide from the world. I was vulnerable in a way that I had never been vulnerable before. There was no longer any doubt, and there would be no miracle. I was facing a cruel decline and imminent death. My wife was weeping beside me. I too was weeping and trying to get my head around the mortal agony and reality of my unalterable diagnosis. The unexpected deaths of perhaps millions of my fellow human beings had been almost a stock-in-trade of my reporting days from foreign wars, famines and natural disasters. Now it was my own turn to die.

I rang Orla and Neasa from the car and told them the bad news. They had been expecting it, but they were shocked and distressed. They had lost their mother, Mary, just a few years previously. I told my daughters, and also those close friends I contacted about the diagnosis, that I could not sugar-coat the news. Motor neurone disease attacks nerves in the brain and the spinal cord. It can impair your ability to walk, talk, eat, drink and breathe. It causes progressive paralysis. It is incurable and terminal.

My type of MND is called Bulbar. It occurs in about one in every five people affected. (According to the Irish Motor Neurone Disease Association, 'in Ireland one person is diagnosed with MND every two days and there are currently over 400 people living with the disease in Ireland.') The first symptom of Bulbar MND is usually a slurring of speech, which was exactly what I had been experiencing progressively for more than seven months before my diagnosis. The speech slurring is caused by impaired tongue movement – again matching my experience since St Patrick's Day. People with Bulbar MND do not experience difficulty walking until late in the progression.

To my daughters and friends I said that my battle was on, that I would probably lose my voice first and get maybe a couple of years before the disease brought me down. I knew that it would take me some time to get my head around the news, but there was no doubt about the eventual outcome. I told my WestAwake comrades that one of my main wishes was that, whenever I departed, I wanted them to carry me to my final resting place.

My WestAwake and Kehoe's Gang friends had been in touch with me almost every day since I had first told them about my early worrying symptoms. I had kept them informed about every visit to my GP or specialist and every scan. I knew when I had met both groups after the COVID restrictions were eased in summer 2021 that there was something serious wrong with me, but their friendship and support had helped me to maintain my sanity and they were, in many ways, 'life-saving' for me.

Sean O'Rourke reacted to my bad news with a text message in which he noted the 'tragically cruel and stupid irony that it starts with your voice, a voice that has literally brought the world to our audiences down the decades'. Jim Fahy sent me the entire seven-verse text of W. B. Yeats's 'The Municipal Gallery Revisited', with its glorious final lines: 'Think where man's glory most begins and ends/and say my glory was I had such friends.'

I waited nearly two weeks before going public about my condition. I was determined that the news of my diagnosis would not emerge in the brutal way that the terminal illnesses of Colm Murray and, earlier, of Minister for Finance Brian Lenihan had come to national attention via newspaper or television reports before all of their family members and all of their wider circles of friends had been told.

I knew that I had very little time before the news reached Dublin media circles. The national newspapers are always eager for stories about RTÉ and its employees. Every journalist wants to be first with the news, whether it's in the public interest or merely of interest to the public.

Only a few months had passed since photographs of a number of prominent RTÉ broadcasters, including Miriam O'Callaghan, David McCullagh and Bryan Dobson, had been splashed across the front pages of the Dublin tabloids after they appeared briefly at an impromptu farewell for a colleague during COVID-19 restrictions. And I remembered how a former girlfriend of mine had been stalked for days by a photographer for an Irish Sunday newspaper bankrolled from London many years ago, solely because she was my girlfriend at the time. I recalled too that the same newspaper had hired a photographer to capture my comings and goings at the RTÉ offices in Washington DC.

More recently, a photograph of my former RTÉ colleague Sean O'Rourke had been published by the *Irish Sun* tabloid and website at the beginning of July 2021 when he sat outside Davy Byrne's pub on Duke Street in Dublin with his arm in a sling after he had slipped while painting at home shortly after he retired. The story, written by the paper's 'Showbiz Editor, Ken Sweeney', was headlined 'RTÉ legend Sean O'Rourke suffers horror lockdown injury' and it said that he had suffered the shoulder injury in a 'home DIY nightmare' that was 'a freak accident'.

It wouldn't take much for people to put two and two together, given the symptoms I had already described. Even my eleven-year-old grandson, Charlie, had made an educated guess about my condition. Orla told me that when she was telling him about my voice problems, he had asked if I had motor neurone disease. He told her he knew about it because they had been learning at school about Stephen Hawking, who had been diagnosed with a crippling disease very similar to MND at the age of 21.

I felt the pressure of needing to disclose this on my own terms, and yet I was still trying to absorb the shock and horror of the confirmed diagnosis and Professor Hardiman's prognosis. I discussed with Claire and my daughters what to do. A few days later, I decided to tweet the news. On the morning of Wednesday, 27 October I posted this Tweet: *Recently I spoke about issues with my voice. I now know why. I have been diagnosed with Motor Neurone Disease. Thanks to all my pals for their amazing support. And the kindness from so many people. Stay safe everyone.*

The tweet quickly garnered 21,400 Likes, 392 retweets and 1,155 comments.

A short time later I was driving home after going for a walk with my pal Sean O'Rourke when I heard Joe Duffy previewing his *Liveline* programme on RTÉ Radio 1 and mentioning my diagnosis. As soon as I got home to Ashford, just after 1.00 p.m., Joe rang me and asked me if I would be willing to do a brief interview with him for *Liveline*. I said that I would. He said that he did not want to put me under pressure and suggested that we pre-record the interview.

I often don't listen to radio interviews that I have recorded, nor read what I have said to newspaper interviewers. On this day, I was so distressed that when we finished the interview I did not switch on the radio to listen to it. I was very glad that Joe pre-recorded the interview because I would have been too upset to talk to him at the start of the programme after hearing how my former colleague, Bryan Dobson, had ended his *News At One* programme immediately before *Liveline*. 'Dobbo', who had soldiered with me at RTÉ for many years at home and abroad, said:

'Before we sign off, I want to take a moment to send best wishes from everyone here in RTÉ News to our friend and former colleague Charlie Bird who has been diagnosed, as you may have heard, with motor neurone disease. Charlie was for many years one of the most familiar voices and faces on RTÉ News, a trusted journalist and a tireless reporter who has continued to contribute to public debate and discussion in the years since his retirement. Behind the scenes he was the very best of colleagues. Charlie, you are in our thoughts at this difficult time.'

I didn't find out until a couple of days later what Bryan Dobson had said and I was blown away by his kind remarks. Neither did I know that Sean O'Rourke had spoken on *Liveline* about me immediately after my interview.

Joe Duffy and I spoke for seventeen minutes at the beginning of *Liveline*. It was my first time to speak publicly about my diagnosis and about my growing fears and uncertainties during the previous seven months. I wanted to break the news myself, and this was my chance to end the speculation and to outline the facts. Even though I had volunteered to be interviewed by Joe, it was a spur-of-the moment decision. I had not rehearsed what I might say on air. I didn't even have a chance to alert my daughters who both were busy at work.

I was too upset to listen back to the interview for a long time afterwards, but I think now that it accurately captured my rawness and fear, as well as my resignation about what I was facing. I told Joe that I was finding it hard to cope with my condition, but that I had to face reality and that I was dealing with it. I said that people experienced knocks every day and that I was only in the ha'penny place compared to people like ten-year-old Adam Terry from Cork, whose scoliosis operation had been delayed, or like the cancer campaigner Vicky Phelan.

I acknowledged that in some instances MND was difficult to detect, but I said that I knew in my heart of hearts that something serious was wrong with me and that I had, in a sense, been preparing for many months for the identification and confirmation of my condition. Since I now knew the final outcome of my condition, I had no option but to confront it.

It was an interview that I could never have imagined I would have to give. My diagnosis had been 'awful bloody news', but I was very fortunate to have the most important people of all supporting me – my beautiful wife Claire and my daughters and sons-in-law and grandchildren. I said that close friends and neighbours, and the support of Joe himself, were keeping me going from day to day. I was not alone in my trial, but I knew that there were many people in dark places who were not getting a light shone upon them. I mentioned the families of people who were dying from COVID-19 and the relatives of the 1981 Stardust disaster who were still awaiting answers about what had caused the fire that killed their loved ones.

I told Joe that I was not sleeping at all and that I was having trouble eating. I said that I had thought about including the Seamus Heaney text message to his wife from his hospital bed – *Noli timere* (be not afraid) – in the tweet I had posted that morning. I knew that my remaining months were going to be difficult but, like everyone else facing hard times, I would have to deal with them and not be afraid.

'Charlie, *Noli timere*, be not afraid', Joe said, ending the interview, 'we're all with you, so many people, most of them who you probably don't know. We're all with you and we're as conscious of people as you are, people who are going through their health challenges regardless of their age at the moment and we're thinking of them. Charlie Bird, you're a hero. Keep going.'

As soon as the programme finished, I began to get phone calls from newspapers seeking interviews. After all the months of turmoil and uncertainty, the news of my MND was finally out. I agreed readily to talk to every reporter who asked, partly because I was so stressed and fearful that I might soon end up in a wheelchair. On the same day I was also approached about writing this book and about letting a TV documentary crew into my home. The *Late Late Show* also contacted me about an appearance. Claire and I had a hollow laugh next day when I got miffed over the *Irish Times* describing me as 'a retired journalist'.

I was still feeling extremely raw and emotionally fragile when the documentary team of John Kelleher, Colm Quinn and Kevin Minogue spent three days filming me at home while Tommie Gorman threw questions at me. I broke down uncontrollably several times while answering Tommie's questions and while I was being filmed reading some of the letters and cards that had begun to arrive through my letterbox from all parts of Ireland. I'm not a deeply religious person, but I was enormously moved by the handwritten messages on the scores of Mass cards I received. I have huge admiration for the hundreds of people who had never met me but who took the trouble to send me those cards and messages. They gave me strength, but they also made me cry like a child.

I might have been better advised to postpone some of the media interviews until I had had time to absorb the shock of my diagnosis but, after a lifetime in journalism, my instinct was never to refuse fellow-professionals trying to do their job as best they could. I was determined to keep fighting, to make my remaining months or years meaningful and to cherish the love of my family and friends. Tommie Gorman's questions for the TV documentary caught me at my most vulnerable and fragile time. I was hopelessly incapable of hiding my fragility and my sorrow when answering his questions about my parents, my career, my children and grandchildren and my wife.

What was upsetting me most, I told Tommie, was my inability to protect my wife and my family from my fate and my grief. What was making me saddest of all during those interviews was that my looming death would mean that I would be leaving my relationship with my beautiful Claire and my wonderful daughters and my cherished grandchildren.

I get upset every time I talk about my daughters and my five grandchildren. I know that I am not going to live to see my grandchildren grow up. I know that I am going to miss so many important occasions in their lives. I had always looked forward to sharing those milestones with them and their parents, but that is simply no longer possible.

My illness has also made me think increasingly about my own parents. They both came from Macroom in West Cork, where one of my grandfathers was the engineer who brought street lighting to the town and where one of my grandmothers ran a hotel in an area that became known as Bird's Corner.

My parents had tough lives, even though an old saying promises that Macroom is 'The town that never reared a fool'. They went to England during the Second World War and lived in Hornchurch in Essex, near London, where they narrowly escaped death in the Blitz and where they often had to spend nights in a garden bomb shelter.

Returning to Ireland, they lived in Sandymount while my father worked in the ESB power station in Ringsend, before moving to Goatstown when my father went to sea as an engineer with the State-owned Irish Shipping Company. My father died on decimalisation day in 1971.

My mother died tragically in 1983 after she was knocked down by a car outside Cornelscourt shopping centre. She had to be strict and frugal when my father was away at sea for long spells and when she was widowed. It hurt me that she never spoke about my progress in RTÉ, but I now know that that was my failing, not hers.

It's a symptom of my ever-worsening condition that I get emotional and weepy nearly every day. The words 'terminal illness' are non-negotiable. The trough of terror, shock, dread, denial and despair into which I had sunk after the confirmation of my diagnosis at the end of October 2021 lasted throughout November and December of that year.

My career as a nationally known public service broadcaster with RTÉ, and my post-retirement documentaries and podcasts, meant that I had lived most of my life – more than forty of my seventy-two years – in the public eye, presenting a professional persona that was sometimes mocked by newspaper columnists and other cynics. My frequent Facebook and Twitter postings, coupled with my commitment to a new post-diagnosis RTÉ documentary and to this book, ensured that the remainder of my life would also be subject to public scrutiny, or at least public interest.

I had grown comfortable in the public eye as my career had progressed, but the prospect of losing my voice completely and being progressively disabled made me vulnerable and afraid of even being seen in public. I knew that I had no hope of living for the one thousand months that are allotted to most people these days, and I was dreading the attrition that the MND would wreak upon my body and my mind, as well as the distress that it was causing my loved ones.

Midway through my trough of despair, just weeks after my diagnosis was confirmed, Vicky Phelan appeared on the *Late Late Show* in late November. I knew that she was the most prominent and outspoken of the hundreds of Irish women afflicted with incurable or advanced cervical cancer following false results from smear tests carried out for the Irish health service by a US laboratory in 2011. Her terminal illness had come to national attention in 2018 when she won a High Court action in Dublin against the US laboratory. 'If I was told sooner, I would not be in a position of a terminal cancer diagnosis,' she told the court.

I didn't see that *Late Late Show* because I was travelling to Inis Oírr with Claire, but I had long been an admirer of how Vicky Phelan had exposed the smear test scandal during and after her High Court action. I had told Joe Duffy on *Liveline* on the day I went public about my diagnosis that I had been watching her trials and tribulations. I said that she was a remarkable woman and one of my heroes. When I saw the reaction to what she had said on the *Late Late Show*, I tweeted that she was an amazing and courageous person and I resolved to try to meet her.

Vicky told the *Late Late Show* that she had abandoned chemotherapy and was instead undergoing end-of-life 'palliative care' treatment so that she could spend more time with her children, 16-year-old Amelia and 10-year-old Darragh, at Christmas. Before I had a chance to contact her, she sent me a message out of the blue. I had asked one of her local TDs, then Labour Party leader Alan Kelly, for her telephone number, but she got to me first. Her message said: 'I hope that you are doing OK and that you are managing to enjoy the small things and not get overwhelmed by it all. I look forward to hearing from you. Warmest wishes, Vicky.'

I knew that her struggle with her own terminal illness had been harrowing and lengthy and also, like my own struggle, very public. It was clear that she had real determination to fight every bit of the way. I was at the start of my trial, still trying to come to grips with my diagnosis. She became my heroine. I knew that I had to meet her soon.

Vicky had spoken in public a number of times, calling on politicians to allow people who have a terminal illness the right to die with medical assistance. I knew that this debate on the 'right to die' was underway in the Dáil and among the general population, and that it had been ruled on in the country's highest courts in recent years. The issue had been on my mind in the months before my own diagnosis because I was finding it so hard to deal with not knowing exactly what was happening to my failing body. This notion of 'assisted dying' had become very real and urgent for me when my diagnosis was confirmed. I even mentioned it to Professor Orla Hardiman at one of our first meetings at Beaumont Hospital.

I met Vicky after I had responded to her WhatsApp message by telling her that I was not coping very well with my diagnosis. Claire and I drove to her home near Limerick in December 2021. Vicky had tea and scones ready for us and it turned out to be a lovely and memorable encounter.

Vicky was so welcoming to us that she immediately put me at ease. It was as if we had known each other all our lives. We just hit it off straight away. We chatted over everything for about for forty minutes. We joked and laughed over a shared physical similarity of having big eyes. We even spoke a little bit about 'assisted dying'. I told her that it had gone through my mind, but that was all that I said on the subject.

A reporter from the *Irish Independent* rang me as we were driving back to Wicklow because Vicky had posted on her Facebook page a photograph that Claire had taken of the two of us standing together, with my arm around her shoulder, just before we left the house. The reporter, Nicola Anderson, asked how we had got on and whether we had discussed 'assisted suicide'. I kicked for touch and told her that we had not discussed the issue in a big way. The photograph of Vicky and me appeared on the front page of the newspaper next morning, headlined: 'Finding solace as if we were friends forever'.

I had not felt able to tell Vicky, or the newspaper reporter, that I had started to research the subject of 'assisted dying' within days of my diagnosis. I had even ordered a book from Dignitas, the Switzerland-based non-profit organization that facilitates assisted or accompanied dying for people whose bodies are incurably diseased but whose minds are still sound. I told no one about the book. I put it on my bookshelf in my bedroom with the spine facing inward so no one would notice it.

These darkest of thoughts had occurred to me secretly even before my diagnosis, during the weeks when my worsening symptoms and uncertainty were distressing me deeply every day. Claire was working from home, and I used to take Tiger for a walk nearly every day from The Murrough, near Wicklow Town, to Killoughter, heading towards Greystones. It's a very popular walk, between the Dublin–Rosslare railway line and the Irish Sea. I had loved that walk for years, and it was close to where Claire and I often swam after leaving our clothes on the stony beach.

The walk used to take me an hour when I was on my own, or up to two hours with the inquisitive and wandering Tiger. One day in October, when I was about fifteen minutes from The Murrough, where my car was parked, I got a totally uncontrollable coughing fit. I was coughing so much that I was convinced that I was about to choke to death. I was so terrified that my mind began to wander.

Just typing these words now takes me back to a place that I didn't want to re-enter. I said to myself that if I did have MND, then maybe one day I would come back down to Killoughter without Tiger and I would swim out to sea and hopefully I would not come back. In the back of my head I reckoned that people would think that I had drowned by accident, that I had been swept away by the outgoing tide. The honest truth is that this awful thought often went through my head fleetingly when I was in that very distressed state in October and November 2021.

I had come to terms with what was going to happen to me. I had grown used to the certainty that my death would come sooner rather than later. A serious illness diagnosis had also recently come to blight the later years of an older friend of mine, the top Sinn Féin official Rita O'Hare, who I have known for almost thirty years. Our friendship had developed over my years covering the

Northern Ireland peace process. We had kept in touch when we both worked in Washington DC and later, after my retirement. We had planned to do a podcast on her life and times in 2021, but had to abandon the idea when our respective illnesses made it impossible. Before I was given my terminal illness news, Rita told me that she had her own health battle on her hands.

By late 2021 my ability to speak clearly was declining with every passing day. I was having to accept the very painful reality that my broadcasting career was over, but my new and unavoidable fear was that I might not even be able to talk to my loved ones and my friends for very much longer.

I knew from Professor Hardiman, and from what I had read about Bulbar MND, that my voice would be gone almost completely by the beginning of 2022. My diction was already becoming incomprehensible to all but my family and closest friends. I knew that even they and Tiger would no longer understand me as the new year got underway.

I was extremely fortunate, however, that an RTÉ commissioning editor had put me in touch with two Irish innovators who were developing cutting-edge technology to clone a person's voice by 'banking' or storing a huge number of that person's recorded words and sounds, so that the words could then be heard via a speaker a few seconds after being typed into a laptop or tablet.

Keith Davey, founder of Marino Software in Dublin, and Trevor Vaugh, Assistant Professor at the Department of Design Innovation in NUI Maynooth, are the men behind the pioneering voice-banking system. It is far more advanced than the artificial computerized voices used by the likes of Stephen Hawking in the past.

My speaking voice was already imperfect when I met Keith and Trevor, but I was also very fortunate that the RTÉ archives contained nearly forty years of radio and TV recordings of my voice. Claire took on the massive project of going through the hundreds of hours of recordings to isolate words that would be used to create the voice bank. She spent six weeks harvesting words and phrases from thousands of my broadcasts that were stored in the archives. Keith and Trevor then fed three hours of clean audio of my recorded words into a computer, where advanced algorithms analyzed and stored them.

The results were miraculous. Claire and I were astounded by the quality of the reproductions. The words I typed on my laptop emerged within seconds through an app. It was almost impossible to notice even a micro-gap between the words. The algorithms had spliced them together seamlessly from the voice bank that Claire had harvested from the recordings of my voice in the RTÉ archives. From a standing start in November, Keith and Trevor developed a voice bank that enabled me to compose sentences on my keyboard that emerged as my nearly perfect cloned voice through my iPad. We hoped that we might also be able to install a similar app on my mobile phone that I could use to communicate with family and friends.

In the depths of my own despair, I began to wonder if this pioneering Irish technology would end the silent torture of people with voice problems everywhere. I can only hope that people with voice issues like mine will get the same opportunity as me, if their voices could be recorded before they deteriorated.

3. SHOW

In the weeks after my diagnosis my family and friends rallied round to support me, and messages from strangers buoyed me, but I struggled badly, trying to absorb the reality of having a terminal illness. But two appearances on *The Late Late Show*, one shortly before and one shortly after Christmas 2021, dramatically altered my attitude towards my disease and towards the remainder of my life.

My appearance on the show on Friday, 10 December 2021, was at a very low point in my illness. Claire and I had been reeling in shock and despair since the confirmation, just eight weeks earlier, that I had MND. Claire and my daughters had wisely dissuaded me from accepting an invitation to appear on the show immediately after my diagnosis was confirmed in mid-October. Claire had the additional difficulty that, as a behind-the-camera RTÉ employee, she was going to be in the spotlight talking about her husband's terminal illness.

The Late Late Show, which is said to be the longest-running TV chat show in the world, has been a constant presence in my life and career. It was one of the first programmes I worked on when I joined RTÉ as a researcher in the early 1970s and I had made several guest appearances on the show during my career as a journalist.

I had worked with Gay Byrne, the show's first and best-known host, when I was a *Late Late Show* researcher, and I was a guest on the show when he presented it for the last time on 21 May 1999 after 38 years at the helm. That was the night that Bono and U2 presented him with the Harley Davidson motorbike that he then went on to ride around the roads of south Dublin in the years after he retired. One of my first jobs as a researcher on the show was to help prepare a programme about the Irish community in London. I had to trace three people and brief them about the programme and then I had to brief Gay and the team about the guests. My three were Liam Brady, then an up-and-coming footballer with Arsenal, champion jockey Jonjo O'Neill and the prolific romance novelist Barbara Cartland.

Gay was a kind and friendly man. He encouraged me throughout my subsequent career. I cannot recall ever appearing on the show when he was the host, but I do remember getting a great scoop from him early in my career as a journalist. I marched into his office one afternoon and demanded an answer from him on whether he was about the leave RTÉ to join a new national commercial radio station that was being set up by a friend of his, Oliver Barry. He said that he was not commenting to anybody, but when I continued to press him, he told me that he was considering a very attractive offer from his friend. He then told me to 'Fuck off' out of his office – but he had given me a scoop. It was the top story on the *Nine*

O'Clock News, immediately before that night's show, and it led to the RTÉ Director General ringing me to find out what exactly Gay had told me.

I was also a guest on the show after Pat Kenny succeeded Gay Byrne as presenter in 1999. I alarmed my RTÉ News bosses and the Garda Síochána on one show by recounting how I had smuggled a quarter of a million dollars in cash into Kenya, via Dublin and Paris, for the Third World charity GOAL. I also appeared on the show a number of times after Ryan Tubridy took over as host in 2009. He interviewed me about life and love shortly before I married Claire in 2016. I brought Tiger onto the show with me a couple of years later when the Irish Society for the Prevention of Cruelty to Animals wanted to highlight the issue of unregulated 'puppy farms'.

The Late Late Show had been a recurring staple of my life since my teenage years, as a viewer and as an occasional guest. The 10 December 2021 programme turned out to be the most important of my several appearances on the show, although for an entirely unplanned and unexpected reason. Although I was stressed and unsure that my voice would hold out, I agreed to go onto the show with Claire to chat generally about the evolution of my illness and about my reaction to the confirmed diagnosis. The recent diagnosis had changed my life, but that appearance on *The Late Late Show* changed the whole direction of what was happening to me as well.

I ought to have been relaxed and calm before the show, even if I was still trying to come to terms with my illness. The RTÉ television building was where I had spent most of my working life. I was on familiar territory, going into a studio I knew so well to talk to a former colleague I had known for years. Claire and I arrived into the TV building with Tiger shortly after 9.00 p.m., even though we were not due on air until about 11.00 p.m. for the last two segments of the show.

I could not relax. I was pacing around with Tiger non-stop in the hospitality room that we were assigned. The ten friends that I was allowed to invite began to arrive in dribs and drabs, but I could only give each of them a cursory greeting because I wanted to spare my voice and my composure. I was also trying to focus on what I might say to Ryan before my voice and emotions would make it too difficult to keep talking to him. The face masks we all had to wear because of COVID-19 added to the uneasy and very unfamiliar atmosphere in the hospitality room. I knew that Ryan would not be keen on allowing Tiger onto the set with me, so a young staff member was press-ganged into walking our dog around the RTÉ campus while Claire and I were doing the interview.

While waiting with Claire in an ante-room, I met Daniel O'Donnell for the first time. He approached us very tentatively when he was leaving the set after his interview. I'm afraid that I replied to him very briefly because I was preoccupied with thoughts of how I would cope during my own interview. I was still petrified about what my disease had done to me and uncertain about what it would do to me in the near and middle future. My mindset was that this was going to be my last appearance on *The Late Late Show* and that I would be dead in a few months.

I spoke briefly to Ryan when he came off the set during the commercial break before our segment. I told him that this was probably the last time in my life that I would be in his studio. I said that I had only one request – that he should be his normal self and shoot straight questions at me without fear or favour. He said that both of us should speak from our hearts.

Once on the set, I was oblivious to the Christmas tree and festive lights all around me. Ryan let me give lengthy answers to each of his questions. I spoke as if it really was my last opportunity to speak on *The Late Late Show*, or on any show. I wanted what I said to be as clear and as honest as it could be.

In reply to Ryan's first question, I said that I was feeling 'so-so, not great' but that what was important was that I was alive and still here. I acknowledged that I cried every day because of my condition, but I said that there were people watching the show who were probably going through the same thing. They and I were going to have to be brave.

I emphasized that I was far from being the only person going through a difficult time. I pointed out that there were thousands of people waiting for hospital appointments or operations. My final wish, I said, would be that Ireland, as a country, should try to make sure that it looked after everybody who was ill. I hoped that the Irish people, collectively, could help Professor Orla Hardiman and others who were trying to find a cure for MND, Parkinson's and other diseases. I wanted to use whatever time I had left on Earth to help other people.

Claire sitting beside me throughout the interview was hugely comforting. She had never appeared on the show before, but her calmness steadied me. I had always been relaxed and casual when I had appeared on the show in the past, but this was entirely different. I could not have done that show without Claire beside me. I remember her gently rubbing my back when I broke down and cried. She also told Ryan about our meeting with Professor Hardiman. She recalled crying all through the long drive home to Wicklow and she said that she then cried all through that night after googling what Professor Hardiman had outlined. I was filled with pride and love when she added: 'Then the next morning I said, I better get up and take control of what's happening . . . any problem Charlie has, I'm on it. We have a great team that are looking after us. There's a nurse, Bernie, who's amazing.'

When Ryan asked me about the future, I was fearful that I probably would have no voice in three or four months. I was losing weight every week at the time and I was genuinely convinced that I would not be alive for Christmas 2022. I was wondering if I would ever see Claire and my grandchildren opening Christmas presents again. I said I would deal with whatever was written in the stars but that at the moment, I was coming out fighting. I had suspected for many months that my symptoms pointed to MND, but I had tried to hide my condition, and my conviction, from my friends and neighbours.

The hardest issue raised by Ryan was about my thoughts on assisted suicide. I was still struggling with the question at that time and I had not made up my mind about it. I had been a long-time supporter of the suicide-prevention services of Pieta House, and I was struggling with the question. What made it so difficult was that I knew I wanted to spend as much time as possible with my family and friends. I wanted Claire and my two daughters to be with me for as long as possible. I wanted to see all of my five grandchildren – Charlie, Hugo, Harriet, Abigail and Edward – grow up.

I had not at that time told Claire or my daughters about my darkest fears. I did not want to add to their worries by hinting that I might not be able to cope with my condition and might want to end it all quickly. I now think that my comments on assisted suicide, and my remarks about not wanting to end up in a wheelchair, might have been too frank and too candid for them and for some viewers. I answered off the top of my head, too, when I revealed the names of the two songs I wanted played at my funeral: Bruce Springsteen's 'Land of Hope and Dreams' and the traditional song 'The Parting Glass'.

After a commercial break, three of my former Newsroom colleagues spoke about our work together. It was emotional to hear from them and some of their tales were comforting and funny, despite the sorrowful state that I was in. After George Lee, Joe O'Brien and Sean O'Rourke had spoken from their socially distanced seats in the front row, Antoinette Keegan, of the Stardust relatives group, spoke to support me from the second row. So too did Austin Hallahan, who had sent me a powerful letter after I went public about my illness, and who was sitting a few seats away with his partner, Edwina. A further few seats away was Karl Hayden, who had become a good friend of mine during the Marriage Equality campaign. In the third row, sending positive energy my way, were my old Newsroom pals Samantha Libreri, Dympna Moroney and Ray Burke. I was glad that I had invited ten friends to sit in the audience. Their presence and encouragement were a great distraction and comfort.

In reply to a question from Ryan, I said, again off the top of my head and without forethought, that I would like to climb Croagh Patrick before I died. I had suggested it to a few close friends after my diagnosis was confirmed, but only a couple of them had promised to accompany me. I think that they and I were not sure how quickly my illness would progress, or even if I would be physically capable of climbing any mountain or hill by the following springtime. I think that I wanted to prove to myself that I could still do it. I felt that I would climb any mountain while I had the energy to do it. I had unwittingly started a campaign that quickly snowballed over the following weeks and months.

I had been thinking about Croagh Patrick now and again because the COVID-19 restrictions had kept me and my west of Ireland friends away from the walks and reunions that we had been planning at the start of 2020, but it hadn't even crossed my mind while I was pacing around the RTÉ Television Centre with Tiger before the show. I didn't realize it at the time, but before the interview was over I had, quite inadvertently, stumbled onto a project that would take over most of my waking hours for the next four months.

I broke down at the end of the show, when Ryan said that the internet had 'essentially melted with love' in reaction to my appearance. Ryan and I shared a tight and lingering embrace when we came off the set as I continued to cry freely. Ryan was getting emotional, too. Everyone, including Claire, stepped back and allowed Ryan and me to cling to one another, crying. He promised that he would do anything he could to help me.

Daniel O'Donnell was standing at his dressing-room door as Claire and I returned to our room to collect our coats. He had watched me being interviewed by Ryan. As I was walking past him, he reached out his hand and pressed something into mine. I didn't look at what he had given me until I returned to our own room. It was rosary beads that he had brought back from the pilgrimage village of Medjugorje in Bosnia and Herzegovina. It was his own personal set of beads, engraved with his name and that of his wife, Majella. He said he had been moved to give them to me after watching my interview. I am not a religious person, but I was so affected by his gesture that I promised myself I would carry the beads with me everywhere for the rest of my life.

Our drive home was sombre, matching the bleak mid-winter darkness, but Claire and I also felt the first hint of the broad public reaction to my appearance. It had been a painful evening, but it had ended with a spark of hope-fulness.

Next morning, I wrote on Twitter that I had cried tears of joy at the overwhelming support I had received during and after my *Late Late Show* appearance. I promised that if I was still mobile in the springtime, I would climb Croagh Patrick to highlight MND and other terminal illnesses. I invited people to join me.

I was feeling much better when I was invited back onto the show a month later, on 7 January 2022, even though my voice and my general condition had deteriorated further by then. Claire had not told me that the entire show was being devoted to me. I was surprised when I arrived into the TV Centre at Donnybrook to be handed a package containing 150 beautiful coloured drawings of footprints that had been posted to me by the boys and girls of Scoil Phádraig, Newport Road, Westport, the nearest town to Croagh Patrick.

In an accompanying letter, the children said they could see the Reek from their classrooms and playground and they promised: 'We will be walking with you in spirit every day'. They said that they had been told that I was sick and they added: 'We know it's not a small sickness like a sore throat or a tummy bug. We understand that it's bigger than that. We think that it is so cool that even though you are feeling unwell, you are going to come and climb Croagh Patrick – it takes a big heart to think about helping others when you are not feeling so great yourself. We learn a lot in Scoil Phádraig about helping others, and doing the right thing even when it isn't easy.'

Each of the coloured footprints they sent me carried the name of the child who had drawn it. 'As you prepare for the climb and especially on the difficult days, we thought you might like to pick a few footprints from children in our school to accompany you on your journey,' the letter said.

The children also promised that every class in the school would take turns to walk a Daily Mile route around the school so as to be with me in spirit as I prepared to climb Croagh Patrick in April. They said that they wanted to share their school motto 'Ar Aghaid le Chéile' – Going Forward Together – with me. The letter was a wonderful boost and I resolved to try to go to Westport in January to walk the Daily Mile route with them.

That 7 January *Late Late Show*, which Ryan Tubridy billed as the formal launch of 'Climb With Charlie', began with the Clew Bay Pipe Band, which includes one of the Scoil Phadraigh teachers, Nicole Gannon, performing outside Studio 5. With Tiger on my lap I told Ryan that I wanted the climb, now fixed for Saturday April 2, to be a major fundraiser for the Irish Motor Neurone Association and Pieta and also to help people with other terminal illnesses like Parkinson's and multiple sclerosis.

I told Ryan about the large number of letters from all over Ireland that had been arriving at my home. I said that I was crying less frequently than before Christmas and that the support of people had been unbelievable and had lifted me a lot, mentally and spiritually.

I said that I had found peace over the past few weeks. I had been crying every day since I got my diagnosis, but I was no longer doing that. I was not as afraid now, or as broken, as I had been when I first got my diagnosis. I wanted to do something, not for me, but for other people.

Claire was sitting in the front row of the audience and Tiger was sitting on my lap for much of the show. But when the floor manager saw that Tiger was obstructing my view of Ryan and of the camera, he took him from me and dropped him onto Claire's lap during a commercial break.

Claire, Neasa and Orla spoke about how I was changing as the weeks passed. Claire also spoke about the voice app that was being created from recordings of my broadcast voice and that I would be using it to communicate when

I was no longer able to speak. We heard a sample and it sounded amazing.

The secret was out now and I realized that the entire show was devoted to me and to the launch of Climb With Charlie. I could only sit back and watch what followed. Vicky Phelan was unable to travel to Dublin for the show, but she sent a video message in which she repeated that she hoped to join me on the climb. Former President of Ireland Mary McAleese and 91-year-old retired broadcaster Mícheál Ó Muircheartaigh also sent similar video messages. All-Ireland hurling winner and now trainer Davy Fitzgerald sent another video message, urging people to climb any local peak for the two charities on the day if they were unable to travel to Mayo.

Donie O'Sullivan, the young CNN reporter from Kerry who became well known after his live reporting on the storming of the Capitol Building in Washington DC on 6 January 2021, sent a video from the United States wishing me well and recalling how he had met me in the RTÉ Newsroom when he had blagged his way in there as a transition-year student.

My friend and sometime Wicklow neighbour John Fitzpatrick, owner of Fitzpatrick's Hotel on Lexington Avenue in Manhattan, New York, interrupted his Christmas and New Year holiday at home to come onto the show and recall how I had arrived into his hotel a couple of days after the 9/11 Twin Towers attacks, having raced to New York from Colombia in South America via Mexico. With all US-bound airline flights banned, I had literally walked into the United States at the border crossing between Juárez in Mexico and El Paso in Texas. I then got a flight from El Paso to Heuston, Texas, and onwards to New York.

Dr Harry Barry, the mental health wellbeing advocate and author, and my former RTÉ colleague and pal Tommie Gorman, also cheered me up with inspiring contributions about the benefits of walking and climbing. The personal trainer Karl Henry gave advice on how to prepare for the climb and on what to wear. The TV presenters Baz Ashmawy and Dermot Bannon also appeared and promised to join me on the climb. The meteorologist and RTÉ weather presenter Joanna Donnelly said that she always brought good weather with her and she forecast that 2 April would be a fine day.

By the end of the show, it had begun to dawn on me that something unique was going to happen on the second day of April, not just on Croagh Patrick but right across Ireland and further afield. Even though my voice was deteriorating rapidly, and I knew that I would soon need to use the app to communicate, I felt a definite spark about the future. I knew that I would be busy for the next few months at least and that I would have little time for retreating into gloom and despair. I had found a new and firm focus – an unspoken and unexpected new year's resolution.

The December programme had not been my last appearance on that show, after all. Instead, it had unexpectedly and unintentionally given Claire and me a new impetus and a noble purpose that would keep us fully occupied seven days a week for the next three months and into the springtime and summer of 2022.

RTÉ's longest-running television programme, where I had worked as a young researcher at the start of my career, became the launchpad nearly fifty years later for the Climb With Charlie project. The *Late Late Show* team, many of whom had not been born when I was working with Gay Byrne on the programme in the mid-1970s, were leaders among the people who helped to kickstart and drive the campaign, perhaps my last major undertaking.

4. MOUNTAIN

'This is no place for seniors or middle-aged men,' warned the writer and surgeon Oliver St. John Gogarty of Croagh Patrick. He climbed the Reek at nearly sixty years of age while researching his 1938 book, *I Follow Saint Patrick*. He recalled resting several times to catch his breath while being overtaken by 'pilgrims in endless procession shuffling up along the precipitous path, which was composed of loose stones, grey and greasy with the fog'.

The Kerry writer and journalist Alice Curtayne (1901–1981) was even more off-putting in a pamphlet that Gogarty purchased at the summit. 'Is there anywhere in the world a more toilsome prayer, a more punishing prayer, a more gruelling or a more humbling prayer than this annual appeal to Patrick?' she asked, adding: 'And is there anywhere a more fearful mountain? Whatever this strange mountain was made for, normally it was surely never meant to be climbed... Nothing ruder than this journey can possibly be imagined: It demands everything the pilgrim has; the last shred of his resolve, the last ounce of his physical reserve, the last gasp of his wind, the uttermost of his capacity for prayer... It would be unnecessary to recommend silence on this journey, so thoroughly do conditions enforce it. The physical distress is too acute, the breathing too laboured for conversation.'

It was a daunting description of what I would be facing in April, but I was determined to attempt it. I had climbed the famous Co Mayo 'Reek', known as 'Ireland's Holy Mountain', three times previously. I climbed it twice in two days when I returned from a foreign assignment some years ago and I climbed it with Claire in 2016 after our wedding that summer. I vowed in 2016 that I would never do it again, but the new urge became much more forceful and persistent after my diagnosis.

Croagh Patrick, with its conical summit, has been a magnet for climbers and pilgrims since time immemorial. Saint Patrick fasted on the mountain for 40 days and 40 nights on his way to the most westerly extremity of his Irish sojourn on Caher Island (Cathair Phádraigh), between Clare Island and Inishturk, in the year 440 AD, according to folklore. During my childhood in the middle decades of the last century, an estimated 60,000 people did the climb each year on 'Reek Sunday', the last Sunday in July.

This annual climb on that last Sunday of July was officially revived as a Catholic pilgrimage by the Archdiocese of Tuam at the beginning of the twentieth century, following the discovery in the Vatican of a Papal document dated 27 September 1432, in which Pope Eugene IV granted indulgences to those who ascended Croagh Patrick on the Sunday preceding the Feast of St Peter's Chains, which falls on 1 August.

'Reek Sunday' pilgrim numbers had fallen over the decades to about 25,000 annually in the years before Covid-19, but growing numbers of people were climbing the mountain all year round, as a physical challenge, if not a spiritual one. Pre-Christian traditions may have related to harvest rituals and to the mountain's conical shape and its vistas over the surrounding landscape. People from Westport and its environs have maintained their own local tradition of doing the climb on the Friday before 'Reek Sunday', called 'Garland Friday'.

I knew very well that the climb would not be easy. I was nearly six months past my seventy-second birthday and I could no longer complete the 10-mile walks that had been my near daily habit. But the preparations were ramping up and I started to plan the climb in earnest. I contacted Fr Charlie McDonnell, the priest responsible for the church on the Croagh Patrick summit. I decided that it would be a fundraiser for two charities: the Irish Motor Neurone Disease Association and Pieta, the mental health and bereavement counselling service.

Even before I had confirmed the climb date on *The Late Late Show* in January, the Chief of Staff of the Defence Forces, Lieutenant General Seán Clancy, rang to offer any support that he or his members could give me on the climb. And within days of my appearance on the show, the bosses at Dunnes Stores said they would support the climb with a fundraising campaign in all their stores countrywide.

I was getting busier and busier with all the planning when I got the shattering news of the death of my dear friend and former colleague, Jim Fahy. I knew that Jim had been unwell since the beginning of winter, but I was shocked to the core by his death. I learned later that he had watched my *Late Late Show* appearance with his family in his bedroom, exactly a week before he breathed his last breath.

Jim was RTÉ's longest-serving Regional Correspondent and he was an outstanding colleague. We worked together in the west of Ireland many times and I spent a month working with him in New York every day after the Twin Towers terrorist attacks in 2001. He had arrived via Canada, having got one of the first flights from Europe to Toronto while US-bound flights were still banned. I'll never forget his kindness and his work rate during those weeks. I delivered the latest news from the search site at the World Trade Center each day, while Jim mined his extensive contacts and connections among New York's Irish community to produce unforgettable, raw and emotional testament from firefighters, police and community stalwarts. His television documentary, *Sept 11th – Stories from the Twin Towers,* won several gold medal awards in the United States for its portrayal of three New York families – two Irish and one Irish-American – whose lives were changed forever by the Twin Towers attacks.

I remembered too that, by an amazing coincidence, Reek Sunday had been the very first event that Jim was assigned to cover after he was appointed RTÉ's first Western News Correspondent in the mid-1970s. This was twenty or thirty years before pictures and voice reports could be fed directly to Dublin from satellite vans or from laptops. RTÉ's regional reporters in Belfast, Cork and Galway had to have their pictures and voice recordings ready by 2.30 p.m. to send them by train to Heuston Station in Dublin, from where an RTÉ messenger would race to Donnybrook to get the material to an editing suite in time for the evening bulletins. Since fewer trains ran on Sundays, RTÉ News hired a light aircraft to collect Jim and his footage at Castlebar Airport and fly him directly to Dublin, where he would be able to edit his filmed report in time for the evening TV bulletins.

I remember Jim telling me how he had raced from Croagh Patrick to Castlebar by car and climbed onto the expensively hired aircraft. He began writing the script for his first big RTÉ News story and he did not look out of the aircraft's window for 10 or 15 minutes. When he did, he was shocked by what he saw. From his years working for the *Tuam Herald* newspaper and later for RTÉ Radio, he knew every highway and byway in Connacht. He saw instantly that the plane was flying south over the Plains of Mayo and Claremorris, towards Tuam and Galway, instead of heading east towards Dublin. He roared at the pilot, who told him not to worry as he was following the railway line. Jim had to tell him that he was following a north–south railway line instead of an east–west one.

After that exciting TV news debut, Jim covered Reek Sunday for RTÉ News almost every year for most of the next forty years. He knew every inch of the climb in sunshine and in rain. He once brought a camera crew and a producer up and down the mountain with him three times in two days to shoot an RTÉ *Nationwide* programme.

Along with my former workmates and many people throughout the West and elsewhere in Ireland, I was heart-broken when I heard that Jim had died after a short illness. We had been in regular contact until the final weeks of his life. From his deathbed he had watched Tommie

Gorman and me on the *Late Late Show* referring to our friendship with him.

Jim's funeral mass was celebrated on Monday, 17 January 2022 in the Cathedral of the Assumption of the Blessed Virgin Mary in Tuam, the seat of the Archdiocese of Tuam, which covers Croagh Patrick. It was one of the saddest and most heartbreaking days of my life. I sat with a large number of former RTÉ News colleagues. I broke down more than once when Jim's daughter, Aideen, recalled in her eulogy how the family had watched the *Late Late Show* in Jim's bedroom on their last night of normalcy after they had learned that his fight could not be won. She thanked Tommie and me for talking about loss on the show and helping Jim on his hardest day. She assured our WestAwake group that Jim's spirit would be with us climbing mountains in future, as he had been with us so many times in the past.

Aideen's comments brought home to me that the climb would be even more meaningful than I had been imagining. I knew that Jim would be with me in spirit every step of the way, on every single one of the steps that he himself had trodden so many times.

Later that week the www.climbwithcharlie.ie campaign went global when I got a lovely message from some Irish people in New York who were organizing a climb there. I could feel that the cause was being taken to people's hearts, and it was a tremendous feeling.

I travelled to Mayo to join the pupils in three Westport schools who were among the earliest supporters of Climb With Charlie. They had sent me their heartfelt support on the paper footprints given to me at the *Late Late Show*. I met them on Friday, 21 January 2022 and it was one of the most incredible days of my life. Claire and Tiger and I joined several hundred children from Scoil Phádraig, the Quay National School and the National School in Murrisk as they promised to continue to support every step of our Croagh Patrick climb.

In the Scoil Phadráig playground they sang a 'special song' for me, composed bilingually around their school motto: *Ar Aghaidh le Chéile*. Their song used the air of the well-known and very catchy 1988 hit by the Scottish duo The Proclaimers, 'I'm Gonna Be (500 Miles)'. Its rousing chorus says:

> *Ar Aghaidh le Chéile is what we say*
> *We're right behind you all the way*
> *We'll make it to Croagh Patrick's top*
> *So come on, show us what you've got.*

Before joining the children on their Daily Mile walk, I thanked them from the bottom of my heart for what they were doing for me. I had been to the South Pole and to the North Pole and all around the world over the previous forty years, but I had never received such a reception. I urged them to be kind, to make people happy and to put their arms around anyone who needed help. I told them that their love and support had lifted me from a very dark place and that I was the happiest man on the planet that morning.

School Principal Fergus Seoighe told the children: 'On mornings when Charlie doesn't want to get out of bed, he can look at all the footprints made by you and Ms McGreal and that will help him.'

I knew that these children would remember this day. I guessed that they would talk about it among themselves and with their families. Some of them might someday decide that they too wanted to travel the world and visit the North and South Poles, or some of them might decide that they wanted to be journalists, or to study medicine or science so that they might find a cure for the disease that was crippling and distressing this man who came to visit their school.

By the beginning of February more than €200,000 had been raised for the two charities and nearly 700 people had pledged to climb a mountain at some 45 locations. We had launched an updated www.climbwithcharlie.ie website on the first day of February. I travelled to Westport again, with Tiger, to record a video of me and him walking towards Croagh Patrick and looking up at the cloud-shrouded peak. We also included in the video a new caricature of me on the peak, drawn by Niall O'Loughlin. I had never met Niall, but he readily agreed to our use of his caricature. I'm sure that his image of me will be around long after I'm gone. The video was viewed nearly 50,000 times in the days after we posted it on Twitter.

The Taoiseach, Micheál Martin, told me that he had been very taken by what I had said on the *Late Late Show*. Climb With Charlie was mentioned by the Tánaiste and Minister for Enterprise, Trade and Employment, Leo Varadkar TD, when he announced government funding of €5 million, via Science Foundation Ireland, for research into MND. His announcement followed a pledge by another government minister, Eamon Ryan TD, Minister for Environment, Climate and Communications, in the Dáil in mid-February that he would seek cabinet approval for increased funding for research into MND and help for sufferers.

I found it hard to believe that our efforts had already come to the attention of the country's top politicians and that my name and my plans were mentioned in the Dáil barely five weeks after we had launched the campaign. I began to think that we might be able to raise a sizeable sum of money.

When he made his pledge, Minister Ryan was responding to a question by a Mayo TD, Alan Dillon, who complained about the paucity of existing resources for MND sufferers in the west of Ireland. Deputy Dillon said: 'As people prepare together at Mayo's Croagh Patrick and countless other hills and mountains around the country to climb with Charlie Bird, it is important to highlight the need to increase funding and support for those living with MND. University Hospital Galway is the western regional centre for neurology but is short of neurology nurse specialists.'

I was shocked and upset by Dillon's claims that MND patients in the west of Ireland were enduring long waits for diagnosis and treatment and that University Hospital Galway had only four nurse neurology specialists when it should have had thirteen, based on its catchment area. I knew that my own wait for diagnosis and treatment had seemed cruel and interminable, despite my medical insurance policy and my contacts. I shuddered to think about the agonies and uncertainties faced by public patients who did not have the privileges that I had. I was anxious to raise as much money as possible to help those who needed it most.

Away from the Dáil, preparations for the climb were gathering momentum. Daniel O'Donnell repeated his offer to climb with me in a video he tweeted. Bono from U2, who I had known since I had interviewed them about their concert at the Lincoln Memorial in Washington in 2009, contacted me to say that I could use an excerpt from one of their songs from that year, 'I'll go crazy if I don't go crazy tonight', to promote the climb. 'You are an eternal spirit,' he told me in an e-mail. 'Your coverage in DC and around the world [is] legend in our house. MND is unfortunately all too well known to us in the U2 family. Let me figure out how best to support you on this heroic climb.'

He added the words of his song's chorus. Like that of the Westport Scoil Phádraig's 'Ar Aghaidh le Chéile', it is very catchy and apposite. It says:

> It's not a hill, it's a mountain
> As you start out the climb
> Do you believe me, or are you doubting
> We're gonna make it all the way to the light?

At a meeting on 7 February, Sligo County Council agreed to record a vote congratulating Vicky Phelan and me for undertaking the climb. The motion, proposed by Cllr Dara Mulvey and seconded by Cllr Joe Queenan, said that our efforts showed 'an amazing degree of concern and empathy for others'. It said that our courage was commendable and should be acknowledged and applauded. It urged as many people as possible to support the climb and donate to the two charities.

South Dublin County Council passed a similar motion a few weeks later, commending and saluting my fundraising and praising the dignity with which they said I was proving an example for other MND sufferers.

The singer and songwriter Damian Dempsey called me 'the warrior Charlie' and said he would climb a local mountain in solidarity with me on 2 April. He also very generously offered to come to my house to sing for me, to cheer me up.

The great flautist Matt Molloy, a co-founder of The Bothy Band and long-serving flute player with The Chieftains, sent me a video of him playing a reel called 'The Mountain Top'. He said that he planned to be on the top of Croagh Patrick with me to raise funds for the two charities and to support one of his musician friends, Noel Kilkenny from Castlebar, who had also been diagnosed with motor neurone disease.

Another singer-songwriter, Imelda May, posted a wonderful video on Twitter, saying that she wished she could join us on the day, but she would be on tour in Wales. She said she would climb some local mountain there, or maybe even just a staircase, to help raise funds for the two charities which, she said, did such special and important work. She urged everyone to join the climb.

On the same day I met the actor Gabriel Byrne and he promised his support. He went on Twitter to say that the climb was 'incredibly worthwhile and important'. He said that what Claire and I were doing was 'courageous and inspirational'. He said that the climb was about solidarity, friendship and joining together to raise funds for the charities.

On 17 February, the transition-year students in Nagle Community College in Cork city raised over €1,000 and promised even more after they climbed Galteemore for the two charities. The Scoil Phádraig children walked 1,000 miles, over 10,000 footsteps, in the month after my visit to them. Someone sent me a poem entitled, 'Light a torch for Charlie'.

Barely five weeks after we had announced it, everybody seemed to be getting involved, from schoolchildren to rock stars and celebrities at home and abroad. From a standing start in the second week of January, our campaign had already gathered a momentum beyond my wildest dreams. I was beginning to feel optimistic about the climb.

The torrential rain that followed Storm Eunice and that came with Storm Franklin did not deter Claire and me from doing a 10 km walk on Sunday, 20 February. On our way we got a great surprise to see a big canvas banner outside our local pub, the Chester Beatty Inn, calling for support for Climb With Charlie. The pub owners, Padraig and Mari Humby, and their staff had shown me nothing but endless kindness over the years, and especially since my suffering began, and I was bowled over by the great poster.

Four weeks before the climb, the total raised topped half-a-million euro (€506,649.59) and 922 people had promised to take part at 110 locations. And the Galway-headquartered fast food chain Supermac's came on board with a countrywide radio campaign supporting the climb.

On Saturday, 5 March, exactly four weeks before the climb, Claire and I trekked halfway up Croagh Patrick. It was challenging and it reinforced my belief that the climb itself would be difficult. But it was a beautiful, clear, if cold, early-spring day and the sight of Clew Bay as we descended was magical.

An amazing song was composed to accompany the campaign, 'Shine A Light', written by Sara Noone and Michael English. It went to number 1 on the iTunes Irish singles charts on the day after it was released. It was sung by Michael English and recorded by the RTÉ Concert Orchestra and a choir that included dozens of my former RTÉ colleagues. It was such a powerful song that it made me cry every time I heard it.

Throughout the month of March, I broke down and cried several times every day. The doctors told me that this was one of the symptoms of MND, but I'm sure it was also due to the emotions raised in me by the love and generosity that was being sent to me from all over the country. People from all kinds of backgrounds and with all levels of incomes were putting money into the fund, from young people in Westport to the financier Dermot Desmond, who I met in mid-March. I was amazed and humbled as the donations kept coming.

By St Patrick's Day, two weeks and two days before the climb, the amount pledged was €567,516.72. Some 922 people had promised to climb on the day at 135 locations. The money pledged topped €750,000 at the beginning of the last week before the climb. A week later I took a few hours away from my Climb With Charlie activities to join my former colleagues in the National Union of Journalists in a protest outside the Russian Embassy in Dublin about the suffering Russia was inflicting on the people of Ukraine.

I am not a religious person. I don't follow any organized religion and, as I will explain in a later chapter, I'm more agnostic than anything else. But I do believe in goodness, and something strange happened to me as Climb With Charlie moved forward and support kept pouring in from all kinds of people. Practically from the outset of this notion of doing the climb, everything seemed to fall into place. My own pilgrim's progress was well underway. I felt during January, February and March that there was some external force or spirit moving me forward in this whole idea every single day. The support of strangers showed me that the world is full of good and decent people.

Throughout those three hectic months of planning there was only one, brief occasion when I felt it might not happen. It was suggested at a planning meeting with the community in Murrisk, at the foot of the Reek, that only my immediate family and close friends should accompany me. Locals were concerned about car parking, stewarding and the need for first aid. But the two people who had played a key role in getting the project underway in Murrisk and Westport were Fr Charlie McDonnell, who is based in the Westport Parish, and Garda Inspector Denis Harrington, who is stationed in Westport. Both men were crucial in linking us up with the people of Westport and with the community in Murrisk. It was because of their interventions that we knew on the days leading up to the climb that everyone was on board to help us, not just in

Mayo but in the almost 240 other locations around Ireland and abroad.

Claire, Tiger and I got a thoroughly warm and friendly reception when we arrived back down in Westport three days before the climb. The schools and communities could not have been more welcoming. Our only big worry was what the weather would be like on the day itself, following two full weeks of unusually warm and dry spring days and nights in the West.

The ability to solve one of our last logistical problems was also weather-dependent. We needed to get all of the musical instruments of the Clew Bay Pipe Band, and all the PA system and broadcasting equipment of Mid-West Radio, to the summit in advance of the climb. Nobody could remember any musical group ever performing on the summit, never mind a forty-member pipe and reed band. And nobody could be expected to climb the Reek carrying delicate bagpipes or a big bass drum. Once again, Fr McDonnell and Inspector Harrington solved the problem quietly and efficiently with the help of the Defence Forces Chief of Staff, Lieutenant General Seán Clancy.

Lieutenant General Clancy had contacted me out of the blue back in December to offer any help needed and also to offer to accompany me on the climb. He even gave me a medal bearing his name to carry with me on the Reek. Now, in addition to the services of the Army Reserve during the Saturday climb, he also deployed an Aer Corps helicopter to provide emergency first-aid flights, if necessary, and to ferry the band and broadcast equipment to the summit on Friday, weather permitting.

We were in luck when the sun shone on Friday. The Aer Corps chopper was able to make a number of flights with the equipment to the summit from the Murrisk field in which stands the haunting John Behan 'Famine Ship' memorial sculpture. All of the equipment got to the top safely. Everything fell into place on that Friday.

That afternoon, the children from Scoil Phádraig appeared at the Octagon in Westport, under the lovely statue of St Patrick in the centre of the town, to sing their 'Ar Aghaidh le Chéile' song again in front of a large gathering of townspeople and visitors. I could not hold back my tears. It was these beautiful children who had sent me the crayon letters and drawings that had greeted me in RTÉ before I went on the *Late Late Show* in January. Less than three months later, here we were on the eve of the climb, and our fundraising had already comfortably exceeded our ambitious target.

Even though it was not yet Easter, throughout the weekend Westport was thronged with people, as if it was high-summer. It carried echoes of the Reek Sundays of the 1930s when, in the words of Oliver St. John Gogarty, it became a town 'into which bus-loads and train-loads of pilgrims had been pouring for two days'. Everywhere I walked, local people and pilgrims stopped me and wished me well on the Reek and on my illness struggle.

At the Hotel Westport, where my family and close friends were staying for the weekend, the *Late Late Show* production team were rigging up a room for a live broadcast when Claire and I sat down for dinner with Daniel O'Donnell and two of my closest RTÉ friends, George Lee and Dympna Moroney. I got a bad coughing fit during our meal, not that

I needed any more reminders of my perilous and worsening health condition. Unexpected and frightening coughing fits like this were happening more often. A happy meal with good friends turned into a bout of terror and embarrassment. I knew that this was an unavoidable facet of my illness, but it always upset me and terrified me. At those moments of distress, it was of little consolation to me that I was raising funds and raising awareness about the dreadful illness that was progressively weakening my muscles.

Despite that scare, my excitement was mounting as more friends and family arrived at the hotel. The atmosphere was really special. The first pictures of the cheering *Late Late Show* Friday night audience beamed to us from Dublin added to the excitement. Claire and Daniel O'Donnell spoke to Ryan Tubridy via satellite link. My first-born grandson, Charlie, was also interviewed from Westport. I was very sorry that Vicky Phelan could not be there with us due to her illness, but her family turned out in force to represent her. It was great to meet her parents and siblings and to hear her sister Lyndsey being interviewed by Ryan.

We worried about the weather during the night, but Saturday dawned sunny and clear, if a little cold, just after 6.30 a.m. Claire and I could see that there was a wisp of cloud on the top of the Reek as we arrived at the car park in Murrisk shortly after 8.00 a.m. Claire had arranged buses for most of our family and friends to be brought out to Murrisk, about 10 km from Westport. Our base was set up at Campbell's, the well-known pub at the foot of the Reek. When we arrived our great pal Inspector Denis Harrington told us that the car park was already full, as was one of the two fields set aside for overflow.

We were told that people had started climbing from 5.00 a.m. It was a huge joy to see my family and close friends already there. I was also delighted to see the RTÉ Director General, Dee Forbes, poised for the climb with former colleagues Joe O'Brien, Dympna Moroney, Carole Coleman, Vivienne Traynor, Eileen Dunne, Fran McNulty and Fergal Keane. Broadcasters Dermot Bannon and Baz Ashmawy were there too, full of good cheer and encouragement, as they would be all day. We had a good laugh when someone shouted that 'the celebs' bus has broken down' to explain their delay in joining us at base camp.

My first task was to do a number of media interviews. As I had little or no voice left, it was a bit strange. The first interview was with a local Mayo TV channel. I had nothing prepared for them, so I tried my best to say a few words and Claire answered some of their questions for me. Then I went to the car park, which was full, and had my photograph taken about a dozen times with people who were just setting off on their climbs.

I then did an interview with my former RTÉ colleague and North West Correspondent Eileen Magnier, who was covering the climb for radio, TV and online for the day. We walked up to the St Patrick's statue, at the start of the climbing path, to do the interview. By this stage, I was using the voice app and it was working very well for me. Every interview I did now involved taking out my iPad and playing my recorded spoken words in response to the interviewer's questions. I was thinking that Eileen must never before have interviewed someone who was non-verbal and able only to nod while their words were coming from an iPad they were holding in their hand.

Again, I got a bit emotional. I had spent my working life interviewing people and I never wanted to be less than fully cooperative with any working journalist. It nearly killed me to be unable to articulate my thoughts and feelings on one of the most important days of my life. I cried with frustration and helplessness on the side of the mountain.

Above me, the mountain reared up, looking higher than ever before.

5. CLIMB

We set off on our climb shortly after 10.00 a.m. Father McDonnell and the Church of Ireland rector, Reverend Jennifer McWhirther, blessed us all at the St Patrick statue and I released a white dove of peace. I could not hide my anxiety about whether I would be able to complete the climb from the many journalists and photographers who accompanied us nearly every step of the way. Living in Wicklow, I was used to hill-climbing, but I wondered how I might cope with a coughing fit, or if my lungs and heart should begin to weaken on the ascent.

I also tried hard to hide my anxiety from my five dear grandchildren, who were skipping along close to me. Orla's children – Charlie, Hugo and Harriet – and Neasa's two – Abigail and Edward – showed no fear, nor did their fathers, Aidan and Rob.

The climb was very tough, both physically and emotionally. Thick black clouds – 'bred on the Atlantic', to use W. B. Yeats's phrase – hit us with a nasty shower of cold rain and sleet before we had reached the halfway point. But I was hugely buoyed as we approached the part of the climb called 'the Shoulder' when I saw dozens of young children from Brackloon National School, which we had visited a day earlier, bunched together with their black and red flags billowing in the wind, waiting for me, and cheering 'Charlie, Charlie'. I cried my eyes out when I reached them and saw that they had spelled out my initials with large stones in the valley below.

Using the tiny bit of my voice I had left, I told them that they were lifting me up the mountain. They had climbed up from the other side of the Reek, where their school is situated, accompanied by their teachers and some of their parents. The fact that they had done this hard enough climb to cheer me on lifted my spirits, and indeed the spirits of the others who were climbing with me. The support and recognition I received from schoolchildren all around the country was one of the most satisfying and enduring accomplishments of the campaign. I was very sorry that my declining health prevented me accepting invitations to visit more schools.

The hardest part of the climb is the cone below the summit. It is covered in shale – loose, hard rocks that give way under your feet. I struggled badly on this gruelling section, despite the proximity of Claire and Inspector Harrington. I would have called him 'my bodyguard', but I had no energy to speak. Stone steps that had recently been inserted on parts of the cone were a help, but I lost my footing at one point and had to climb on all-fours, as did some others.

I was putting all of my energy and all of my concentration into just putting one foot in front of the other at this stage. Some people were already descending near us and saying things like, 'You're nearly there' and 'Ten more minutes', but I could not look at any of them and I did not know if I could believe them. I was afraid to look up, or to look anywhere except down at my feet. I kept telling myself that if I just kept putting one foot in front of the other, I would make it to the top, but I was struggling for strength and for air. I was determined not to let down my family and friends, or any of the thousands of people who had given up their day to climb for charitable causes. The words of my fellow south Dubliner Samuel Beckett came to mind: 'I must go on. I can't go on. I'll go on.'

I was concentrating so hard that I was nearing the summit before I realized it. I had been trudging upwards in my own bubble, not daring to look up. It was the wild cheering that alerted me. I was completely exhausted when I finally saw the white chapel that told me we had reached the summit. It had taken us just over two hours. For as long as I live, I will never forget the sights and sounds that greeted us. Scores of friends and family members were already there, whooping in their yellow day-glow campaign tee-shirts. Among the friends and strangers waiting at the summit for my arrival was Bridget Larkin, aged 62, who had travelled from Ballycumber in County Offaly. 'Only for Charlie Bird, I would never have climbed it. It's my first time,' she told one of my friends.

The Clew Bay Pipe Band, who had helped launch the climb campaign on the *Late Late Show* at the beginning of January, were playing Patrick Kavanagh's 'Raglan Road' to welcome me to the top. It was time, as Kavanagh's poem says, to let grief be a fallen leaf, but I could not help crying for most of my stay on the summit.

Daniel O'Donnell and Ryan Tubridy tried to comfort me with tight hugs and embraces. My grandchildren and my daughters and Claire came close to console me. I had never previously had such close and emotional moments with my grandchildren. I think that they will always have these moments etched in their minds and hearts after I'm gone from this Earth. I love all five of them dearly. I will never forget those moments together either.

The five months since my diagnosis and the three months of the Climb With Charlie campaign had been very tough, but these moments were special and unforgettable. I think that everyone at the summit felt the same. And the Heavens agreed – just after we reached the summit, the clouds moved away and disappeared and the sun came out.

History was being made all around us. An estimated 6,000–7,000 people completed the climb, almost certainly a record for a day in early spring. Never before had a group of musicians as numerous as the Clew Bay Pipe Bank played at the summit. Never in recent history had so many people lingered at the summit on any day other than Reek Sunday. 'This, ladies and gentlemen, is Ireland at its best,' Ryan Tubridy told the crowd, 'a beautiful country, generous people and we are all here because of Charlie Bird . . . when we are asked to do something good, we stand up and are counted . . . we will never forget what we did here together as family and friends . . . thank you, Charlie, for bringing us together like this . . . it's been beautiful. God Bless Ireland. God bless The Bird.'

Daniel O'Donnell said that it was a privilege and a great honour for him and for everyone else to be gathered at the summit 'on this very special day'. He recalled meeting me in the corridor outside the *Late Late Show* studio in December 2021 and being moved by my vulnerability and my strength to do something to help others. He said it was amazing what 'one man and a good woman can do'.

'This is incredible', he added. 'Charlie's journey has been amazing. There has been no story that Charlie has ever told in all his travels that will top his own story of today. As I was walking up and looking around me, I was thinking how one man has united Ireland. I thought if the man who is dividing the world could see this man that is uniting Ireland . . . Charlie, I want you to know that what you are doing is beyond incredible and we stand in amazement and we just stand in awe of you and we are privileged to be with you.'

Claire spoke briefly to thank all of the climbers, volunteers, family members and friends who had completed the climb and who had helped prepare for it over the previous nine weeks. She said she wanted to thank, in particular, the people of Mayo and Fr Charlie McDonnell and Inspector Denis Harrington.

I had to use my iPad and my voice bank to address the crowd. It was another 'first' as my voice boomed out over the holy mountain via the sound system that the Aer Corps had ferried to the top the previous day. As my natural voice was practically gone, I had already prepared and recorded in the days before the climb the words that I was going to transmit once I reached the summit:

So, we have made it to the top of Ireland's holy mountain. This is not just a special moment for me, but what is happening is a tribute to the tens of thousands of people right across Ireland and abroad who have extended the hand of friendship to Climb With Charlie.

Yes, last October when I was diagnosed with a terminal illness, motor neurone, it was a devastating moment for myself and my wife Claire and my family as well. But something amazing has happened since then, and I mean it from my heart: something spiritual has been moving me forward.

Yes, I had a mad idea when, off the top of my head, I told Ryan Tubridy that I wanted to climb Croagh Patrick and what is amazing me now is we have people all across Ireland, in almost 150 locations, and in many places abroad, including the United States, Canada, England, Australia and Dubai, climbing with me. I just want to say here my great colleague Jim Fahy was going to climb with me and Jim, who knew this mountain so well, sadly passed away. But the support that I have received has lifted me in a way which I cannot express in words. But today is not just about me, it is about everyone who has a terminal illness.

And after the last couple of years that we have all gone through with the pandemic, we know that many people have their own personal mountains to climb every day. And what I would like everyone to do today is to extend the hand of friendship, or an elbow, to the people standing beside them.

Remember, we never know what is around the corner for any of us. I have said this before and I mean this: I have no idea how long I am going to survive for, but for every moment that I am around, I am going to continue to extend the hand of friendship.

As a journalist for forty years, I have come across the spirit of generosity of the Irish people many times. But the outpouring of support that I have received over the past few months has stunned me beyond belief. I have received hundreds and hundreds of letters of support from all over Ireland. And all of these people are in my thoughts today. Even though I still cry a lot with my motor neurone, crying is not that unusual. Most times that I cry now is as a result of the kindness that is being extended to me every day. I have made amazing new friends over the past few months and at some stage in the not-too-distant future I am going to thank these people publicly. And these people have been so generous to Climb With Charlie.

In Westport, I have made so many new friends as well. Father Charlie McDonnell is now one of my great pals, as are Harry Hughes, Denis Harrington and Matt Molloy. I have been touched with incredible kindness and the people who have climbed the Reek with me today are showing me so much kindness. But that kindness is being shown all over the country as well. I also want to thank the incredible group of volunteers who came on board to help me.

And all the money that is being donated, and I mean all, is being divided evenly between the two charities that are close to my heart: Pieta, the national organization that helps people with thoughts of self-harm and suicide, and, of course, the Irish Motor Neurone Disease Association, the only voluntary organization in Ireland that looks after people with this dreadful disease. Also, so many organizations are helping us today, the Gardaí, the army, the local mountain rescue team. And so many volunteers from the Westport area.

So here today, on the top of Croagh Patrick, I am lighting five candles.

The first is for my new-found friend and a most remarkable lady, Vicky Phelan. Vicky had hoped to wave me off for the climb but because of the current state of her illness, she could not make it. But members of her family are climbing today. Vicky, you will always be in my thoughts, and indeed the thoughts of most of the people in Ireland.

The second candle is being lit for everyone who has a terminal illness. We need to show our love and support for all of these people.

The third candle is being lit for everyone whom I describe as being in a dark place. People who every day are struggling to climb their own personal mountain.

The fourth candle is for everyone in the country who has helped in the battle against the pandemic.

In a way, I see today as a time of celebration for everyone. We have all gone through a tough time over the past few years.

And lastly, the fifth candle I am lighting for the people of Ukraine, and shining a light on the genocide they are going through.

We have always known this – the people of this country are so thoughtful, generous and kind. So here, on the top of Croagh Patrick today, I would ask people with me to have a few minutes in support of the people of Ukraine.

Thank you, everyone, for your support and stay safe, and take it easy going back down the Reek.

Another historic and incredible moment came immediately after I had finished my remarks. A man at the back of the crowd held up his mobile phone and shouted that Vicky Phelan wanted to pass on a message. Daniel O'Donnell called for the phone to be passed to him and he held it to the microphone so that Vicky's voice could be heard loud and clear. Her voice and words boomed out across the mountain. 'Hi Charlie, fair play to you,' she said. 'You made it to the top. Good man. I'll tell you one thing, you are some man.'

Addressing Daniel, she added: 'Isn't he some man, Daniel? I mean, to do what he is doing with that condition that he has and to rally everybody around him is just . . . I mean, the photos that I've seen from all around the country and all around the world today have been just unbelievable. I've never seen anything like it, never.'

I had no voice to be able to respond to Vicky. Daniel told her that even though she had been unable to join us on the climb, she was with us in spirit and in everybody's heart. He said that what she had done over the past number of years had been unbelievable. He thanked her and told her that her fight was not over. 'We know that there will be many days and months and, please God, years ahead,' he said.

That was an unforgettable moment, but the most poignant moment of the day was when my daughters and their children joined Claire and myself in the small church on the summit to light the five candles that Fr Charlie McDonnell had got from a Westport artist Catherine Roddy and placed before the altar. Some people were still climbing, while others had begun their descent as I shared this private and sacred moment with my nearest and dearest. It was certainly one of the most amazing moments of my life. I hope my grandchildren remember it all their lives.

Since dawn, the day had been a rollercoaster of emotions and standout moments, but none was as special as when I gathered with Claire, my children and my five beautiful grandchildren to light the five candles in that chapel. I had cried much of the way up the mountain and for most of my time on the summit. Now, my tears flowed again.

My eyes were still full of tears and the hairs were standing on the back of my neck when I went back outside to hear another new pal of mine, Matt Molloy from The Chieftains, playing his own tune, 'The Mountain Top', accompanied by the Clew Bay Pipe Band. Daniel O Donnell sang, Matt Molloy played the flute and the Clew Bay Pipe band's lovely music boomed out across the mountaintop.

I knew that I would never forget these moments. On a beautiful, clear April Saturday, hundreds of people were lingering at the top of Ireland's 'holy mountain', talking or singing or simply praying privately. And they were all there because of a mad notion that I had blurted out off the top of my head on the *Late Late Show* on a dark December night. I wanted the moment to last forever. I could not believe what I was seeing and feeling.

While the music was playing, I walked through the crowd to go to the edge of the summit, where the Irish tricolour was fluttering in the wind above the blue-and-yellow flag of Ukraine. I wanted a moment on my own near both flags. I was very moved to see the flag of the suffering people of Ukraine fluttering on top of Croagh Patrick, close to the most westerly point of Europe.

Then, standing at the sign that says simply, 'Croagh Patrick: Ireland's Holy Mountain', with beautiful Clew Bay and its 366 islands far below me, I thought about how the mad idea that had started with my impromptu remark had now come to pass. I had no doubt but that some unknown spirit had pushed me and guided me from Studio 5 in the RTÉ Television Centre to the peak of this ancient pilgrimage site less than four months later.

My friend Harry Hughes, owner of the Hotel Westport and author of several books on Croagh Patrick, came up to me and showed me the remains of an ancient church on the summit. He said to me: 'Charlie, what happened today on the Reek will go down in the annals of Croagh Patrick.' Would I have exchanged those historic moments for a cure for my MND? That's a hard question to answer.

Our descent was difficult. Like everyone else, we found it more treacherous than the ascent. We were again blessed that our 'bodyguard', Inspector Denis Harrington, stayed close to us throughout. Daniel told me that he had to rush back to Dublin, but he stopped at the St Patrick statue to join Michael English in a rousing rendition of the hit song 'Shine a Light' in front of hundreds of well-wishers at the Mid-West Radio roadcaster.

I got another rousing reception from family and friends when we finally got back to our base camp at the back of Campbell's pub. We spent time with family and friends, but we didn't linger there too long.

I was so exhausted that all I could do when we got back to the hotel was to soak for a while in a hot bath. Even though I had decided against getting any politicians involved in the campaign, I was chuffed to see, when I checked on my phone, that Taoiseach Micheál Martin was among the first people to tweet congratulations about my endeavours. Another was President Michael D. Higgins, who, as Head of State, is above politics, but whose recognition of the climb as First Citizen sealed the achievement. It was such a thrill and such a great honour to know that they had watched how the climb had become a day of celebration right across the country and abroad.

We reviewed the events of the climb in Matt Molloy's pub later that night, and on Sunday I went to the St Patrick statue at the Octagon in Westport to record a message of thanks to all of the people who had taken part in all of the climbs in Ireland and other countries. The love and kindness that we had experienced on the mountain had spread outwards across the island of Ireland and to places much farther away.

Grief and sadness overwhelmed me a short time later when I was told that one of those tens of thousands of climbers had died tragically on Saturday. At the very time that we were resting, talking and singing on the Croagh Patrick summit, tragedy struck a little over 200 km south of us when a young mother of two children, Cora O'Grady, died suddenly while climbing Galtymore mountain in County Cork with her children in a Climb With Charlie event. She was aged 51 and she left behind her son Luke, aged 11, and daughter Lily, aged 8 years. She died near the summit of Galtymore just as I was preparing to go into the church to light my five candles. I cannot forget and I will not forget that she died while fundraising for me.

'Cora's last achievement was raising money for a good cause, out in nature, climbing with the people she adored. That act alone sums up our Cora,' her cousin Jerome told her funeral mass in the Church of Our Lady Conceived Without Sin in Mitchelstown on the following Friday. 'We lost a bright light, an absolute beaming, shining light, who brought so much fun and joy and a real sense of devilment to so many people in so many ways,' he added, speaking on behalf of her family. 'Everything Cora did, everything Cora said, was about Lily and Luke. She absolutely idolized them.'

Cora lived in Luí na Gréine, Ballinwillin, in Mitchelstown, north Cork, not far from Macroom, where my grandparents came from. Galtymore, as its name suggests, is the highest point in the Galtee Mountains, Ireland's highest mountain range, close to the Cork/Tipperary border in the Golden Vale. Galtymore is 918m high, compared to Croagh Patrick's height of 764m. Cora collapsed suddenly near the summit. The paramedics were unable to revive her. She was much closer to Heaven than we were when she died.

Cora and her family and friends have been in my thoughts every day since her death. Claire and I expressed our sympathies with Cora's family and friends when we spoke on the *Morning Ireland* programme on RTÉ Radio 1 on the Monday morning after the climb. Later, we and the Irish Motor Neurone Disease Association wrote to her family, too, but we did not travel to her funeral for fear of intruding on their grief or creating a media spectacle.

Alongside Cora, those foremost in my thoughts in the days and weeks after the climb were my former colleagues Jim Fahy and Colm Murray. I imagined them smiling down on us as we trudged up and down the mountain. Colm's widow, Anne, was among a large group of former Newsroom friends and colleagues who climbed Howth Hill at the same time as we were on the Reek. I was delighted that the group included my former boss, Ed Mulhall, editors Pat Brennan, Mary Butler and Bethan Kilfoil, and colleagues Sineád Crowley, Samantha Libreri, Dyane Connor, Doreen Dermody, Glenda Sheridan, Daniel Quinn, Amy Ní Riada and Gavin Jennings.

In a voice app message broadcast on *Morning Ireland* on the Monday after the climb, I said that the previous Saturday had been a remarkable and beautiful day, not just on Croagh Patrick but all over Ireland. I said that the atmosphere on the Reek had uplifted me and that I was still pinching myself at the memory of the history-making performances of Daniel O'Donnell and the members of the Clew Bay Pipe Band on the top of the mountain. I said that the importance of the climb was not just to raise funds, but also to help raise awareness about the work of Pieta and the IMNDA and about extending the hand of friendship to those who needed kindness and support.

Claire told the same programme that as the money raised had gone above and beyond what we had expected – at that time it was already over €2 million, more than double the target – we would need to put a better plan in place for how to spend it. She said that our initial thoughts were to help build a respite centre close to Beaumont Hospital for people with MND who had to travel long distances for their appointments at the hospital. She revealed that we would like to call it 'The Bird House'. The amount of money and awareness generated for MND and for Pieta meant that 'we need to sit down and develop a plan of how we feel we should use this money'.

She went on to say that she had been amazed and overwhelmed by the help and support of so many people, not just on the mountain but also in the weeks leading up to the climb. 'We cannot believe we have raised so much money. The nation is just so generous and so kind. It's been unbelievable.'

Claire said that the climb had been hard and difficult, but that Saturday was 'the most beautiful, emotional and inspiring day I've ever experienced'. She said that she saw that people wanted to embrace me and to cheer me on my way up the mountain, to show their love and kindness to me.

On his show, directly after *Morning Ireland*, Ryan Tubridy also described the weekend as 'like no other I've ever had in my life'.

There was something very beautiful happening on Croagh Patrick on Saturday. Everywhere I looked, I saw joy and I saw happiness and I saw a lot of tears and I saw a lot of love . . . there's something about the Reek. It's a special place. It emits some class of spirituality. The climb was tough, while the alternating rain and sunshine, as well as people's human kindness, made it almost biblical. I saw people falling and other people would go up to them and give them a hand.

There was a lovely sense of community, humans at their best, Ireland at its most gorgeous.

That shale part of it was tough. I would like to thank the number of people I slipped down through the rocks and landed on. You just land on people, particularly people who had sticks because they were able to prop themselves up, so I'd land on them. Thankfully, there's not a whole heap of me to land on anyone, so I don't think I caused them any physical pain . . . maybe psychological scars, but certainly you were a great help and it was a joy.

Ryan said that his show had been 'inundated with e-mails from people', many of whom had watched the climb on Twitter, Instagram or Facebook and who had felt that they were part of the experience and had donated money. He said that the climb was 'mission accomplished' for me and that all of my friends and other people who had promised to accompany me had delivered on their promise. 'So thanks, everybody, for such a lovely welcome and for being part of that story', he added.

Besides Croagh Patrick, walks took place in just under 240 locations in Ireland and abroad. More than 220 of the walks were in Ireland – 25 in Cork, 25 in Donegal, 21 in Mayo, 18 in Kerry, 18 in Wicklow and multiple locations in other counties. In the rest of the world, there were 6 in the United States, 5 in Spain, 2 in England, 2 in Australia, and walks also took place in New Zealand, Singapore and South Africa. I was stunned by the willingness of so many people in Ireland and around the world to join me in my climb, wherever they were.

The actor Colin Farrell sent me an e-mail from California a few days after the climb. He wrote:

I caught the coverage in the *Irish Times* and it was amazing to see the well-earned support out en masse to will you on.

It's amazing what you're doing. Simon Fitzmaurice was a dear friend of mine, Charlie, so I have the height of respect for the struggles you must be facing while fully acknowledging I know nothing of them. But the symbolism of one foot in front of the other to climb that mountain is no small thing.

I received a beautiful message from Daniel O'Donnell. He and I had never met before the *Late Late Show* had serendipitously brought us together, but he had since become a great friend. He was a steadfast companion on the day of the climb, even lingering with people long after our descent when he had been due to rush off to a meeting in Dublin. I had carried the rosary beads that he gave me in my pocket to the top of the Reek.

He told me later: 'Climb With Charlie is an event that will live in my memory for as long as I live. To stand at the bottom of Croagh Patrick and look up and see the thousands of people making their way up the mountain and feel the sense of community and togetherness was amazing. To eventually stand at the top, shoulder to shoulder with you and Claire, while the Clew Bay Band played so beautifully, was one of the most emotional experiences I've ever had. I feel privileged and honoured to have been part of something so special. Thank you, Charlie, you are an incredible human being.'

My accidental encounter with Daniel at RTÉ was so fortuitous, and the messages we exchanged with one another subsequently were so powerful, they added to my feeling that some new spiritual force was moving me. I now count Fr Charlie McDonnell of Westport as one of my good friends and I have become more than willing to accept the many personal blessings that he has given to Claire and me in God's name. I accept them in the spirit in which Fr Charlie has given them to us.

After the dust had settled on our climb, and after the proceeds had been presented to the Irish Motor Neurone Association and to Pieta, I could not stop thinking about how my unusual and unexpected quest had been driven and guided by some mysterious and supernatural force. I was reminded of Gabriel Conroy's belated epiphany in James Joyce's magnificent short story *The Dead*, a story whose resonances were increasing for me with every passing month: 'Better pass boldly into that other world, in the full glory of some passion, than fade and wither dismally with age.'

Like hundreds of thousands of people before me, I had made the pilgrimage. I had now become, in the words of Joyce's sometime friend Oliver St. John Gogarty after his own 1930s climb, 'a worthy person'. I could not have done any of this without Claire's love and her constant, steadfast support. I have been beyond lucky to have enjoyed her love since the first day we met. We have had seventeen blissfully happy years together. Her care and courage helped me to cope with my illness and guided every single day of our Croagh Patrick campaign. Her support drove every step of my climb to the top of the mountain.

In the weeks and months after the climb, I sometimes wondered if my motor neurone affliction was the price I had to pay for the love of Claire and for the transcendental peace and serenity that I experienced on the holy mountain.

I will never know the answer to that question.

6. LETTERS

Letters and cards began to arrive by post a couple of days after I went public about my diagnosis. The postman delivered further huge bundles after my *Late Late Show* appearances and after the Croagh Patrick climb. Most of the letters were addressed simply to 'Charlie Bird, County Wicklow', or 'Charlie Bird, c/o the Chester Beatty pub, Ashford, County Wicklow'. But other, novel addresses included: 'Charlie Bird, Ireland'; 'Mr Charlie Bird, ex-RTÉ, Somewhere in Wicklow'; 'Mr Charlie Bird, Irish Broadcaster, County Wicklow' and 'Mr Charlie and Claire Bird, Greatest RTÉ Journalist Reporter (retired), County Wicklow, Ireland'.

After my December *Late Late Show* appearance a letter arrived addressed simply to: 'Mr and Mrs Charlie Bird, The nation knows who he is, County Wicklow'. Among the letters sent to me via RTÉ in Donnybrook was one addressed to 'The Main Man Charlie Bird, RTÉ, Donnybrook, Dublin 4' and another that said 'Charlie Bird, RTÉ, A Great Irishman'. Many envelopes carried apologies to the postman or woman for not having a full address and pleas to deliver them anyway, if possible.

Many of the cards and letters, including Christmas cards and Mass cards, were sent anonymously or with no return address, but I read every single one of them and I replied to as many as I could. I got a beautiful letter from Colm Murray's widow, Anne, offering support and inviting me to ring her for advice at any time. Letters and cards arrived from nearly every county in Ireland and from parts of England, as well as from New York, Mozambique and the Philippines. Two serving government ministers sent me handwritten, personal letters.

'All good wishes to you from across the Atlantic,' wrote Bernadette Tuohey from New York. She said that a Mass would be offered for me in Saint Patrick's Cathedral on Fifth Avenue and added that her running team in New York was organizing a mountain climb on 2 April, to be with me in spirit on the Croagh Patrick climb.

A Redemptorist Missionary priest, Fr Brian Holmes, wrote to me 'from a little village hidden away in the mountains in a remote corner of Mozambique' to wish me peace and courage and to recall our meeting in Brazil twenty years previously when I was doing a report on slave-workers on farms there.

A lay missionary named Helen wrote from the Philippines to say that it was my coverage of the false imprisonment of the Irish Columban priest Fr Niall O'Brien and the other 'Negros Nine' men in 1983 that had prompted her to devote her life to community work for justice. 'Your reporting so many years ago from a remote island when the world was a much larger place directly influenced the path I chose in life,' she wrote. 'I have always been grateful to you for that and how you opened eyes, ears and hearts, not least mine, to the daily realities for so many Filipinos.'

I was amazed and humbled by the sheer number of letters that kept arriving and by what people said in them. That letter from Helen in the Philippines made me pause and feel a little proud and grateful that my work as a journalist had helped to shape the career of someone I didn't even know. I could never have imagined that my work as a reporter could have inspired this. I was always focussed on the present when I was reporting. I was providing 'today's news today'. Nearly forty years later, I was gratified and shocked to find a letter dropped through my letterbox telling me that my reporting had determined a person's career path and that her life choices had been so fulfilling.

I received a number of very generous and helpful letters from the partners or siblings of people who had been afflicted with MND. These accounts were harrowing, in part, but they also offered solace, support and valuable information when Claire and I were still struggling to absorb the enormity of my diagnosis.

Several people wrote to say that I had helped them because of the public way I had spoken about my illness. They said that most men don't talk or indeed cry in public and that what they appreciated about my reaction to my illness was that I wasn't going to hide from what was happening to me.

A schoolmate from my pre-teenage years, Patrick Salvadori, wrote to me from Hungerford, in Berkshire, on the day after a friend rang him from Dublin with the news of my illness. Patrick and I used to cycle to school together each morning from the top of Kilmacud Road to the Christian Brother's School in Oatlands, Stillorgan. He told me that he had never forgotten how I had stood up for him when one of the teachers was being cruel to him and how the memory of my gesture all those years ago helped him in his daily work as a teacher, mentoring children and young people.

A woman whose husband had been stranded in Baghdad after the invasion of Kuwait in 1990 wrote to thank me for contacting her to tell her that I had met him in Baghdad and that he was OK. She recalled that 'not everyone was so sympathetic to our plight at the time'. She said that she was caring alone for her one-year-old daughter at the time and 'amidst all the worry and anxiety of those few months my meeting with you that day always stood out as one of the positives of that time, so for that I thank you.'

A card from Monkstown in Dublin had no sender's surname and no return address. It read: 'Dear Charlie, my youngest sister persuaded me over 10 years ago to spend a few hours collecting for a homeless charity that she was director of – my experience was that most people ignored us, but you gave me €5.00 and made my day. Thinking of you and Thank You – Fiona.'

Another card that had no name or return address came from 'a nun in the West', who promised that she and her friends would climb Croagh Patrick with me. She said she was inspired by my fortitude. She told me: 'When the earth shall claim your limbs, then shall you truly dance.'

Several people offered to put me in touch with faith-healers. Others sent me relics, rosary beads, miraculous medals or holy water. A number of people urged me to petition particular saints of the Catholic Church. I was also advised to change my diet and to research the work of some MND specialists in the United States.

One of the first people to write to me was the champion showjumper Cian O'Connor, whose forfeiture of his Olympic gold medal in 2005 I had reported on extensively on RTÉ News after the International Equestrian Federation ruled that his horse, *Waterford Crystal*, had a banned substance in its body at the Games. He made no reference to my laying siege to him in 2005 but said that his heart went out to me and he invited me to his stables in County Meath for a walk and a chat.

A man in Mayo wrote to say that my plea on the *Late Late Show* for people to help each other had moved him powerfully because he had been saved from a suicide attempt by his two sons ten years previously.

Some of the letters that moved me most were from schoolchildren. Several of these letters had very worn €5.00 notes attached to them and were sent to my home address. 'I will give you some of my Christmas money. I hope your climb goes well,' wrote Aoibheann Lacey, aged 8. 'I hope you get a medicine to cure your illness. Hope you get well soon. Lots of hearts and kisses,' she added.

Hannah, aged 6, wrote: 'I want to give you some of my money I got from my granny. I hope you enjoy your climb. I hope you feel better soon. I will pray for you that you don't feel sad anymore.' Ten-year-old Seamus said: 'Dear Charlie, I can't imagine how hard it is for you. Hope you'll get better.'

Several more euro notes – €10.00 and €5.00 notes – arrived from the children of the Holy Family National

School, Templetouhy, Thurles, County Tipperary. Even better than the cash donations were the wonderful handwritten and typed notes from the children themselves: Caoimhe Lawlor, aged 13 and from the village of Errill in County Laois, told me she had two older sisters and she attached a €10.00 note to her letter. Conor Leahy, also aged 10, said he had seen me on TV. He asked after Tiger and attached a €5.00 note. Another 10-year-old, Cillian Russell, also attached a €5.00 note and said that his schoolmates would climb the nearby Devil's Bit mountain for me on 2 April. J. P. Everard also wrote to me from the same school.

The twenty-five children in third and fourth classes in St Finian's National School in Waterville, County Kerry, sent me individual handwritten letters onto which they had stapled their own beautiful drawings of Croagh Patrick, or of Tiger and me climbing the Reek. They told me that they would be supporting me by hiking the 16 km (10 miles) from Glencar to Glenbeigh on the Kerry Way, along with 27 schoolmates from fifth and sixth classes.

Beautiful messages from separate schools arrived on the one day. Seven children from St Gabriel's School in Limerick sent me a brilliant letter, wishing me love, strength and endurance for the walk. The letter was addressed simply to: 'Charlie Bird, Croagh Patrick Walk, IMNDA, Climbwithcharlie'. Someone in An Post had helpfully added: 'Try Wicklow'.

Twelve children from fifth and sixth classes in Scoil Mhichíl Naofa, Dún Géagáin, Baile 'n Sceilg, Contae Chiarraí, sent me a terrific bilingual letter, saying that I filled them with *misneach* (courage). They added: 'We will climb Cnoc na dTobar which overlooks the town of

Caherciveen. It is 690 metres high and it is an ancient pilgrim path. It is a very special mountain in the heart of the Iveragh Peninsula. We are excited about this challenge and will let you know how it goes for us. We will follow your hike to Croagh Patrick with great interest. You are a legend. *Treise leat! Go n-éiri go geal leat agus guimid gach beannacht ort ó Chiarraí Theas.* We're extending the hand of friendship, *a chara. Ar aghaidh linn le chéile.* We are going to make it all the way to the light.' A P.S. added: *'Suil againn go bhfuil Tiger go maith.'*

One person, writing from West Kerry, wrote to me after the Croagh Patrick climb and said that she wanted to thank me personally 'for the motivation you have given me to keep going in life. I suffer from depression, and on the day of your walk I was pretty low, but watching you getting up that mountain I had to take a bit of action, so I got out of bed and climbed the stairs and have been doing that almost every day since. You are an inspiration to people like me. I will keep you in my prayers, Charlie, and don't forget my door is always open.'

The scores of people who had climbed Bear Mountain on the western bank of the Hudson River in New York State with Team Ashling sent me an enormous banner emblazoned with the Climb With Charlie logo and caricature. On the back of the banner were more than 120 signatures and handwritten goodwill messages. Bear Mountain, coincidentally, is on the opposite bank of the Hudson River to the Iona Island Bird Sanctuary!

Several other people wrote to say that they found watching the climb on TV or online inspiring, and some people sent me paintings or photographs of the Reek.

Among the first batch of letters I received was one from a man named Austin Hallahan. I didn't recognize the name. The letter was handwritten and it filled four A4 pages. As the letter was just one of a bundle that was delivered to my home that morning, I scanned the pages hurriedly, thinking that I would read it in full later in the day, when a line at the bottom of the first page jumped out at me. The words were: 'It was you who saved my life.'

I went back to the top of the page and began to read the letter slowly. It began:

Dear Charlie,

This has been my umpteenth time starting this letter to you. I crumpled up so many pages to start again that I'm afraid Greta Thunberg might mention the heap of paper here beside my desk, and all start with 'Dear Charlie'.

What can I say to you Charlie? Like everyone, I'm in shock that something like this has happened to you. You are one of the 'good guys' and this just doesn't seem the way things should go.

I know saying things like that probably doesn't help you with 'accepting and getting on with things' – but just for a brief moment indulge me in my reminding you of how and why you are one of the greatest human beings I know and know of.

I was a terrified, vulnerable and lost young lad. I was at death's door and edging closer to it. I really did not see any way out of the chaotic and turbulent place I was in. This was all leading to a place of no return, a journey that may have started from childhood but would be concluded by the lies and 'Walter Mitty' persona of that [person]. I had said my goodbyes, wrote letters and sent my Mam flowers.

I wanted to be taken seriously on what I believed to be an awful and terrible truth and I reached out to you. I can't remember how I got in touch or even how I was able to convince you to meet me, but for whatever reason it was you who met me and not any other journalist, it was you who saved my life.

Because of you, I'm here today. A grown man and most importantly a great father to my two boys.

That day, it was the concern you showed. You assured me and I believed all will be alright.

What I have carried with me since our brief meeting is the kindness you showed me. You didn't have to do all the things you did, but because you took the time, I got through the most difficult time of my life.

What I learned from you and about myself that day has got me to here and will stand to me for the rest of my life. You brought a calmness to my raging storm and showed me the way back from that darkened door.

This letter, I realized, was taking me back twenty-three years to a summer Saturday in Buswell's Hotel at the corner of Kildare Street and Molesworth Street in Dublin, opposite Leinster House. I had gone there to meet a man who had contacted me on my mobile phone and said that he had information for me that was so sensitive, it could not be discussed on a telephone.

This was just a few weeks after RTÉ News had begun to run the stories that George Lee and I had unearthed on the National Irish Bank overcharging and offshore accounts scandals. It was not unusual for us to get anonymous tip-offs via our phones. Although I hadn't had a weekend off for months, I reluctantly agreed to meet the man because he was so convincing and because I thought he might be a whistleblower with valuable information.

Buswell's Hotel, normally teeming with politicians, lobbyists and business people on weekdays, is quieter on Saturdays. The young man and I had no trouble identifying each other when I walked into the lobby. We sat in a quiet corner and the man began to talk. I soon realized that he was not a whistleblower, but a very young man suffering deep mental turmoil. His talk jumped from a mention of his girlfriend and of the flowers that he had sent his mother to details of another friend who was in the IRA. After we had spoken for a while, I was convinced that his contacting me was a desperate cry for help.

I managed to convince him that he should return to his family immediately. I was only somewhat reassured when we parted. I could not stop thinking about his inner torment. He had insisted that our conversation was confidential, but I immediately got on to directory enquiries to try to get a telephone number for his family's business.

I rang the number and asked to speak to the man's father. He came to the telephone, but he ended the call as soon as I said, 'This is Charlie Bird from RTÉ'. He obviously thought it was a prank call. I rang again a few minutes later, but the same man answered and again hung up when he heard the name 'Charlie Bird', even though I said quickly that I had met his son a short time earlier and that I was worried about him. My third call was answered by the young man's sister, but she too cut short the call before I could say anymore.

I was panicking. I felt helpless and I feared that I had been drawn into something that could end in tragedy. I contacted the RTÉ Correspondent in the region that covered the man's hometown and got the telephone number of the local Garda superintendent. This man grasped the seriousness of my call. He contacted the family and convinced them to listen to me when I called again. This time, the man's sister listened to my urgings and she assured me that the family would find her brother and help him. A few days later the man's mother rang me to thank me for what I had done on the previous Saturday and to tell me that all was well.

I hadn't got a story in Buswell's Hotel that day, but by listening to that troubled young man and taking his anguish seriously, I now know that I had done something far more important than getting any journalism scoop. He wrote to me some time later:

Dear Charlie,

You probably don't remember me, but a couple of years ago I had arranged to meet you . . . You were worried about me, you rang my dad at the family business . . . well to cut a long story, things have only been better for me since. I've been meaning to write to you ever since.

He told me that he was good at playing music and he sent me a CD he had made 'for people who at some time in my life did something nice for me or helped me out *in some way'*. He added: '*Thank you for taking the time out to meet someone you had never met, listening to me and taking a weight off my shoulders . . .*'

More than twenty years passed before Austin wrote to me again, prompted by the news of my illness and diagnosis.

Charlie,

I have thanked you so many times in my life, especially times, moments with my kids. I could not imagine all of my life, thus far, not happening, but I could not also have imagined any life beyond the next day before we met and talked.

Some people know our story, others do not. I look back on that vulnerable and broken young man that I was and see, maybe not a different person now, but a steadier, happier and peaceful man now. If I was to take a quick glimpse back on my life from the last 20 years, I cannot believe all the things I would have missed out on.

Being a parent eclipses any other experience I've ever had by far, but being given the chance to live in California and move back is something I pinch myself over. While there, I made it. I made the most wonderful friends. I climbed up the work ladder, right to the top through hard work and no college degree needed! I officiated at my friend's wedding in a beautiful grove in the woods under the Californian sun. I joined the police force, albeit for one day only – a story for another time – sat underneath the Golden Gate Bridge many a time and thanking you and the universe for getting me here.

Pinching myself. Counting my lucky stars. Sitting in awe of life. Nourishing wonderful moments with my boys. Moments in time. All possible because you took the time to meet me.

Thank you Charlie.

Words are really not enough. Now what can I do to help you?

Austin sent me a voucher for a health retreat in Wexford. He said to give it to my daughters if I did not use it myself. He gave me his phone number and said he would love to meet me again for a chat, even though he knew that I was a private, family man and that my voice and energy were fading. His letter continued:

I am so sorry that this has happened to you Charlie, I really am, and when my boys, Conor (15) and Roan (12) are a little older I will tell them all about our brief moment in time and the impact you had on my life. That I promise you. Please feel free to reach out.

Life has its up and downs but – actually scrap that last piece, it has no downs – it is life, and I'm glad that you have had such an impact on it.

From my heart, Charlie, thank you.

Austin's letter moved me so much that I invited him to join me on the *Late Late Show* on 10 December 2021. Accompanied by his partner, Edwina, he spoke bravely about our meeting in Buswell's Hotel in 1998. He told me later that he was not one bit nervous about going on the programme. He said he wanted people to know what

I had done for him when he believed that he was lost and broken.

It is hard for me to put into words how I felt when I realized that I had helped to save another person's life. To this day, I feel how very courageous Austin had been to go so public about the events in his life before I first met him. It was a huge step for him to admit in public that he had been on the verge of taking his own life. I thought long and hard about publishing his letters, but he was clear and positive that he wanted me to do so in order that it might help others.

Following his *Late Late Show* appearance, he has since told me, three people came up to him in his shop and poured their hearts out to him there and then. Each of them had similar stories of abuse. They all spoke about the shame they carried and the hurt and lonesomeness of harbouring this secret – until hearing him on the *Late Late Show* that night made them feel ashamed no longer. He said they talked openly and at length about their experiences, not worrying about who might overhear them. He had known those people for years and had had no clue of their sufferings. 'They thanked me for speaking out and showing no shame,' he said. He said that he felt very honoured that they shared their stories with him, and that they showed the far-reaching ripples of my decision to help him all those years ago.

He told me: 'Even though I didn't think what I had said that night was anything too compelling or enormous, it was to them, and so, because of you, because of you caring for a complete stranger 25 years ago, ultimately you have helped three more people that I know of here locally to deal with what they have gone through and to feel some kind of comradeship with someone like me. I cannot imagine how tough it has been on them, but it really warms my heart to know that they can come to me and just talk about it. So I just wanted to let you know that your good and kind deed continues to ripple through the lives of many we will never meet and some we will. Thanks Charlie.'

As with the letter from Helen in the Philippines, I was reminded again that some of my work was continuing to reverberate decades later. My good deed of listening to Austin in his hour of need had continued to bear positive fruit for people that I had never met and that I never would meet.

Before his appearance with me on the *Late Late Show,* Austin told his two sons, about our meeting in Buswell's Hotel nearly twenty-five years ago. He said that they both wanted to meet me, to thank me. He sent me a WhatsApp video message from himself and the boys sitting in his car. In it, he spoke about how important it was to keep talking to each other, especially as a parent. He continued: 'You know I wouldn't want anyone else to go through what, say, my parents went through and we talked about the miracle of meeting you on that day and how it could have turned out so differently, and all the things we've done in the meantime since they were born.'

Austin said in the video message that the boys wanted to thank me and they promised to read my 2006 book, *This is Charlie Bird*. I had devoted two pages in that book to the Buswell's Hotel meeting and its sequel. Austin held the book up to his phone's camera and said that it had been on his bookshelf for many years but that he himself had not yet read it.

Conor, the eldest boy, aged 15, was sitting in the front seat. He said: 'Hello. Thank you so much. I've heard this story and it's incredible. It could have [gone] so many other ways and it was just by luck . . . what you've done is amazing. Thank you so much.'

Roan, aged 12 and sitting in the back seat, added: 'Thank you, Charlie. That story actually made me cry. I wouldn't be here if it wasn't for you, so thank you so much.'

Austin said that the Buswell's Hotel story had had an impact on so many people in so many ways. He knew the enormity of what had happened in the hotel that day and the impact on other people of him talking about it publicly. Recently, he told me further details about the crisis that precipitated his cry-for-help to me all those years ago. He was barely into his twenties at the time. He was working happily in County Mayo and he had a girlfriend there. He took a week's holiday, intending to rent a car and drive around Ireland with two friends after a brief visit home. 'Life was good,' he said.

He had eight siblings, but the family member he was closest to was his mother. He said that he had a special relationship with her and that he and she were the only two people in the family who played the piano. He told me: 'We were both self-taught and so we helped each other in figuring out how to play songs on the piano. When I was living at home I played for hours every day. Once I had moved out of the house, Mom missed the sound of the piano being played, so she had arranged for me to record some of her favourites on a few CDs so she would always have the sound of the piano in the house.' It was one of those CDs that he sent me a few years later.

Austin said that both his parents were very trusting. One particular local man who called to their home regularly used to talk about his very famous relatives in America. From his earliest teenage years Austin was in awe of this man, who soon began to tell him stories of his active membership of the IRA and of his gun-smuggling exploits. He felt honoured that this man, a prominent figure in the town, shared family stories and dangerous secrets with him. On the weekend that he was about to begin his holiday, this man told Austin over a cup of tea that something 'huge' was about to happen.

What that man told Austin was indeed 'huge', but it was a complete fantasy. He said that the IRA was planning a series of massive bomb attacks that would destroy much of London and bring the British government to its knees. Even though the IRA had declared a new ceasefire a year previously, it had not surrendered its sizeable stockpiles of guns and explosives at that time. This man said that the plans for a new bombing campaign in London were very well advanced and that the attack was imminent.

Austin told me that he was shocked and numbed, but that he had no reason to disbelieve the story. The man had been a regular and trusted visitor to his home since childhood. He had a responsible and respected position in the local community. He had previously told Austin shocking stories. Some of his claims about his famous American cousins were true. Austin said he was dazed and panicky, thinking about his sister who was nursing in London and about two friends who had just moved there, but he was unable to tell his parents about the trusted family friend who had another life that involved blowing up London and killing people.

Terrified of telling the local Gardaí (some of whom were in the IRA, according to the man), and paranoid that the IRA would find and kill him, Austin spent a sleepless night at home and bought flowers for his mother before taking a bus to Dublin to try to alert a national journalist or someone in authority about his secret information. He contacted a few newspaper journalists and had spoken to two Sunday newspaper reporters before he contacted me through the RTÉ Newsroom.

By the time I met Austin in Buswell's, he had attempted to kill himself by cutting his wrist and ingesting a large number of paracetamol tablets that he had bought in various pharmacies in Dublin. He felt powerless to stop what he believed was going to happen in London. He decided to write down what he knew and then take his own life. He wrote individual farewell letters to both his parents and to each of his eight siblings. He also wrote a brief note to the family friend, saying that he despised his murderous patriotism. And he left a note of apology to whoever would find his body in a Dublin hotel room.

I knew none of this when I sat down with him. He hadn't eaten or slept properly for two days and, I learned later, he had severe stomach pain from the paracetamol tablets, which had made him lose consciousness but had not killed him. He was clearly in deep mental turmoil and he broke down and cried as he told me his story. He believed that he had secret, advance knowledge of an atrocity that would kill very many people. He was an emotional and physical wreck.

From my knowledge of the IRA and from my professional contacts with its spokesmen, I knew that the notion of a new London bombing campaign was nonsense and that no member of the IRA would speak as recklessly as his family friend had. I told him that in my work I had met IRA leaders and that I had been chosen by them as the journalist through whom they issued their ceasefire statements in 1994 and 1997. I assured him that what he feared would not happen and that he was going to be OK. I knew that the notion of the IRA bombing London again so soon after restoring its ceasefire in 1997 was so absurd that I did not even need to contact my bosses about it. I knew that it was nonsense. I happened to be the right man in the right place at the right time.

I knew very little of this when I met Austin for the first time in Buswell's Hotel. I just saw a very troubled young man whom I felt compelled to help. Like me when I feared that I had a terminal illness, he was distressed and powerless. Helping him was the only thing on my mind. Fate and fortune had dictated that he would be able to face a new and better tomorrow.

Recalling that moment in Buswell's nearly twenty-four years later, Austin told me in early 2022:

'I really cannot put into words the gushing feeling of relief and stupidity I felt for the next few minutes. I felt physically weak and just dazed. It took me a few minutes to fully comprehend what you had just told me and then the realization of what an idiot I was to believe this [family friend]. I could have hugged you there and then as you had not known fully what I had gone through in the past 48 hours, but we were in public and I don't think I had the strength to even get up.

I knew you were going to reach out to my family, but I didn't care at that point. Charlie Bird had just saved my life. No other person or journalist could have said the things you said because you had the authority to dispel all the lies that I believed. I would never have believed anyone else if they had told me the same thing. By some form of fate or meeting the right person at the right time, I was freed from the fate that I thought was the only option left for me.'

I had made him promise me in Buswell's Hotel that he would go straight home and contact me when he got there. He told me that he slept on the bus going home and that 'the feeling of liberation outweighed the feeling of embarrassment of what I had done and nearly succeeded in doing'. He told his parents every detail of his forty-eight hours in Dublin and of his shame that he had not confided in them sooner. His family were in shock.

He never spoke to the family friend again, but he told me he has forgiven him now. He quit his job in Mayo and began a new career, working with people with disabilities. The paracetamol had damaged his liver. 'Because you asked those questions [in Buswell's Hotel], and because you broke the silence and reached out to my family, I was able to get medical help in time to save my liver and save my life,' he told me.

He said that whenever he was struck by the awesome beauty of life in the years since that day, he always thought of me and thanked me 'for being exactly the right person to have met that day and to tell me the information that only you would have'. He said he often thought about me during his years in California, looking forward to having a pint with me and filling me in on how his life had turned out there. He said that I had been a rock and a steadfast friend and that he would be grateful to me eternally.

He also took to sending me a little audio clip of his piano playing every day, to let me know that he was thinking of me as my illness progressed. He told me: 'If I had not met you, my life would surely have ended all those years ago.' But the meeting had been as life-changing for me as it had for him, because it brought me a friend when I most needed support in my darkest times.

A woman wrote to say that she hoped that publishing the letter she had sent me might help somebody else who was suffering.

Charlie,

Thank you for sharing your journey with the nation. You are an inspiration. I am a 46-year-old Mum of two girls, aged 9 & 11. After enjoying six years in remission, I received the devastating news last year that my cancer had returned. I am now Stage Four. Terminal.

I've always been an optimistic person, but I now live in a dark place full of fear and worry for my girls (both of whom have additional needs). I feel so alone. When I heard you say in an interview you 'cry every day', I froze. It struck a chord with me. I put on a brave face to all around me, but I secretly cry every day. It's so draining and relentless. I feel like I'm going

*through the motions of living but not making the
most of the time I have. Watching you climb and
seeing you achieve what you had set out to do has
inspired me to get off my backside and live my life
to the most with my girls.*

*So tomorrow when I cry, I'll know someone else
out there is doing the same . . . I'm not alone. Thank
you. I will keep you in my thoughts, Charlie Bird.
God bless you.*

This woman later told me that Stage Four cancer was
a lonely journey, but that she had felt part of something
when I mentioned, on the top of Croagh Patrick, that I
would light a candle for all patients with terminal illnesses.
She asked me not to publish her name, but she said that
she was happy for me to use her letter in this book.

She added: *'Perhaps someone in a similar situation will
read it and not feel alone.'*

Throughout the whole Climb With Charlie campaign I
often spoke about helping people in dark places, and
especially those with suicidal thoughts. Letters like the
woman's above made me happy that some of my work
might have been of value. And Austin Hallahan's letter
helped me to put this issue front and centre of my whole
project. I hope that Austin and his two beautiful young
teenage children, and any others who were moved by my
climb, are part of my real legacy.

7. STARDUST

'You're about the first person that's listened,' June McDermott told me in summer 2017.

We were sitting at her kitchen table in Edenmore, north Dublin, more than thirty-six years after her two brothers and one of her sisters were killed in the Stardust fire tragedy in nearby Artane. William, George and Marcella McDermott were among the forty-eight young people who died in one of the worst mass fatalities in the history of the Irish State when fire engulfed a St Valentine's Day disco in the Stardust nightclub in the early hours of 14 February 1981. Some 214 other local youngsters were seriously injured in the fire, many with permanent disfigurements.

June and her mother Brigid and her sister Selina were talking to me for a documentary I was making for RTÉ Television about the unanswered questions that they and the other victims' families had been asking in the decades since the fire, which had been one of the first major stories I had covered after joining the RTÉ Newsroom in 1980.

I'll never forget the phone call I got from my boss in the early hours of that morning in February 1981. He told me to rush to the scene of a bad fire outbreak in a disco in Artane on the northside of Dublin. I was living in Bray at the time, in County Wicklow, and I didn't know exactly where I was going after I crossed the River Liffey. But as I passed by the City Morgue on Amiens Street, I saw an image that will never leave me – ambulances were already arriving with victims' bodies inside. That sight and the scenes that I witnessed a short time later in Artane have haunted me in the 41 years since that night.

I was one of the first reporters on the scene of the catastrophe. It was freezing cold and all of the water from the fire hoses that the firemen had been using was frozen on the ground. The whole thing was like a horrible dream. It was and still remains one of the greatest losses of young lives in the history of the State. Well over one in every four of the estimated 811 young people who were in the ballroom when the fire started ended up dead or seriously injured.

Although I had been a senior researcher on high-profile RTÉ programmes like *Seven Days* and *The Late Late Show* for nearly a decade, I was something of a rookie news reporter when I arrived at the scene of what was clearly an horrific disaster that was without precedent in Ireland in the television age. Inexperienced and thrown in at the deep end just a few months after joining RTÉ News, I said in my report from inside the charred and still smouldering shell of the building that a government inquiry would have to examine important issues about emergency exits and emergency lighting. I was careful with the wording I used, but I was very naive to expect prompt or definitive answers from any government inquiry.

The country's biggest political party at the time, Fianna Fáil, postponed its annual Árd Fheis, which was due to begin that morning, but the survivors and relatives of the victims claim that they were neglected or treated with near-indifference by the political establishment for most of the following four decades. 'It seems that our leaders shed crocodile tears' was how Christy Moore put it in his 1985 song 'They Never Came Home' – a song that radio stations refused to play for fear of libelling the Stardust owners.

Most of the victims were teenagers. Half of those who died were aged 18 years or younger. None was older than 28 years. Four of them were only 16 years old and eight others were aged 17. The dead and injured included siblings like the McDermotts and some young couples. Almost all of them came from Artane and the nearby neighbourhoods of Beaumont, Bonnybrook, Coolock, Darndale, Donaghmede, Edenmore, Kilbarrack, Kilmore and Raheny. Some of them were their family's main breadwinner. Five of the dead had to be buried in a communal grave as their remains could not be readily identified.

'Their coffins were closed at the undertakers,' Brigid McDermott told me, referring to the remains of her children: William, aged 22 years, George, 19 years, and Marcella 16 years. 'I wanted to see them. They would not let me see them. I don't even remember burying them. I know I was there, but I don't remember burying them.'

Brigid's daughter Selina was aged 11 when she lost her two older brothers and sister in the fire. 'I just woke up and they were gone,' she said. 'From age 11 I had no childhood. I straight away became a carer for my mother.'

The family told me that they got no help from doctors, social workers or TDs. I was stunned when June said: 'You're about the first person that's listened.'

Within a week of the fire, the Dáil and the Seanad voted to establish a Tribunal of Inquiry, headed by a High Court judge, Mr Justice Ronan Keane. It sat for 122 days and heard from 363 witnesses, some 160 of whom were in the building when the fire occurred. Its main conclusion, that 'the fire was probably started deliberately', shocked and dismayed the survivors and the bereaved when it was published in June 1982.

I remember being shocked and confused by the Tribunal report. I had not been assigned to cover the hearings in the Law Society premises in Blackhall Place, Dublin, but I knew from my colleague Kieron Wood, who reported from the Tribunal, that the families were surprised and upset. Their pain was compounded by the knowledge that a file of photographs of the charred victims had been distributed among the legal teams and had been seen by journalists. I often wondered how the families must have felt when the file with the harrowing photographs of their dead loved ones was being handed around.

I got to know a brother of one of the victims fairly well. Peter Hobbs, who lost his 21-year-old brother Brian in the fire, worked for a stockbroking firm close to Leinster House and he used to fill me in on the annoyance of the relatives and the survivors whenever we met. Peter, from Whitehall, was a lovely man. My regular chats with him kept me informed of the suffering of the many families involved and their outrage that it was the young people who were being blamed for starting the fire.

Mr Justice Keane's Tribunal report had concluded, without offering any evidence whatever, that 'the fire was probably caused deliberately, the most likely mechanism being the slashing of some of the seats with a knife and the application of a lighted match or cigarette lighter to the exposed foam, or the ignition of newspaper on or under the seats.' The Tribunal report also exonerated the Stardust owners of legal responsibility for the blaze. Its conclusion enabled them to sue Dublin Corporation successfully for compensation of almost £600,000.

A Stardust Victims Compensation Tribunal established by the Houses of the Oireachtas in October 1985 made 823 awards, but no further funding was provided for follow-up medical treatment or counselling until more than twenty years later. Brigid McDermott astonished me when she told me that the counselling she was offered following the deaths of her three children amounted to being told to sit in a room and do some knitting and sewing. I could not believe that the State's succour to a woman who had lost three children in one of the worst disasters in its history was to knit and sew.

Before talking to the McDermotts, I had spent the more than thirty-five years since the disaster moving from one breaking news story to the next, never having much time to dwell again on the grief and suffering of the survivors and the victims' families after the media interest in their disaster had waned or ended. My work would not allow me to become obsessed with one particular disaster. I could not involve myself in any cause or campaign without damaging my own reputation and RTÉ's legal obligation for impartiality, but I could not forget the horror of the fire or the images of the charred bodies. And I often experienced flashbacks to the image of one survivor, holding up his two heavily bandaged hands when I reported from a hospital ward in the days after the fire.

Dublin City Council dedicated a section of a public park in Bonnybrook, Coolock, to the Stardust victims in 1993. Centred around a bronze statue of a young couple dancing, it features forty-eight pillars and forty-eight water jets representing each lost life. Outside the victims' neighbourhoods, the Stardust story had effectively disappeared, but I continued to be bothered that the truth about the cause of the fire had never been credibly established. Whenever I met bereaved relatives, I was moved by their determination to continue to fight for the truth.

Fifteen further years of near-futile campaigning by survivors and relatives followed the public park dedication before the government appointed a senior counsel, Paul Coffey, to conduct an independent examination of the case submitted by the Stardust Victims Committee for a reopened inquiry in July 2008.

His report ran to 76 pages and almost 24,000 words. It offered hope to the families. He said that the 'inescapable' conclusion of his independent examination was: '*prima facie* the Tribunal's finding of fact that the fire was probably started deliberately is on its face a mere hypothetical explanation for the probable cause of the fire and is not demonstrated by any evidence that the fire was started deliberately'.

He said that the Tribunal finding was 'demonstrably flawed' and added: 'I am satisfied that the Committee has established a *prima facie* case that the Tribunal's conclusion as to the cause of the fire cannot be demonstrated to be objectively justifiable.'

His criticism of the Tribunal's finding went further. 'The Tribunal,' he wrote, 'has placed on the public record a finding of probable criminal wrongdoing which is *prima facie* speculative and fraught with evidential and logical difficulties. Moreover, insofar as it is stated to be a "finding of fact", the finding is so phrased as may well give the mistaken impression to a reasonable man or woman in the street that it is a finding established by evidence that the fire was started deliberately and not a mere hypothetical explanation for the probable cause of the fire.'

Paul Coffey recommended that, as the Tribunal had been established by the Oireachtas, the government should consider correcting the public record by placing on the record of the Dáil and the Seanad an acknowledgement of the Tribunal's findings that there is no evidence that the fire was started deliberately and, instead, that the cause of the fire is unknown.

He also recommended that any new inquiry conducted after a lapse of nearly thirty years would only serve the public interest if it could find evidence that would establish the cause of the fire forensically, rather than speculating hypothetically.

The Coffey Report led to a Dáil vote in February 2009 that the 1981 Tribunal verdict was hypothetical and that none of the people in the nightclub had been responsible for the blaze. In the absence of a scintilla of evidence that the fire had been started maliciously, the arson verdict was overturned and the public record was corrected. The government's motion that night also pledged renewed medical and counselling care for survivors and bereaved families. Eight TDs spoke in favour of the government motion, only two of whom were from Dublin southside constituencies.

Nearly eight more years passed before continued campaigning by the families led to a new Dáil vote in January 2017. This motion, supported by twelve TDs, called for a new, independent assessment of potential fresh evidence, following a Programme for Government commitment to examine any new evidence 'which would be likely to definitely establish the cause of the fire at Stardust'.

By this time, I had been retired from RTÉ for five years, but I was asked to look back on the Stardust disaster in a series called *After the Headlines* that I was making for the station. We arranged a meeting of the families and the relatives at the Skylon Hotel in Drumcondra and once they knew that I was involved, they gave us their full co-operation.

I went back to the site of the disaster to do some filming for the documentary. It was my first time there since the night of the fire. I was dumbfounded to find that there was nothing there – no plaque, no memorial, no mention of the dead and no trace of the tragic fire. I was no longer constrained by the imperative of impartiality that applies to news reporters and I readily agreed when the leading campaigner for the families, Antoinette Keegan, asked me to unveil a simple banner with the names of the forty-eight young people who had died there.

The government's new, independent assessment was carried out by a retired judge, Pat McCartan, who had been a TD for Dublin North East between 1989 and 1992.

After meeting with representatives of the Stardust Victims Committee and examining a dossier that they had prepared, he advised the government that 'there is no new or updated evidence disclosed in the meaning of the terms of this Assessment and no new [inquiry] is warranted'.

His fifty-page report acknowledged that the grief of the bereaved and of the survivors was compounded by the likelihood that the cause of the fire would never be established, but his recommendation that no new inquiry was warranted added to the families' grief. It was also severely criticized when the report was debated in the Dáil on 14 December 2017.

Ten TDs spoke during this debate and the only ones who did not criticize the McCartan Report were the Minister for Justice and Equality, Charlie Flanagan TD, and the Minister of State at that department, Finian McGrath TD. Six of the TDs who spoke, including the two ministers, referred to the *After the Headlines* documentary that I had presented on RTÉ television two nights before the debate.

In the programme, which my former boss Ed Mulhall had suggested that I make, I looked back on the night of the tragedy and spoke to survivors and relatives. Listening to several of the families who had lost children in the fire brought home to me how and why they had felt so abandoned by the State and so let-down by the justice system for thirty-six years. I was deeply affected by their grief and their dismay and I fully understand how, to this day, they feel that they haven't got justice for their loved ones.

As well as the McDermotts, I also interviewed Patricia and Edward Kennedy, who told me that their marriage broke up after they lost their daughter Marie in the fire. They said that they were silently blaming each other for letting her go to the disco. Only now, thirty-six years later, were they able to talk about it for the first time. 'We used to call her the dancing queen,' said Patricia. 'She died doing what she loved – dancing,' Edward said.

I'll never forget the fortitude and dignity of Gertrude Barrett, who spoke to me in Glasnevin Cemetery at the grave of her son Michael, who was 17 when he died in the fire. 'Everything died with him,' she said. 'He had the world at his feet, like the other forty-seven. They had hopes. They had dreams.'

Gertrude said that every day was a struggle, but she visits her son's grave every Sunday and she lights a candle there: 'You don't often even feel you have a right to anything, to go out and get your hair done, or to dance or laugh or sing. The question is why? And I'm thirty-six years asking why? Why I was never, and all the other families, allowed follow the procedures of a democracy? We should have been allowed to get a solicitor, sue the owners of the nightclub, get your justice, get your compensation with some semblance of normality out of unimaginable grief. You could have moved on where you're stuck in time. Nothing has moved. I'll put it this way: as long as I'm above ground and I breathe air I won't be giving up, because he was my child.'

Three members of Antoinette Keegan's family also died as a result of the fire. Mary, aged 19, and 16-year-old Martina died in the fire. Their father, John, died of a broken heart afterwards. 'It killed him as well. He was a family man,' his widow, Christine, told me. She recalled how she and John had to change out of their funeral clothes after burying Mary and Martina to visit a third daughter, Antoinette, who was in intensive care in hospital and unaware that her two sisters were dead. During her two weeks on a life-support machine, Antoinette was not permitted to listen to a radio, read a newspaper or watch television. Anyone going to visit her was told to tell her that her two sisters were still alive.

Antoinette told me: 'It's like I've been trapped in it. I can't get out of it because the truth hasn't been put out there and I won't give up until the truth is out there. It's like what they're saying happened didn't happen. I know what happened and I can never escape that memory until I get the truth, because my two sisters were killed that night and forty-six others were killed and all the people that were injured. It will never leave me. It'll always be there.'

After being discharged from hospital, Antoinette slept every night with the lights and radio on, but nightmares would waken her. She recalled being embarrassed for a long time that, as an 18-year-old, she used to run into her parents' room and ask if she could get into bed beside them. She said nobody who was in the Stardust on the night of the fire was ever the same again.

The survivor who spent the longest time in hospital, Jimmy Fitzpatrick, needed multiple skin grafts to rebuild his hands and arms, which were extensively burned. He said that the families had been let down by the State and by their fellow citizens. He pointed out that media interest in the tragedy waned, fizzled out and went away. 'It isn't at rest. It isn't all over now. How can they let it rest? The families never got closure. I didn't get any closure either,' he said.

The families of the five young men who were buried in a communal grave because their bodies could not be identified had to wait until 2007 before DNA tests allowed formal identification. One sibling, Andrew Loughman, told me: 'My mother, for years and years and years, if there was a knock at the door or a ring at the doorbell, she always thought maybe that's Eamonn – maybe he banged his head, he went to a hospital, got up, walked out, got a bus to the country, didn't know where he was, his memory gone. She lived with that for years, thinking that one day, because he wasn't identified, it could be him.'

It was these testimonies that had made me return to the scene of the fire for the first time in thirty-six years. I found it incredible that there was not a single sign or notice on the building to say that forty-eight young people had lost their lives there and that scores of others had been injured. It was as if the tragedy had been airbrushed out of history, even at the place where it happened.

Listening to the families made me acknowledge that, like the rest of the media, I too had moved on after the tragedy and had given it little further thought over the years. I had acknowledged in one of the *A Living Word* broadcasts I did on RTÉ Radio in the late 1990s that sometimes when the cameras move away from a story, we forget that there are real people who have to live with their grief and their loss.

I was privileged that so many of the families trusted me to listen to their heartbreaking stories. As a news journalist, I had had to maintain a degree of distance from their campaigns. My retirement from daily news reporting allowed me to temper my professional detachment and to share their harrowing memories, to show that the passage of time had done nothing to ease their torment.

The fortitude of the Stardust families continues to inspire me when my own daily struggle with motor neurone disease threatens to overwhelm me with despair. The uncertainty and the need for answers that I experienced during the seven months between the onset of my first symptoms and my diagnosis were unbearable. I cannot imagine how the Stardust families have managed to face each day for more than forty years with so many unanswered questions about how their loved ones died.

I ended the *After the Headlines* documentary by saying that it was only now, at the end of 2017, that I truly grasped the damage that events like this left in their wake. When the truth is never fully revealed and questions are left unanswered, the families and survivors are given a life sentence of grief, torment and anger. I hope that we never see the likes of it again in Ireland, but if we do, the victims' families must be treated with the fairness, care and humanity that was so sadly lacking in the case of the Stardust fire.

I marched with the families and Christy Moore in a protest at the Office of the Attorney General to demand new inquests, but it was not until 2019, some thirty-eight years after the tragedy, that the Attorney General confirmed, following the renewed campaigning by the families and the media, that fresh inquests should be held because there was 'an insufficiency of inquiry as to how the deaths occurred'.

In February of that year, on the anniversary of the fire, I was honoured and privileged to be asked to unveil a permanent plaque in Artane carrying the names of the forty-eight people who had died. I told their relatives and survivors and other campaigners that the cause of the fire should not still be a mystery and that the State authorities should find the answer and should pay for a proper memorial.

I think they are a remarkable group of people. I have urged them not to give up their fight. I think that if a similar tragedy happened in Ireland today, the country and the world would be convulsed. The country was convulsed for a time after the fire in 1981, but it was subsequently swept under the carpet. The families and friends and relatives of the deceased have lifted that carpet up.

I am convinced that it is one of the darker stains on recent Irish history that the truth about the fire has never been established. I hope that the truth will eventually come out. I'm not certain that the political system wants to establish the truths that the families deserve, but I know that they will not give up their campaigning and I will support them for as long as I live.

I addressed another anniversary vigil at the site in 2020, followed this time by the journalist Eamon Dunphy and by Antoinette Keegan. She reminded the large crowd that the three investigations to date into the cause of the fire had all been inconclusive. 'We have never got any truth from them,' she said.

The 40th anniversary of the tragedy in 2021 was shortly before I first began to notice changes in my voice and my tongue. The relatives and supporters asked me to contribute to a short commemorative video by reading out the names of the forty-eight people who had died. Before enunciating the forty-eight names, I said that I thought it was of crucial importance that everybody in this country knew what happened on that night.

In one of the last recordings of my voice before it began to deteriorate, I said that some progress was being made because of the determination of the families who had been involved tirelessly, year-in, year-out. I added that they should not have had to fight so hard to try to get to the truth and that I hoped we were belatedly on the verge of getting to know what really happened on that night.

The commemorative video, called *Stardust: 40 Years On*, also featured Antoinette Keegan. 'It was like being in hell,' she said as she recalled how the melting ceiling had fallen onto the dancers and how there had been a stampede as they tried to escape via exit doors, many of which were locked and chained. She spoke of her two sisters, Mary, who was 'great, bubbly', a scholarship girl who had recently excelled in her Leaving Certificate exam, and Martina, who was 'absolutely gorgeous, a stunner, like Marilyn Monroe'.

Twelve days before the 41st anniversary of the fire in 2022, Dublin City Coroner's Court was told that the owner of the Stardust nightclub, Eamon Butterly, was seeking to exclude 'unlawful killing' as a possible verdict in the forthcoming resumed inquests. The coroner, Dr Myra Cullinane, told a preliminary hearing that Butterly's barrister was seeking to delay the inquests pending a ruling 'as to whether the verdict of unlawful killing is one open to the jury'.

Counsel for the families, Seán Guerin SC, told the hearing that the Butterly request was 'objectionable'. He said it was 'just unthinkable that the court would exclude a verdict that is permitted by law before the evidence has been heard.' Seán Guerin told a further preliminary hearing a week later that the families were 'appalled and extremely anxious' at Butterly's threat to seek a judicial review to delay or prevent the inquests. Dr Cullinane refused Butterly's request after studying the coroner's powers. A judgment on Butterly's High Court challenge to Dr Cullinane's ruling was awaited in autumn 2022.

The Taoiseach, Micheál Martin, met the families on St Valentine's Day 2022, the 41st anniversary of the fire. He promised them 'all the relevant resources and supports you need' for the inquests. The meeting took place at the site of the former Richmond Hospital, where some of the victims had been taken after the fire and where a memorial bench, designed by artist Robert Ballagh, was unveiled.

I broke down when I sat on the memorial bench with Antoinette Keegan. We had become close friends; she has been in contact with me almost weekly since I told her of my illness. She had lost her two sisters in the fire and both her parents had gone to their graves prematurely as a result of it. She has been a tireless campaigner and longstanding chairwoman of the Stardust Victims Committee. I had been with Antoinette and the other relatives at the site of the disaster on the previous day for a candlelit vigil. I became very emotional at times on both days. I was recalling the trauma of the fire and fearing that these were the last Stardust gatherings that I would be able to attend.

My voice had been getting weaker every day and I had planned to use my voice bank app in public for the first time at the candlelit vigil at the disaster site in Artane. A year earlier my voice had been perfect at the commemoration, but now I was carrying my little speech in my iPad. I decided to speak spontaneously, however, after the welcome I got from the families and the introduction I got from Antoinette. She said that I had been a huge supporter of the campaign for a full inquiry 'from the morning of the tragedy until now'. She said that I was a great friend and a legend to all of the families.

The Stardust families are my heroes and they are entitled to justice. I am convinced that if the fire had happened in a more affluent part of Dublin, there would have been a proper inquiry and the cause would not have been swept under the carpet. I have no idea how much longer I'll be alive, but I will continue to support them as long as I have breath in my body. I have three things on my 'bucket list' – to climb Croagh Patrick for charity; to try to see the Northern Ireland peace process endure; and to see justice for the families of those who never came home from the Stardust disco.

Relatives of each of the forty-eight victims attended the 2022 candlelit vigil. I read out every victim's name as Maurice McHugh, who lost his 17-year-old daughter Caroline in the fire, presented a member of each family with a candle featuring their loved one's name. Christy Moore sang an *a cappella* version of his song 'They Never Came Home'. He was convicted of contempt of court over the song in the mid-1980s. Antoinette Keegan pointed out that the only other person ever brought to court in relation to the Stardust fire was her father John, who was given a suspended sentence for assaulting the nightclub owner, allegedly in self-defence, and bound to the peace for a year while being denied legal aid.

Antoinette Keegan epitomizes the quiet dignity and unquenchable fortitude of the Stardust families. She has spent her entire adult life trying ceaselessly to uncover why her two beloved sisters died at a St Valentine's night disco. She was one of the first people to greet me when I descended from Croagh Patrick in April 2022. She had travelled to Mayo with a group of friends. She said she wanted to be with me there, even though a back ailment prevented her from doing more than a little of the climb. I was deeply honoured. I broke down again as we hugged each other. It was another special moment for me.

One of Antoinette's friends, Lorraine Smyth, summed up that day for me. She had had to climb her own personal mountain of a cancer diagnosis, but she had travelled from Wexford that morning to be with Antoinette and me at Croagh Patrick to raise money for other people with health worries.

Whenever I have listened to Antoinette Keegan speaking year after year at public events, or as she did on the *Late Late Show* with me in December 2021, I have always been reminded of the privileged and carefree life that I had before the onset of my motor neurone symptoms.

My suffering and my uncertainty about what the future holds for me have given me a glimpse of the unbearable and never-ending pain that Antoinette and hundreds of her neighbours have been enduring every single day and night over the past forty-one years.

8. WASHINGTON

Going to Washington DC as RTÉ's US Correspondent in 2009 was probably the biggest mistake of my career.

I applied for the job partly because I had become bored of loitering around the Kildare Street Gate of Leinster House in search of political stories. RTÉ News had a very strong team of political correspondents and reporters working inside Leinster House and my own beat as Chief News Correspondent no longer carried the excitement of the 1980s and 1990s – which had featured the Haughey 'heaves', the Progressive Democrat dramas, the collapse of the Albert Reynolds government and Haughey's eventual, grandiloquent exit.

I also shared the unease of my bosses and some of my colleagues after some people during the previous general election campaign had sought to shake my hand rather than that of the Taoiseach, Bertie Ahern, when I covered his countrywide canvasses. RTÉ is obliged by law to be objective in its news reporting. Assigning the Chief News Correspondent to the incumbent Taoiseach for the second general election campaign in a row might have left RTÉ vulnerable to a charge of illegal partisanship.

Robert Shortt's four-year term as US Correspondent was coming to an end in autumn 2008. RTÉ had a strict policy that nobody could serve more than one term in the role. I was at a career crossroads in Dublin and I decided, with some reluctance, to apply for the Washington job. Even today I can recall some of the cold sweats I broke out in when I wondered if I was doing the right thing. I had reported for RTÉ News from the US several times and I had always enjoyed working there, but moving to Washington full-time, late in my career, was ill-judged and I came to regret it.

One of the main reasons for my unease about the move was that I was in love. Our from-a-distance admiring had become a relationship and it was clear that Claire was a once-in-a-lifetime love. We often laughed when Claire later told me about one of the first times she had seen me. It was in November 1991, during what turned out to be the last of a number of 'heaves' within the Fianna Fáil party against the leadership of Charlie Haughey. I was working at the Kildare Street Gate of Leinster House, doing 'live' inserts into the evening TV News bulletins while a marathon meeting of the Fianna Fáil parliamentary party continued inside the building.

After the pubs closed, a large crowd of Saturday night revellers joined the crowd of Fianna Fáil supporters and reporters outside Leinster House and they began good-humouredly chanting 'Ooh Ah, Charlie Bird, Ooh Ah, Charlie Bird' in mock imitation of one of the chants that Irish soccer supporters had made famous during the previous year's World Cup finals in Italy. Emboldened, they followed this up with another soccer terrace adaptation:

'There's only one Charlie Bird, one Charlie Bird, one Charlie Bird'. One of the Saturday night revellers, unknown to me, was my future wife.

Claire also told me later in our relationship that she and a friend often went to the main RTÉ canteen on what she called 'The Bird Watch'. I would, of course, have noticed and admired her on those occasions, but I was either too shy to approach her or I may have been in another relationship at the time. My life changed forever after I asked her out.

The Washington vacancy arose at a time when my relationship with Claire was going from strength to strength. We had been together for about two years and we had found true happiness together, but I had itchy feet professionally and I went to the US when I was offered the job. Claire travelled to Washington with me to help me settle into my new posting and I was so happy when she stayed on with me for about ten days. I remember feeling very alone on the day that she headed back home. I can vividly remember the taxi pulling away and Claire looking back at me as I faced into starting my new job. Then, over the eighteen or so months that I stayed in Washington, we phoned each other every day and Claire travelled back and forth to stay with me more than half-a-dozen times.

We visited all the tourist sites along the Mall, from the Capitol Building down to the Lincoln Memorial. I got goosebumps standing on the spot where Martin Luther King had made his famous 'I have a dream' speech in August 1963 and at the War Memorial that carries the names of the almost-60,000 US soldiers who died in the Vietnam War. But the streets in Washington's political and business hubs, where RTÉ's office is located, are deserted each weekend when the office-workers go to their homes outside what they call the Beltway. The area becomes like a ghost town. I often did not see another person on the street when I had to go into our office on a Saturday or Sunday.

If I wasn't working on a weekend, I used to cycle for miles on the bicycle paths around DC. I purchased a bike and when Claire came over for a few days we used to hire a bike for her and head off out to Mount Vernon, the home of George Washington. We used to race each other along the 30-mile route, even in searing heat. These were magical days for me. Everywhere you look in Washington and the surrounding areas is steeped in history, including many Civil War sites.

Another highlight of my leisure time was a trip to the Soldiers' National Cemetery in Gettysburg, in Pennsylvania, with Paddy Whelan, who owned Hoban's Irish Bar on DuPont Circle. I had developed an interest in Abraham Lincoln and I had read many of the books about him, so that trip out to Gettysburg was a real treat.

I also used to regularly meet Denis Staunton, the Washington Correspondent of the *Irish Times*, for a meal and a chat. Friends from home called from time to time. I had a great couple of days with Peadar and Bríd Póil from Inis Oírr when they called over.

But nothing prepared me for how unhappy I would become when Claire was in Ireland. I was also badly missing my two daughters. I had worked in the US for RTÉ News several times over the previous thirty years, including for weeks after the 9/11 Twin Towers attacks in

New York in 2001, and I had always thrived there, but I had never covered the country's domestic politics. Before I formally took over the posting, I covered some of the Democratic Party primaries when Hillary Clinton was in the battle of her life with Barack Obama. I also covered the historic Presidential election day and night in Chicago in November 2008 when Obama defeated John McCain.

I will never forget the morning of the vote. Chicago was in the heart of Obama country. We went out very early in the morning, at around 6.00 a.m., to watch people form queues outside polling stations. I interviewed an elderly black lady who told me that she was casting her vote for the first time in her life. She said she was voting for Obama. It really was a spine-tingling moment – on that very cold November morning in Chicago, Illinois, this woman was not just voting for the first time in her life, she was voting for the man who was the first person of colour to run for the office of President of the United States of America.

Later, I had the privilege of being in Chicago's Grant Park when the result was announced and Obama walked onto the platform with his wife Michelle and their two daughters, Malia and Sasha, to deliver his historic acceptance speech. It was another spine-tingling moment for me and for the tens of thousands of people who were there.

My eighteen months in Washington coincided, more or less, with the first year-and-a-half of Obama's historic and ground-breaking presidency. My first assignment, after I had taken over the role in January 2009, was to report on his journey from Chicago to Washington DC for the inauguration. Obama was sworn in as the 44th President of the United States on 20 January 2009. It was a bitterly cold morning on the Mall, but the crowd of 1.8 million people was one of the largest gatherings ever seen in Washington. It was a day that I will never forget. Even though I wasn't overly excited about my Washington posting, I was watching history in the making. Witnessing Barack Obama become the first black person to become President of the United States was one of the standout moments of my career.

One of the pre-inauguration concerts at the Lincoln Memorial at the top of the Mall in Washington featured U2, who were the biggest rock band in the world at the time. I went to the band's hotel to interview them before the concert. When I had finished the interview, a producer in the RTÉ Washington office, Lesley Steinhauser, asked if she could have her photograph taken with Bono and the lads. Bono turned to her and said: 'Yes, you can have your picture taken with us, if we can have our picture taken with Charlie.' That photo of me with my arms around Bono and The Edge has hung on a wall on the stairway of my home since I returned from Washington.

In February 2009, I travelled to Mexico and Cuba with Micheál Martin, who was Minister for Foreign Affairs at the time. We travelled south on the Irish government jet, but my cameraman, Harvey Cofske, and I returned from Cuba on commercial flights after spending a few free days touring rural parts of the island. We were able to return there a few months later and I was able to report from the notorious Guantánamo Bay prison camp, despite our being shadowed non-stop by US military personnel. It was a tightly controlled and unpleasant experience. We were accompanied by 'minders' at all times and we were not allowed to go near any inmates, even though we could hear some of them shout out to us as we passed by. I felt very uncomfortable throughout the visit, not because we were in any danger but because every step we made was so regulated.

In my early months in Washington, I also managed to secure an interview with Hillary Clinton in her office in the State Department, after she had been appointed Secretary of State. It was quite a lengthy interview and we ended up laughing together. I cannot remember what question of mine sparked the laughter, but members of her staff suggested afterwards that we might have been flirting mildly with each other.

Despite my welcome in the State Department, my transition from being a big fish in a country of not many more than three million people to being a mere sprat in a country of more than 300 million was not easy and I had trouble settling into my new role, especially when I did not have a big story to cover every day.

But it was not as if my days of being a big fish in a small pool were entirely over. One Irish newspaper submitted a Freedom of Information request to RTÉ News about my expenses, including a question on whether I or RTÉ was paying for my shirts to be cleaned. And one of the Dublin tabloids hired a photographer to sit opposite the RTÉ offices in Washington to take pictures of my comings and goings. He missed a scoop on the day he failed to follow me when I had lunch near the Capitol Building with Rita O'Hare, the former IRA and Sinn Féin activist who had become, because of her flaming red hair, the famous 'An Bean Rua' in the peace process talks on both sides of the Atlantic.

A Belfast-born, lifelong Republican, Rita O'Hare was an early member of the civil rights movement in Northern Ireland and she was imprisoned in Northern Ireland and in the Republic of Ireland for IRA activities during the 1970s. She has been unable to visit Northern Ireland since jumping bail there in 1972.

I first met her in early 1994, shortly after Section 31 of the Broadcasting Acts had been removed by the coalition government. She was hosting a Sinn Féin press conference at Dublin Airport, prior to Gerry Adams's departure to the United States when President Bill Clinton had very controversially granted him a visa. The huge international interest in the visit meant that the press conference was a fairly chaotic media scrum, but she and I established a working rapport there that has endured.

Although banned from entering Northern Ireland, she had been editor of the widely-read weekly Republican newspaper *An Phoblacht/Republican News* and was General Secretary and Press Officer of Sinn Féin. As the nascent peace process got underway, I was in regular contact with her and I got to know her fairly well. I saw her going to and from secret meetings with government officials, including staff in the Taoiseach's Office, and I chose not to report those meetings so as not to endanger the delicate, evolving talks. I had noticed her meeting senior people in the Albert Reynolds and Bertie Ahern governments in the strangest of places, but I respected, and I continue to respect, the confidentiality of those talks.

Even though the bulk of the world's media attention on Sinn Féin was about the roles played by Adams and

McGuinness, I know that 'An Bean Rua' was central to all of the important developments in Dublin, London and Washington. And while she did not play a visible role at the Stormont talks that led to the signing of the Good Friday Agreement in 1998, because she couldn't travel to the North of Ireland, it's beyond doubt that she played a key role in the Republican movement's participation in the path to the peace process.

She was also a regular visitor to the residence in the Phoenix Park in Dublin of the US Ambassador to Ireland, Jean Kennedy Smith, one of the youngest members of the famous Kennedy clan, and another key player in the peace process. As the Sinn Féin representative in the United States for twenty years following the signing of the Good Friday Agreement in 1998, Rita met and was photographed with most of the top politicians in Washington DC, including Presidents Bill Clinton and Barack Obama, and Joe Biden when he was vice-president. One well-known piece of television footage shows Bill Clinton getting out of a car to go over to greet her.

I met Rita in Washington a number of times for a chat and a gossip. If MI5 or any other branch of the British intelligence services was monitoring our meetings, they would have heard nothing sinister. The peace process had brought an end to Provisional IRA violence. 'An Bean Rua' had become a friend of mine. I hope that someday the key role she played in the peace process and the Good Friday Agreement will be fully told.

Away from my lunches with contacts and fellow-journalists, I was increasingly homesick because I was missing Claire and my daughters. Claire had not been happy about my move, but our relationship blossomed even more during our transatlantic relationship. I will never forget the day, in early 2010, when I asked Claire if she would move in with me. I was standing outside the Apple building in New York's Times Square and she was driving along the quays in Dublin when I phoned her. I asked her if she would like to move in with me where I was living in Ashford, in County Wicklow, and she said of course she would. Within weeks she had changed the curtains in one of the bedrooms, much to my confusion when I arrived home. She also brought the ashes of her much-loved dog Garby and she began a campaign for me to get her a replacement puppy. I resisted for a long time before relenting.

The broad Atlantic Ocean divide strengthened our love and made me resolve to cut short my time in Washington.

One big story that bridged the Atlantic Ocean and made headlines at home was my attempt to interview the disgraced and fugitive former chief executive of the collapsed Anglo Irish Bank, David Drumm. The recent collapse of Anglo Irish Bank had precipitated the disintegration of Ireland's entire commercial banking network, necessitating a multi-billion-euro taxpayer-funded rescue. Drumm, until recently Ireland's best-paid and most visible bank boss, was now Public Enemy Number One. He had fled to the United States, and my bosses sent me to Cape Cod to try to find him.

We traced him to a big house in an exclusive area. Harvey Cofske miked me up and he began filming from outside the compound while I walked up to the front door. My knocks on the front door went unanswered, but I could see Drumm through a window and I shouted to ask him why he was ducking down. He said that his children were with him and he asked me to leave. I told him that the taxpayers of Ireland had questions for him to answer.

I abandoned the attempted doorstep because of his pleas about his children. RTÉ has very strict policies about conducting interviews with or near children. People have often asked me why I did not persist, but we could not have victimized the children because of their father's notoriety. Nonetheless, my shouted questions through the letterbox of this exclusive Cape Cod property have been shown and re-shown countless times on Irish TV over the years.

Another domestic drama that followed me across the Atlantic was when my colleague and pal George Lee resigned from RTÉ and was subsequently elected a Fine Gael TD in a by-election in Dublin South in May 2009. It was a double domestic drama in that it involved an RTÉ staff resignation and in that it became front-page national news in Ireland. George and I had been close friends since we worked together on the National Irish Bank scandals in 1998 – the overcharging of customers and the secret offshore accounts that were canaries in the mine of bank management malfeasance a full ten years before the commercial banks caused Ireland's economic collapse. I have never previously admitted my role in George's jumping ship, but I was the one who suggested to the Fine Gael hierarchy that they should approach him about running for them in Dublin South. I remember suggesting to the party press officer Ciaran Conlon, over a coffee, that George would be a great addition to their economics team and that he had the potential to be a brilliant Minister for Finance.

This happened at the same time that Fine Gael were seriously trying to lure me to run for them as a candidate in a Dublin constituency. Maybe they sensed that I was unsettled in Washington, because I remember getting a phone call out of the blue inviting me for a chat on my next visit home to Dublin. During that next visit home I was asked to meet Frank Flannery, who was the party's Mr Fix-it and another member of the hierarchy. We met in the Davenport Hotel on Merrion Square, not far from Leinster House.

I remember looking over my shoulder as I walked into the hotel. Even though it was part of my job to meet political apparatchiks all the time, this was a furtive meeting and I knew that I was being disloyal to my bosses, at least potentially. The carrots the Fine Gael team dangled in front of me were juicy. They said that they felt that I would be a shoe-in for a Dáil seat in one of the Dublin constituencies. They even said that if the timing was right, I might be a presidential candidate for the party. Still, I never seriously considered abandoning journalism for politics. It was never an option for me.

At our next meeting, in the same hotel, they showed me the results of their research, suggesting that I had a good chance of winning a seat in the Dublin South Central constituency. I still have these research papers at home. They emboldened me to ask if I might expect a ministerial job in a future Fine Gael government. The apparatchiks told me I might have a chance of getting a junior ministry, perhaps in Overseas Development – hardly Minister for Finance or the keys to Áras an Uachtaráin, but prestigious nonetheless, with a desk inside Government Buildings, instead of pounding the pavement outside.

I returned to Washington and I quickly told the Fine Gaelers that I had no intention of following George Lee into politics. He and I were in almost daily contact. I knew about his intention to leave RTÉ even before his bosses did and now I learned of his disillusionment after Enda Kenny had failed to add him, in January 2010, to the Fine Gael economics team that already comprised Michael Noonan, Leo Varadkar, Richard Bruton, Simon Coveney and Kieran O'Donnell.

George's bombshell resignation from the Dáil after only eight months as a TD in February 2010 caused a media frenzy at home. I invited George to come to Washington to get away from the furore. He spent several days with me before heading down to New York. While he was staying with me, I had to give a speech to an Irish group in a hotel in Dupont Circle. After my speech, several people asked me questions about George. None of them knew that at that moment George was sitting in the hotel's coffee bar downstairs, waiting for me.

The biggest story I covered during my time in Washington was undoubtedly the 2010 earthquake in Haiti. I still find it hard to comprehend the loss of life and the devastation I witnessed when I spent a week reporting from there immediately after the disaster. I had reported on earthquakes in Turkey and Pakistan, but I had never seen anything like the death and destruction that I encountered in and around Port-au-Prince, the capital of one of the poorest countries in the world.

The earthquake, in the early hours of 12 January, was one of the worst-ever humanitarian disasters anywhere in the world. The United Nations has estimated that the quake killed 220,000 people and injured 300,000 others. Some 1.5 million people were left homeless. The quake had only lasted for a few seconds, but it had been suffered by some of the world's most vulnerable people. Nobody I've ever spoken to in Europe or in the US has been able to grasp those figures. People I ask usually guess the number of fatalities at around 20,000 to 50,000 people, maybe 10 per cent of the total.

It was impossible to fly from the US to Port-au-Prince in the days after the earthquake because so many buildings and roads near the airport had been destroyed, but my cameraman Harvey Cofske and I were among the first foreign journalists to reach there, thanks to my Irish connections. We got there via Kingston in Jamacia after I spent hours lobbying the Irish Third World agency Concern in Dublin and the former Irish government press secretary P. J. Mara, who was now working for the businessman Denis O'Brien, who controlled much of the mobile phone network in Haiti through his company Digicel.

The destruction we saw on arrival almost defied description. I saw a collapsed building where four or five stories had been sandwiched together, trapping and killing people inside. On our first night we slept in the ruins of a destroyed hotel that had just one room still standing, close to the swimming pool. It soon began to fill up with other journalists who were arriving from all over the world. The next day, Concern organized for us to stay with their staff in the ruins of another building in the grounds of their office in Port-au-Prince. Early on the second morning, when we had finally got to sleep, the ground and the remains of the structure started to shake wildly from a massive aftershock. The tremor went on for so long that I feared we were going to be killed. I did a telephone interview with Gerry Ryan on 2FM that morning, our last chat before he died.

A few days later I was interviewing Denis O'Brien down near the market square when shots rang out nearby and his security team had to bundle us into a car to escape. O'Brien, who at the time was also one of the largest shareholders in Independent News & Media, successfully sued the *Irish Daily Mail* over its reporting of his interview and his contacts with me in Haiti. A High Court jury in Dublin awarded him damages of €150,000 for defamation after the tabloid accused him of hypocrisy. I had to attend the court myself to disprove some of the paper's assertions.

The death, devastation and abject poverty that I had seen in Haiti may as well have been on a different planet from the Washington easy wealth, luxury and privilege that I returned to. The ready access to a warm shower and to food and transport was in stark contrast to the hand-to-mouth existence of the majority of the survivors of the earthquake in Third World Haiti. I could not tell Claire about everything I had seen. My day job left me little time for reflection.

One of the highlights of the Washington year is always the visit to the Oval Office in the White House of the Taoiseach to present a bowl of shamrock to the President of the United States on St Patrick's Day. I had covered a number of visits by previous Taoisigh, but the 2010 reception, less than two months after I had got back from Haiti, was probably the most interesting.

With former Garda detective Willie McGee viewing a 1979 *Irish Times* newspaper in which the ransom gang exchanged a coded message with the Department of Agriculture. (Credit: *Irish Times*)

On the Patrick Kavanagh bench at the Grand Canal in Dublin on our wedding day in May 2016. (Credit: Karl Hayden)

With the WestAwake Gang on the Promenade in Galway in June 2021. From left: Sean O'Rourke, Tommie Gorman, Michael Lally, Ray Burke, Jim Fahy. (Missing is Joe O'Brien, who took the photo) (Credit: Joe O'Brien)

With the Kehoe's Gang on Duke Lane, Dublin, in July 2021. From left: Ray Burke, Joe O'Brien, Dympna Moroney. (Credit: Claire Bird)

With Vicky Phelan at her home near Limerick in December 2021. (Credit: Claire Bird)

With Joe Duffy in The Chester Beatty Inn, Ashford, Co Wicklow, in December 2021. (Credit: Claire Bird)

With my five grandchildren before the climb. (Credit: Dee Forbes)

With children from Scoil Phádraig, Westport, at the Octagon in the town on the eve of the Climb. (Credit: Gerry Mooney)

With the children from Brackloon National School on 'the Shoulder', nearly halfway up the Reek, after we had been soaked by a shower of rain and hail. (Credit: Gerry Mooney)

The Struggle (Credit: Gerry Mooney)

With Ryan Tubridy and Daniel O'Donnell on Croagh Patrick. (Credit: Michael McLaughlin)

With Claire, Neasa, Orla and my grandchildren in the chapel at the summit, after I had lit the five candles. (Credit: Michael McLaughlin)

Overcome with grief at the Irish tricolour and the flag of Ukraine at the summit. (Credit: Brendan St. John)

With Claire, Tiger, Fr Charlie McDonnell and Garda Inspector Denis Harrington after a planning meeting. (Credit: Charlie Bird)

With Antoinette Keegan at the Stardust Commemoration in February 2022. (Credit: *Irish Independent Newspapers*)

With Antoinette Keegan at the end of the 2022 commemoration in front of the wall bearing the names and photographs of the 48 Stardust fire victims. (Credit: *Irish Independent Newspapers*)

Reporting from in front of the Capitol Building in Washington DC in January 2009 on the day that Barak Obama was inaugurated as President of the United States of America. (Credit: Lesley

My daring exchange with President Obama in the Oval Office of the White House during the St Patrick's Day visit by Taoiseach Brian Cowen and Minister for Foreign Affairs Micheál Martin in March

Meeting the biggest rock band in the world, U2, in Washington, 2010. (Credit: Charlie Bird)

In the media pool in the Garden of Remembrance in Dublin for Queen Elizabeth's historic visit in May 2011. I'm standing directly above the Queen and President McAleese. (Credit: *Irish Times*)

In the RTÉ Radio Centre preparing for my *Saturday With Charlie Bird* programme in September 2011. (Credit: RTÉ)

With Taoiseach Enda Kenny and contributors to my book *A Day in May* at the book's launch in the National Gallery of Ireland in May 2016. (Credit: Karl Hayden)

At the launch of the Vote Yes campaign in the Pillar Room of the Rotunda Hospital in Dublin on March 9 2015 before the Marriage Equality Referendum. (Credit: Karl Hayden)

At the South Pole in January 2011. (Credit: Crossing the Line Productions / RTÉ)

Encounter with the elephant seals in South Georgia. (Credit: Crossing the Line Productions / RTÉ)

Taking a dip at the North Pole. (Photo credit: Crossing the Line Productions / RTÉ)

Out on the frozen sea with an Inuit guide. Taken near Grise Fiord off Ellesmere Island in a remote part of the Canadian Arctic. (Photo credit: Crossing the Line Productions / RTÉ)

With John Fitzpatrick at the Eithne and Paddy Fitzpatrick Memorial fundraiser at Sleepy Hollow Country Club, New York State, in May 2022. (Credit: Jimmy Higgins)

With Claire and Tiger on the Darkness Into Light memorial walk in Bray in May 2022. (Credit: *Irish Independent*)

Laughing with relief with Ryan Tubridy after my choking scare during the Late Late Show in May 2022. (Credit: Andres Poveda / RTÉ)

Unveiling The Warrior sculpture in the grounds of Westport House in County Mayo in June 2022. (Credit: Conor McKeown)

Sharing a laugh with President Higgins and Tiger after I presented him with a copy of Climb with Charlie in Áras an Uachtaráin in June 2022. (Credit: Maxwells Photography)

Handing over two cheques, for €1,688,000 each, to Lillian McGovern, chief executive of the Irish Motor Neurone Disease Association, and Stephanie Manahan of Pieta, in Merrion Square, Dublin, on Tuesday 26 July, 2022. (Credit: Mark Maxwell /Maxwells

With Peadar Póil in front of the chair with my inscribed wording after its installation on Inis Oírr in summer 2021. (Credit: Claire Bird)

Brian Cowen was Taoiseach at the time. The normal drill on these occasions is that the President and the Taoiseach have a private meeting in the Oval Office before the White House pool of reporters and camera crews are admitted to throw questions at the President from behind a rope barrier. The cadre of Irish reporters accompanying the Taoiseach are normally also admitted and they are expected to throw questions at the Taoiseach.

On this occasion, I was one of the lucky ones. I was standing close to where President Obama was sitting and as events unfolded, I got the opportunity to fire a question at him. At the time he was trying to get his health care bill through Congress and I jokingly asked him if he got his health care bill passed, would he consider visiting Ireland? He responded by throwing his head back and laughing loudly with some funny comment. As he was looking at me, I stretched my hand out to shake his. This was completely against the rules, but Obama stood up and shook my hand and then he put his arms around me, to the utter horror of the Oval Office staff.

Taoiseach Brian Cowen and Minister for Foreign Affairs Micheál Martin could only look on in bemusement, but a White House pool journalist told me that I would be in big trouble for shaking the hand of the president. I had broken all the rules of White House security and protocol. In the end, nothing happened, and the handshake did not over-shadow the reporting of another big day in Irish-US relations. It was an amazing moment. I don't know what compelled me to do it, but I'm glad I did. It's a treasured memory.

One of the White House pool photographers, Doug Mills, had captured the entire sequence of my exchange with

President Obama. A couple of days later I contacted Doug and he e-mailed me the full series of nine photographs. In the background Taoiseach Brian Cowen and Minister Micheál Martin can both be seen clearly laughing at my cheeky encounter with President Obama. The photographs are among the most treasured of my forty years in journalism. They sit on a wall in my home as a reminder of that memorable day in the Oval Office of the White House.

Despite the excitement of these unforgettable professional highlights, I was never far from recurring bouts of homesickness. The St Patrick's Day visits of politicians and journalists whom I had worked with so closely in Dublin only heightened my sense of isolation. In that month, too, the birth of my first grandson made me miss home more and more. I was working in California at the time and Orla could not contact her sister Neasa with the news of his birth, so I got a Newsroom colleague to send a taxi to Neasa's home to ring her doorbell to waken her. I gave her the news via the taxi-driver's mobile phone and I paid him with my credit card. The new arrival was named Charlie, after me, and I could not wait to see him. My feet were getting itchier. I knew that I would face severe criticism both within RTÉ and outside the station for coming home early, but I never regretted the decision.

My itchy feet and loose tongue soon caused the worst row I ever had with my boss, Ed Mulhall, the managing director of RTÉ News and Current Affairs. We had worked very closely together, day-in, day-out, for many years and I still hugely regret our temporary falling-out. Our professional relationship had been almost symbiotic. Nearly every day he suggested stories or angles for me to pursue; nearly every day his hunches were fruitful. We also lived close to one another in Bray and our children attended the same Educate Together school at the same time.

Instead of confessing to Ed that I had not settled in Washington, I began to tell visiting colleagues or Newsroom pals with whom I was in contact that I did not see myself completing my four-year term in the US. I was being honest, but I was far too candid and unprofessional and my loose talk soon came back to bite me.

My habit during short visits home was to drop into the Newsroom to chat with colleagues and to call into Ed for a sit-down chat in his office. My loose talk had, of course, reached his ears and we had a blazing row – the first and worst row we ever had. I had not realized how upsetting it must have been for him to hear of me telling others that I would not see out my term in Washington. And, of course, it looked very bad for RTÉ management to have appointed someone to what was probably the most sought-after posting in Irish journalism only to find that the appointee did not really want to be there. It was an awful meeting, and it still gives me the shivers to recall it.

We argued heatedly for about ten minutes before things cooled down. I apologized for the trouble I had caused. Ed then told me why he was so uncharacteristically upset – just days earlier he had been told that one of our most popular and respected Newsroom colleagues, Colm Murray, had been diagnosed with motor neurone disease. I knew nothing about MND before it afflicted Colm.

Colm's illness shattered everyone in RTÉ and everybody in his huge network of friends and colleagues in horse racing, sports and politics. It made my prima donna-like behaviour over the Washington job seem so trivial and nonsensical. With Ed and Joe O'Brien, I went to visit Colm as his condition deteriorated, and I attended his funeral in Clontarf and in Sutton Cemetery. When my time came, I tried to cope with it with the same dignity and grace that Colm had shown me.

The Irish newspapers gave me a lot of flack about my short time in Washington and about the documentaries I made for RTÉ Television about my work there. With the benefit of hindsight, I realize that I should not have taken up the job, especially so late in my career. At the time, the reasons I gave myself for quitting were that I was having to conduct a transatlantic relationship with my future wife and also that I was missing my daughters and my first grandchild. I have no doubt now, however, that my mistake was going there in the first place.

After my fraught meeting with Ed Mulhall, my days in Washington were numbered. I covered a State visit by President Mary McAleese and the enormous oil spill in the Gulf of Mexico, but after less than eighteen months in the US I was back in Dublin by the end of May 2010, loitering once again outside the gates of Leinster House and reporting on another political 'heave'. This time it was a Fine Gael heave, as Richard Bruton attempted to oust the party leader and future Taoiseach, Enda Kenny. His effort was no more successful than the early anti-Haughey heaves in Fianna Fáil.

I had come full circle, back to my old patch. But my sixtieth birthday had passed and I had begun to catch glimpses of the finishing line of my RTÉ career in the distance. My own brief flirtation with Fine Gael had not been real. I was only testing the waters. But the dalliance, however brief and unconsummated, did show that I was unsettled in Washington and perhaps beginning to get tired of covering the political beat from the outside.

Nearly half a century has now passed since RTÉ first sent me to work in America. I was working as a researcher on the current affairs programme *Seven Days* when I was sent to Boston in early 1976 to help prepare a major television documentary on the 1776–1976 bicentennial celebrations of the United States. I spent a month in 'Southie', in the heart of the huge Irish community in Boston. My producer and I rented an apartment on Swallow Street, near the old harbour and Dorchester Bay. It was a real eye-opener for me as I had only been outside Ireland once before and my transatlantic flight to Boston's Logan Airport was only my third time on an aeroplane.

Dorchester teemed with Irish people, newly arrived emigrants and the offspring of the tens of thousands who had sailed from post-Famine Ireland to Boston in the second half of the nineteenth century. Every face I saw reminded me of four lines from a recent Horslips song: *'You can move to Boston/Take a job in a small hotel/But that won't be the answer/You'll still hear St Patrick's Bell.'*

My producer in Boston was John Kelleher, who had worked on a number of award-winning RTÉ series, including *Strumpet City* and *Hall's Pictorial Weekly*, and who was now a producer/director on the station's flagship *Seven Days* programme. He later made a memorable documentary on Charlie Haughey for Channel 4 in the UK and he made eight cinema films, including the 1986 comedy *Eat the Peach*. He also worked as Controller of Programmes for RTÉ Television and he was Ireland's Director of Film Classification from 2003 to 2009, significantly modernizing Ireland's film censorship regime.

John contacted me again early in 2021 to suggest making a TV documentary on my *Ransom '79* scoop and podcast series. We were discussing how we might adapt the story for television when my deteriorating health meant that we had to abandon the plan before we had even started to sketch it out. Almost immediately after my diagnosis, however, RTÉ commissioned John and his team to prepare a 75-minute documentary on my career and illness. It was entitled *Charlie Bird: Loud and Clear* and it was broadcast on 13 June 2022. At the same time, John reimagined how to televise the *Ransom '79* story and he began work on a drama-documentary version. After nearly fifty years our working relationship had come full circle, but my motor neurone affliction, more deleterious with every passing day, severely limited my involvement in the project.

Colm Murray had been hale and hearty when I went to Washington in 2009, but he was in terminal decline when I returned to Dublin less than eighteen months later. We had worked together happily for years until his career was ended abruptly and cruelly. Nobody could have known then that my own career would end in the same way.

9. RETIRE

Two of the most significant and symbolic broadcasts of my career were made from the Garden of Remembrance on Parnell Square, at the north end of O'Connell Street in Dublin city centre.

Dedicated to the memory of 'all those who gave their lives in the cause of Irish freedom', the Garden is one of the most hallowed places in Ireland. It stands on the site of the nineteenth-century Rotunda Gardens and Rink, where the original Sinn Féin party was established in 1905 by Arthur Griffith and Edward Martyn to work for Irish self-determination. It is also where the Irish Volunteers were founded in November 1913 to defend Ireland's Home Rule aspirations and it is where the captured GPO volunteers from the 1916 Rising were taken and ill-treated at the end of Easter week.

The Garden site is also where Charles Stewart Parnell and the Irish Parliamentary Party met, and where the Land League and Conradh na Gaeilge (the Gaelic League) had offices, and it is adjacent to where Thomas Clarke and other IRB leaders resolved in September 1914 that there should be an uprising in Ireland during the world war that had recently begun.

At the Garden's official opening during the 1916 jubilee celebrations in April 1966, President Éamon de Valera said: 'The purpose of the Garden is to remind us of the sacrifices of the past, the struggle and suffering over the centuries to secure independence. The design is symbolic, representing Christian sacrifice and suffering, faith and hope, resurgence and peace.' He added that it was also a challenge to future generations to prove worthy of all the sacrifices made in the past and to maintain Ireland as a separate nation. And he said that he hoped that future visitors to the Garden would remember not just the leaders of the 1916 Rising but also the nameless ones, the unknown men and women who bore the burden of every battle.

My two RTÉ News reports from the Garden, some seventeen years apart, bookended what I regard as the most important phase of my reporting career. De Valera's hopes about future generations were finally realized in the Garden as the twentieth century gave way to the twenty-first. It was at the Garden's sunken, cross-shaped water feature, whose green tiled floor is broken by warlike designs of swords and shields, that 800 years of Anglo-Irish conflicts gave way to reconciliation and mutual recognition when Queen Elizabeth spoke there in May 2011. The day's symbolism was reinforced by the Garden's centrepiece – a giant sculpture by Oisín Kelly, based on the ancient Irish legend of the Children of Lir, who were reborn as humans after being transformed into swans for 900 years.

I have said many times that the standout parts of my long reporting career for RTÉ News were my coverage of what became known as 'the peace process', the years of unprecedented talks between the Irish and British governments and the IRA and Loyalist paramilitary groups. The 'process' took nearly eight years of tortuous on-off negotiations, and several interventions from the White House in Washington, before the signing of the Good Friday Agreement in Belfast in April 1998 brought an end to thirty years of murderous violence that had spread from Northern Ireland to many parts of the Republic, as well as to England and continental Europe.

It was close to the Garden of Remembrance in August 1994 that my first IRA contact, a man calling himself 'Brendan', gave me, through an intermediary who I still dare not name, a small piece of paper and a miniature Dictaphone cassette recording of the IRA's announcement of its first historic ceasefire of the era called 'the Troubles'. Up to the beginning of that year, RTÉ had been prevented under Section 31 of the Broadcasting Act from interviewing any IRA or Sinn Féin spokesperson. This legal prohibition had been in place since the outset of 'the Troubles' and it had resulted in one RTÉ journalist being jailed briefly and another losing her job over interviews with IRA leaders. It had also caused the sacking of the entire RTÉ Authority in November 1972.

I was heavily involved in the campaign for the removal of Section 31 during my time as Father of the Chapel (chairman) of the RTÉ branch of the National Union of Journalists during the 1980s, shortly after I had joined the Newsroom. We had picketed Dáil Éireann during our annual protests. I had worked alongside Kevin O'Kelly, the RTÉ journalist who had been jailed in 1972 when he refused to identify an IRA leader he had interviewed for a radio programme – the programme that led to the sacking of the RTÉ Authority. O'Kelly was imprisoned for contempt of court after he refused to identify the IRA chief of staff Seán Mac Stíofáin as the subject of his radio programme during the IRA leader's trial in the Special Criminal Court.

My live radio report from close to the Garden of Remembrance was broadcast as a newsflash just after 11.00 a.m. on the morning of 31 August 1994, nearly twenty-two years after O'Kelly's jailing and just a few months after the Section 31 broadcasting ban had finally been abolished by the Minister for Arts, Culture and the Gaeltacht, and future President of Ireland, Michael D. Higgins. The broadcast included the opening lines of the four-paragraph IRA statement that broke the peace talks deadlock. These words were:

Recognising the potential of the current situation and in order to enhance the democratic peace process and underline our definite commitment to its success, the leadership of Óglaigh na hÉireann have decided that, as of midnight, Wednesday 31 August, there will be a complete cessation of military operations.

Even though the IRA statement was typewritten, my contact, 'Brendan', had demanded that both it and the cassette tape should be destroyed after use. The statement, one of only three, had been written in Long Kesh prison and smuggled out. The whereabouts of the other two copies are unknown. The tape recording was of a woman's voice reciting the statement against the background noise of a hairdryer, an IRA precaution to make it harder to trace where or when the tape had been recorded. I quietly defied 'Brendan' and held onto the statement and the audio tape because I recognized their historic significance. They are among the items relating to the peace process that I have donated to the National Museum of Ireland.

The first IRA ceasefire lasted for eighteen shaky, uncertain months. Despite its fragility and the painfully slow pace of political progress in Northern Ireland, the Irish and British governments worked to consolidate their recent rapprochement. Nine months after the August 1994 ceasefire, I reported from Baldonnel military aerodrome in west county Dublin when Prince Charles arrived there to begin the first official visit to Ireland by a member of Britain's Royal Family since Irish independence.

The collapse of the ceasefire just eighteen months later was one of the worst days of my reporting career. It was Friday, 9 February 1996 and I had left the Newsroom unusually early to go home to try to fight a heavy head cold. My mobile phone battery had gone down. I had been the IRA's sole contact in RTÉ since 1993. My boss at that time, Joe Mulholland, and his BBC counterparts had decided then that the exploratory moves towards an IRA ceasefire and the likely imminent abolition of Section 31 of the Broadcasting Act made it imperative to open a line of communication with the illegal organization. As Sinn Féin's director of publicity Rita O'Hare observed later: 'RTÉ was the main source of broadcast news in the Twenty-six Counties and therefore key to people getting accurate information.' It was RTÉ's future Northern Editor,

Tommie Gorman, who did the dangerous and risky work of setting up my contact with 'Brendan'.

But on that Friday evening in February 1996, vital time was lost as my Newsroom bosses tried to contact me to say that 'Brendan' had rung my office extension and had said that he needed me to ring him urgently because the IRA had decided 'with great reluctance' to end its ceasefire. I had no quick way of contacting 'Brendan' when my bosses alerted me on my home landline and said that he had used a codename, Eksund, that I knew to be authentic. I wasted more time trying to reach senior Sinn Féin members before I drove in panic to the house of a leading Republican figure in Dublin.

Just as I arrived at the house, 'Brendan' got through on my recharged mobile phone. He asked me why RTÉ had not broadcast the IRA statement. I said that my bosses could not be sure that it was authentic. 'It's for real, Charlie,' he said. 'You can go with it.' I raced back to RTÉ and I was ushered into the broadcast studio where the *Six-One News* was coming to a close. I told the programme anchor Bryan Dobson on air that the IRA ceasefire was over. A few minutes later a huge IRA bomb exploded at Canary Wharf in London's Docklands, killing two men, Inan Bashir and John Jeffries, and causing millions of pounds worth of damage to surrounding buildings. I'm still haunted by the thought that those men might still be alive had I been at my desk and had my mobile phone been even 5 per cent charged when my IRA contact tried to talk to me more than an hour earlier. I had been the only person that the IRA had sought to contact to announce the end of the ceasefire.

Regrets and recriminations rang out on both sides of the Irish Sea after the Canary Wharf bombing, but within four months I was at Buckingham Palace when President Mary Robinson went there to meet Queen Elizabeth. It was another ground-breaking moment in the peace process – one head of state meeting another – even though political and diplomatic realities meant that Mrs Robinson's status during the visit was as President Mary Robinson, not as President of Ireland.

A military band played 'Amhrán na bhFiann' while President Robinson inspected an armed forces guard of honour in the inner square of Buckingham Palace. Only a few of the people present would have been familiar with the English language translation of the Irish national anthem's opening words: *Soldiers are we.* A little over five years had passed since the IRA had fired mortar bombs into the nearby back garden of the British Prime Minister's residence in Downing Street. I made eye contact with the Tánaiste and Minister for Foreign Affairs, Dick Spring, a TD for the Republican county of Kerry, who had won the third of his three international rugby caps playing against England. With a silent nod to each other we acknowledged the significance of President Robinson's visit.

I was once again the conduit for the IRA's announcement of the restoration of its ceasefire in July 1997. I was asked to meet 'Brendan' in Dundalk, close to the border with Northern Ireland. He changed our meeting point to a local car wash at the last minute after he had spotted a Garda checkpoint outside our arranged meeting place at the Fairways Hotel. I copied the statement into my notebook from a page he gave me. He then took back the original and he corrected my note, insisting that I write that the statement was issued by 'the leadership of Óglaigh na hÉireann' rather than by the leadership of the IRA. I later got Taoiseach Bertie Ahern to sign that page of my notebook.

'Brendan' was the most tight-lipped of the four IRA spokesmen I dealt with. Initially, he never elaborated on whatever script he gave me and he refused to answer any of my questions. I used to joke that I was merely a postman delivering messages for the IRA. He became a little more forthcoming as the peace process progressed and on occasion he even asked me for my opinion on what he had just told me. His three successors were far more relaxed and I was able to garner more background information from them on what was going on in 'the Republican family', as some called the IRA/Sinn Féin team.

I believe that all four IRA spokesmen that I had dealings with were serious players. None of them was a mere messenger boy. I knew that the information they were giving me was correct. If any of them had ever misled me, I and RTÉ News would have ceased dealings with them, as would all of the other media organizations if they had been misled. I remember Bertie Ahern, as Taoiseach, telling me once when we were on the road together that I might soon be getting a call from what he called 'your friends'. I got the call soon afterwards.

Eight more years were to pass after the 1997 ceasefire restoration before I was given the final IRA 'dump arms' statement to broadcast at the end of July 2005. I had to drive to Belfast to be given this statement. Unlike the anonymous August 1994 statement with its tiny typeface, this one was printed boldly on notepaper headed *Óglaigh na hÉireann* in green ink and it was accompanied by a DVD on which a veteran Republican, Séanna Breathnach (Walsh), recited its contents. It said:

The leadership of Óglaigh na hÉireann has formally ordered an end of the armed campaign. This will take effect from 4pm this afternoon. All IRA units have been ordered to dump arms. All volunteers have been instructed to assist the development of purely political and democratic programmes through exclusively peaceful means. Volunteers must not engage in any other activities whatsoever.

I was surprised to get another call from my IRA contact within weeks of the 'dump arms' announcement. I was on annual leave, but the call made me abandon holiday plans and go into the Newsroom to ask my bosses if I could bring a cameraman with me to a secret rendezvous where my contact promised me 'something big'. I was sure that I was going to witness IRA volunteers dumping arms or destroying bomb-making equipment, but I was stunned after being driven around border counties in a van with blacked-out windows for several hours to find myself face-to-face with the alleged former head of IRA 'engineering', Jim Monaghan, who I had last seen in a heavily guarded courthouse in Bogotá, the capital of Colombia, four years previously.

The big story that the IRA was giving me was an interview with Monaghan, who had jumped bail in Colombia with two captured colleagues, Martin McCauley, an explosives expert, and Niall Connolly, Sinn Féin's representative in Cuba. They had been arrested while travelling on false passports in Colombia and they were on trial for providing bomb-making expertise to the Farc guerrillas who were fighting government forces.

I guessed that Monaghan had only returned to Ireland in secret a few days previously. He was frustratingly disciplined as he spoke only to protest his innocence of the bomb-making accusations. He declined to give any hint as to how he and his two comrades had managed to escape from Colombia and make their way back from South America to Ireland clandestinely.

Nonetheless, the interview was another scoop and it angered the Irish government and police, not to mention the law enforcement authorities in the United States and South America, and those Sinn Féin supporters in the United States who were vehemently opposed to the IRA giving any succour to the anti-government Farc forces.

I supposed that the IRA had arranged the interview for me in return for some human kindness I had shown to the three men when I was covering their trial in Bogotá. I had done them a small favour at the start of their trial after a handwritten note had been passed to me from Niall Connolly. In tiny, neat handwriting that was almost as small as the writing on 'the comms' (communications) that the 1981 IRA hunger strikers were smuggling out of the H-Blocks in the early 1980s, he wrote:

Dear Charlie,
  Sorry we won't be able to do an interview as the time is not right. We think if things have cooled next

month we could talk to you. We are interested, but
the time is not right . . . if you get a chance could you
send in three jumpers as it's very cold, and phone cards.
   Thanks,
   Slán, Niall Connolly.

I went to downtown Bogotá when the court rose and
bought three heavy jumpers and some phone cards for the
men, but the interview had to wait for another four years.
The date on the top of Niall Connolly's note to me was
in the European style, 11/9/01. In the United States of
America, it was September 11, 2001 – the day of 'Nine
Eleven'. My bosses sent me hotfoot to New York and I
did not return to the 'Colombia Three' trial for some time.
   My contact with pseudonymous IRA spokesmen petered
out after my surprise 2005 meeting with Jim Monaghan
while 'the secret army', as one historian called the IRA,
evolved into a self-styled twenty-first-century felons' club.
The nature of my work meant that I had met many men
who had condoned murder and indiscriminate violence
and that I had undoubtedly come face-to-face with some
men who had committed or who had sanctioned multiple
murders. It was an odd and unpleasant thought, but it
was a necessary part of bringing the whole story to the
people of Ireland, and preserving it for future generations.

Sudden, violent deaths and catastrophic injuries that
nobody would sanction or condone continued to over-
shadow my work during the following year, 2006, when
I travelled all around Ireland for a twelve-month series of
RTÉ News reports on road traffic accidents. It was an

initiative of my boss, Ed Mulhall, the managing director of RTÉ News and Current Affairs. He assigned me to the story because he wanted RTÉ News to highlight, through its Chief News Correspondent, the grief and pain behind the tragedies that were happening on the roads of every county in Ireland nearly every day of every week.

I had reported on death and grieving in many parts of the world over the previous thirty-five years for RTÉ News, but I found that this year-long series of reports brought me closer to the reality of sudden death and its consequences for bereaved families than any work I had done at home or abroad over the years.

The number of people killed on Irish roads had been declining gradually from an appallingly high total of 640 in 1974, but by the early years of the new century about 400 lives were still being lost every year in crashes in the Republic. Some 396 people had died on the roads in 2005 – an average of more than one every day – and thousands more had suffered horrific or life-changing injuries when Ed Mulhall decided that RTÉ News should focus on this carnage to help generate greater public awareness of the consequences of road traffic accidents.

My reports featured prominently on the *Six-One News* and the *Nine O'Clock News* throughout the year. They carried accounts of the tragic stories behind some recent fatal road traffic accidents. Families and friends of people who had been killed gave harrowing interviews, as did a number of young men who had been badly injured or paralysed for life, and also some Gardaí and medical and ambulance personnel who'd had to deal with the aftermath of the crashes.

John Drea from Athlone spoke to me on camera in a cemetery less than 48 hours after the funeral of his 20-year-old daughter, Siobhan. A mother of a three-year-old daughter named Leah, Siobhan had been killed in a crash near Athlone with her friend Mikhaela Ardelama, aged 24, from Romania. A County Cork mother, Abina Moynihan, gave me an interview at the spot where her daughter Ciara was fatally injured and another daughter, Lisa, was injured.

Two other families, the Cawleys from Blanchardstown and the Martins in Wexford, gave harrowing interviews about losing a daughter and a mother. Erin Cawley, aged 22, died after a car driven by an uninsured driver crossed the central barrier of the M50 and smashed into the Cawley family car on a Sunday morning. Mona Martin was killed near her home a month before Christmas when her car was hit by one driven by a young man.

I also spoke to a hospital Emergency Department consultant, Aidan Gleeson, and an ambulance driver, Sean O'Donnell, about having to deal with the injuries people sustain in crashes. In the National Rehabilitation Hospital in Dún Laoghaire, I interviewed a long-stay patient, 19-year-old Richard Alcorn from Donegal, who had suffered life-altering injuries in a car crash. He nearly broke my heart when he told me, 'I miss home'. In a nursing home in the Phoenix Park I spoke to David Cullen, from Portrane, County Dublin, who was paralysed from the neck down when he crashed near his home after taking his father's car on an impulse. His mother told us that he would need 24-hour care for the rest of his life. I cannot forget his reply when I asked him about his friends. He said: 'You don't really see much of them anymore.'

Some of the reports dealt with the scourge of drink-driving. We filmed a Garda team breathalysing people at a mandatory checkpoint and we reported that between 400 and 450 people, on average, were being caught driving while under the influence of alcohol every week. Former government minister and medical doctor Jim McDaid spoke sincerely and at length about his own guilt after a drink-driving conviction and of how he might have killed or maimed someone while driving after drinking.

Our news reports at the end of each month carried a roll-call of the names, ages and home counties, or home countries, of all the people who had been killed on the roads during that month, accompanied only by pictures of the crash scenes and the sombre violin and piano music of Arvo Pärt's composition 'Spiegel im Spiegel'.

RTÉ sent a 45-minute DVD compiled from the monthly reports to every secondary school in the country with a recommendation that it be used in classrooms as part of Leaving Certificate or Transition Year programmes. The Road Safety Authority subsequently asked me to make a video on the dangers of using mobile phones while driving. Our RTÉ series won a Law Society Justice Media Award for Television News. The citation said that the Award was given 'for this searing road safety campaign series that caused many people to question their own driving habits; that shone a spotlight on the new [drink-driving] legislation; and that set as its goal the saving of lives.'

Dympna Moroney, now the Series Editor for RTÉ Television News, was my producer on the series. She has remained one of my closest friends since that time. She is one of the inner-Cabinet that I consult on important matters after I have spoken to Claire and my daughters. Samantha Libreri, a brilliant young Newsroom reporter, also worked with me on the series. She too has remained a constant friend.

I hope that the RTÉ News series of reports on road traffic accidents prevented further deaths and injuries and I hope that its reporting on the peace process in Northern Ireland helped bring an end to thirty years of murderous violence. I'm proud to have been involved in reporting those phases in modern Irish history. Bertie Ahern, as Taoiseach, offered me the job of Government Press Secretary after the 1997 General Election and the boss of Ireland's top-selling Sunday newspaper personally tried to head-hunt me on another occasion with the offer of a big salary, but I resisted both approaches – my first love, and my life, was broadcasting, and all of my broadcasting had been for RTÉ.

More than a decade after my retirement from RTÉ News, I was still being awakened regularly by a nightmare of the type that afflicts many news reporters. It was always the same nightmare: I was standing in a public telephone kiosk in Finglas, north Dublin, frantically trying to dictate an important and urgent story to a copytaker in the Newsroom, but my words were disappearing into the ether and the copytaker was not able to hear me. This was only a slight variation, though equally frightening, on the daylight nightmares I used to experience regularly during my working life: losing my script in the RTÉ Newsroom computer system just minutes before bulletin time.

Looking back, I think that the prospect of retirement had first started to cross my mind even before my ill-judged spell as RTÉ's Washington Correspondent. I suppose the first time that I realized that the end of my career was looming was when I covered the funeral of former Taoiseach Charlie Haughey in June 2006. I had been reporting on his often controversial career since even before he became leader of Fianna Fáil in 1979. Outside his funeral Mass in the Church of Our Lady of Consolation in Donnycarney, in his Dublin North Central constituency, it was obvious that an eventful era in the State's history had ended. Haughey and his so-called 'mohair suit' contemporaries, who had succeeded Fianna Fáil's founding generation and some of whom, including Haughey himself, had become corrupt, were increasingly disappearing from the political stage.

A younger Fianna Fáil politician had contributed greatly to the wear and tear I was feeling after more than thirty years in frontline journalism. I wasn't burnt out, but I was definitely worn out after Beverley Cooper Flynn, a Mayo TD and daughter of one of Haughey's more prominent Cabinet colleagues, took a libel action against RTÉ News over my reporting of the National Irish Bank's offshore accounts scandal in the late 1990s. The case went on for more than three years in the highest courts in the land. It was before the High Court for 29 days over a six-week period from 6 February 2001 and it only ended in the Supreme Court on 28 April 2004. Even aside from the three days that I spent in the witness box, the entire saga was a harrowing experience that gave me some of the bleakest days of my career. I lost well over a stone in weight while the case was before the High Court. I still shudder when I recall walking through the doors of the Four Courts during the trial and the subsequent Supreme Court deliberations.

The consequences of our losing that case would likely have been career-ending for me and my immediate superiors. To this day, the prospect of ever having to go back through those doors nearly makes me physically ill.

I had also been seriously rattled, and taken to hospital with back and cheek injuries, when I was physically assaulted by two or three men while covering a riot involving Republican and Loyalist thugs on O'Connell Street in Dublin in February 2006. It was obviously a random attack, but it was also undoubtedly due to my fired-up attackers recognizing a prominent TV news reporter at work. The price I paid for my public profile might have been much higher that day had I not been rescued mid-attack by two Special Branch officers. My back injury required several months of physiotherapy.

My Washington DC foray, described in Chapter 7, lasted from late 2008 until June 2010. As it was my own decision to cut short my term in Washington, I knew that I would get flak in some of the Irish newspapers on my return. I was also unsure about the reception I might get from my Newsroom colleagues, some of whom had eagerly sought the Washington job, or how I might be received in Dublin media circles generally. The national mood, too, had darkened during my time in Washington because of the economic collapse and the ensuing emergency budgets, wage cuts and tax increases. The humiliating economic bailout by the Troika (the International Monetary Fund, the European Central Bank and the European Commission) was widely rumoured and was imminent.

One of the reasons that I had gone for the Washington job was to get a break from the daily routine of reporting from outside the Dáil, but on my first day back in the Newsroom I was assigned to cover a big political story. The Fine Gael party, which had attempted to recruit me during my time in Washington, was in the midst of a Fianna Fáil-type 'heave' when I returned to Dublin. Richard Bruton was making a vain attempt to depose Enda Kenny as party leader. The RTÉ political team were, unsurprisingly, not enamoured by the return to the Government Buildings/Leinster House beat of the Chief News Correspondent.

Before the lunchtime news on my first day back in Dublin, I found myself embroiled in a row that was not of my own making. The political staff resented my being parachuted by my bosses into a story that they had been covering. The mid-summer heat that I had left behind in Washington DC was mild compared to the rising temperatures generated by my return to the political beat in Dublin. Things had changed in my absence, and I should not have expected to slip back seamlessly into my old role. As Bob Dylan sang, 'You can always come back, but you can't come back all the way.'

Another 'turf war' with a senior member of the political staff at – of all places – a North–South 'peace process' ministerial meeting at the government's Farmleigh House in the Phoenix Park in Dublin a month later further detached me from day-to-day Newsroom assignments. I was very relieved when I was invited to present the two-hour *Marian Finucane Show* on RTE Radio 1 while she was away on holiday in 2010, and again in March and May 2011.

Stepping into Marian Finucane's shoes for a two-hour programme was a very big challenge, even though I had anchored shorter programmes during my early days in the Newsroom. The series producer, Anne Farrell, and her team helped me enormously and I was soon chosen to host the key RTÉ Radio debate between the seven candidates who were contesting the 2011 Presidential election, even though I was a relatively rookie radio host. I continued to present the programme occasionally over the next fifteen months.

My growing commitments to RTÉ Radio meant that my disengagement from the Newsroom became something of a long goodbye. In September 2011, I was given my own RTÉ Radio 1 show, *Saturday with Charlie Bird*, that ran until the end of May 2012. It was on the eve of the first *Saturday with Charlie Bird*, an outside broadcast from Letterkenny, County Donegal, that I got my first bad health scare and a foretaste of what I would experience with my motor neurone symptoms just under a decade later.

I was about to leave my home in Ashford to drive to Letterkenny on Friday, 16 September 2011 when my GP, Ian O'Grady, rang me to say that my latest routine blood test had revealed concerning levels of elevated white blood cells. He said that I needed to see a consultant straight away. I told Claire and my daughters. I was in shock. I started to Google 'elevated white blood cells'. I was dreading leukaemia or lymphoma throughout the drive to and from Letterkenny and all through my very first *Saturday with Charlie Bird* show. It was a presentiment of the post-traumatic shock syndrome that I would be diagnosed with ten years later.

While waiting for my GP to fix an appointment with a consultant, I did a pre-arranged interview on the following Monday morning with a journalist from the *Sunday Times*.

We did the interview in the RTÉ canteen, but I was totally distracted throughout. I kept looking at my phone to see if my GP had managed to arrange an appointment for me. I should have told the journalist, Eithne Shortall, why I was distracted, but I didn't. Her two-page article on the following Sunday, flagged on the paper's front page with a photograph of me, contained a couple of snide remarks, due, I suppose, to my not giving her my full attention.

'This media-wary reporter,' she wrote, 'considering himself several times bitten [by newspaper journalists] is definitely more than twice shy.' She added: 'Sitting in his home ground of the RTÉ canteen, he fidgets with his hands, darts his eyes around the room, and starts his answers by repeating the questions . . . Charlie Bird is nervous . . . Though careful not to come on too "woe-is-me", he is wary of the print media.'

My GP told me later in the day that he was having trouble finding a suitable consultant to examine me. I was surprised, but then I remembered that I had interviewed Professor John Crown, a consultant oncologist at St Vincent's Hospital, Dublin, and a member of the Seanad, while I was filling in for Marian Finucane during the summer. I contacted him and he rang me back within an hour to say that he had traced my blood test results. He said that they were not as bad as I had feared and did not indicate any serious illness.

Professor Crown sent me to another consultant specializing in blood disorders. He told me, after further tests, that I had a very, very mild form of Non-Hodgkin lymphoma. He explained that blood tests were now so sophisticated, they showed up even the slightest abnormalities. Further annual blood tests showed that my condition had not worsened. The consultant said more than he could have known when he told me that it would be something else that would eventually kill me!

The *Saturday with Charlie Bird* show occupied me for a year, but the Newsroom had been my home for so long that I continued to be bothered that I had not managed to slot back in there successfully when I returned from my spell in Washington. I had come back from the US with my tail somewhat between my legs and I had not wanted to return to the Government Buildings/Kildare Street beat, but that was where I had been sent.

For the first time in my career, I was uneasy and unsettled. I had worked so hard during my thirty years in the Newsroom that it had become my second home. My illness and the passage of time have brought home to me that my dedication to my work, and my time away from home, had undoubtedly affected my first marriage and had meant that I did not give enough time to my daughters, Orla and Neasa, when they were young and daily growing. I had been absent at critical times in their young lives. I had been largely oblivious to their constant worries over my having to deal with IRA men, often in the so-called 'Bandit Country' north of the border. I had not fully appreciated the effect on them of the marathon and high-profile Beverley Cooper-Flynn libel action and of the 'Love Ulster' rally assault, even though they were young adults by then. My work had been consuming most of my time and energy for nearly forty years.

I began to think that I needed a new challenge. I was heading towards my sixty-third birthday. My next 'roundy birthday', in the words of the RTÉ Radio 1 DJ Ronan

Collins, would be my seventieth. I kept thinking of one of the favourite sayings of my father: 'Man's allotted span is three score years and ten.' That saying had always stayed in my head. Now it was at the forefront of my mind. I had to plan for a new future.

One of RTÉ's responses to a drastic drop in income following the country's economic collapse was to offer staff an early retirement deal. Several of my long-serving colleagues had opted to take it. My closest friend and Newsroom colleague, Joe O'Brien, was also seriously considering the severance deal. I agonized over what to do. I was at a crossroads. I needed a new challenge. If I retired at 63, instead of the mandatory 65 years, I could work on new projects of my own choosing. I thought about new broadcasting ventures that I planned to pursue, but it was still with a very heavy heart that I decided to retire early. It was like the end of a long marriage. RTÉ really was my second family.

The RTÉ Director General, Noel Curran, rang me a day or two after I left and asked to see me. He had previously been Head of TV Programmes and he had authorised my documentaries on my time in Washington and my trips to the Arctic and Antarctic. He said he had not known about my taking early retirement and he asked me why I had left. Even today, I am not all that clear about why I left when I did, but when you make your own bed, as they say, you have to lie in it. And that is what I did. Of course, we can all be done without. Graveyards are full of people who thought that they were indispensable.

I've had to return to the RTÉ complex in Donnybrook many times since I retired and I have always felt very strange and uneasy there. Claire works in the TV building and I often used to drop her off in the morning or collect her after work, before COVID-19 forced her to work from home. The longer I was away from the place, the more uneasy I felt going back there. It always felt like I was going back to a marital home that I had left voluntarily or prematurely.

I loved every day of my thirty-eight years in RTÉ. I have often said that when I got the chance to join the national broadcaster back in 1974, it was, for me, akin to winning the Lotto. I had failed every exam I had ever done, including my Inter Cert and my Leaving Cert. I had never gone to university. The opportunity to get a job in RTÉ was something that I grabbed with both hands. In a way, that is why I worked so hard there. I wanted to prove to myself that I could make a go of it. I was lucky to find a job that suited whatever talents I had been given. I worked like a demon to repay my employer's trust in me. In the many, many talks I have been asked to give over the years about my career, I have never been afraid to say that I clawed my way to the position of Chief News Correspondent by my fingernails.

I remember the first story I did for the TV News after I joined the Newsroom in 1980. I was as proud as punch when my name appeared across a report I did on the Irish Countrywomen's Association. The name Charlie Bird seemed to me to be in bright lights when I saw it on the screen. I also vividly remember that around that time the late Derek Davis came up to me in the Newsroom and put his arm around me and told me in his lovely Northern brogue that I should change my on-screen name. He said viewers wouldn't take seriously a reporter with a name like Charlie Bird. He said that I should change my name to Charles, so that people would take me more seriously. I thanked him for his advice, but I remember thinking that, while I was born Charles Brown Bird, I had always told people that I was Charlie Bird and I wanted to stick to that name.

I was always very proud when my reports made it onto the TV bulletins and even prouder when they were headline reports. By the mid-1980s I had become well known as a TV news reporter. Over the years I was given a number of different titles. The first was Chief Reporter, and then Special Correspondent, and later I was given the title of Chief News Correspondent, which would remain with me until I moved to the US as Washington Correspondent. I retained the title of Chief News Correspondent when I returned from Washington.

I did my last TV reports as RTE's Chief News Correspondent in the spring and summer of 2011. In March, I reported on the end of the marathon Moriarty Tribunal of Inquiry, which found that political corruption in post-colonial Ireland was not confined to members of Fianna Fáil but had infected some in Fine Gael, too.

I spent four days in May reporting on Queen Elizabeth's historic visit to Ireland. I was in the Garden of Remembrance in Dublin on 17 May for her moving and memorable visit and speech there. Over the following days I reported on her visits to the War Memorial at Islandbridge, Dublin, and to the Rock of Cashel in Tipperary. On 21 May, I reported from the Mansion House in Dublin where people were paying their last respects to former Taoiseach Garret

FitzGerald. Two days later, on 23 May, I was back in Tipperary, on its border with south Offaly, reporting on the visit of President Barack Obama to the village of Moneygall, one of his ancestral homes.

My last television report for RTÉ News was less than a month later, in mid-June 2011. It was the funeral of former Minister for Finance and Fianna Fáil deputy leader Brian Lenihan, who had died aged only 52 after a short illness. President Mary McAleese and Taoiseach Enda Kenny led the large congregation at the funeral Mass in St Mochta's Church, Porterstown, west Dublin, before burial in St David's Church graveyard in nearby Kilsallaghan.

Brian Lenihan was one of the third generation of his family to be elected to Dáil Éireann. He was the scion of a family of Fianna Fáil royalty. The 2011 General Election, just four months before his death, swept Fianna Fáil from power and ended its reign as the most successful political party in democratic Europe. His funeral was a day on which, in more ways than one, 'the old order changeth, yielding place to new', as Alfred, Lord Tennyson wrote in 'Morte d'Arthur'.

My last day working for RTÉ was Sunday, 26 August 2012, when I presented a two-hour radio programme in the Marian Finucane slot while she was away on holidays. In my closing remarks I said that you're always told that you're great when you are going out the door. In an interview for an item on the TV News bulletins that night, I said that I was not retiring but had decided to move on to pastures new and to take up new challenges. I told reporter Samantha Libreri that I was not disappearing off the radar and that I hoped to be in front of a microphone and camera again in the coming months. My nearly forty years of reporting the news ended with my retirement from RTÉ being the subject of a TV News report on the Sunday-night bulletins.

RTÉ had been such an important part of my life that when the COVID-19 lockdown was imposed on 12 March 2020, I was the first person to ring the Head of News to offer to help in any way if there was a staff shortage in the Newsroom. I did not want to work as a news reporter, but I offered to work as a car driver for reporters or camera crews, or in any other support role.

Even though I left RTÉ a couple of years prematurely in 2012, my RTÉ family and friends have been with me every step of the way since I got the diagnosis confirming my terminal illness. They are like any loyal family. I still feel very strongly about the importance of public service broadcasting. I know how dedicated my former colleagues are and I still get annoyed when people criticize 'you lot out in Montrose'. I used to reply by saying that everyone who comes through the door in Montrose comes from every county, village and hamlet in Ireland. I always was and I always will be so proud of my RTÉ family.

I have been gratified and consoled beyond words to be told that my long RTÉ career has left a mark. I had never met the station's current Director General, Dee Forbes, before 2022, but she was one of the first people to write to Claire and me when I was diagnosed with MND, offering any help that we might need. She was also one of the first people to volunteer to join the Croagh Patrick climb and she also enthusiastically joined the RTÉ staff who performed the 'Shine a Light' song in the run-up to the climb. She and her sister, Aodhdín Forbes, climbed the Reek together on 2 April 2022 and they reached the summit some time before me. We had a chat and a laugh about that when we met on the evening after the climb. One of my fondest memories of the day was that Dee Forbes and so many of my former RTÉ colleagues joined me on the climb, or on their own hike to Howth Head. And, of course, Ryan Tubridy and his *Late Late Show* crew were prime movers behind the whole climb project.

In the end, I believe that the most important and emblematic of the reports that I did for RTÉ News during my final month in the Newsroom was undoubtedly the visit of Queen Elizabeth to the Garden of Remembrance. Almost seventeen years after my meeting with the IRA's 'Brendan' outside the Garden in August 1994, I was back there again, working as a reporter inside the Garden, witnessing Queen Elizabeth's historic visit to the memorial site for all victims of the fight for Irish freedom.

It was the first time in more than one hundred years that a serving British monarch had come to Ireland. It provided one of the most spine-tingling moments of my forty years in journalism when Queen Elizabeth bowed her head as the strains of 'God Save the Queen' rang out over Dublin's north inner-city, the heartland of Sean O'Casey's powerful plays about the Easter Rising and its aftermath. It was a powerful moment, and one of the most-watched television broadcasts in Ireland that year, drawing a near-record 710,000 viewers to the *Six-One News*. The memory of that moment will be with me until the day I die.

I mentioned my reporting from the Garden of Remembrance in a short essay I wrote for the book *Reporting the Troubles 2*, which I was honoured to be asked to launch in Belfast in March 2022 in the presence of former Taoiseach and Good Friday Agreement signatory Bertie Ahern. In the book I recalled visiting Belfast in 2019 for a conference on the IRA ceasefires and being delighted to see Republic of Ireland number plates on almost all of the cars parked in the huge Titanic Centre car park – clear evidence that the peace process was working and that the island of Ireland was now being shared by all of its people.

One of my dying wishes, as I said at that book launch, is that the peace process will continue to go from strength to strength for both communities. I hope and pray from the bottom of my heart that all the people who died during 'the Troubles' did not lose their lives in vain.

The era known as 'the Troubles' – from the deployment of British soldiers in Derry in August 1969 to the IRA's 'dump arms' decision nearly thirty-six years later – spanned more than half of the reign of Queen Elizabeth II and almost the entirety of my long reporting career. Her presence in the Garden of Remembrance in May 2011 was the centrepiece of one of my last and one of my most important reporting assignments.

I can look back now and be immensely grateful that my work allowed me to witness some of the most historic moments in recent Irish history - and few more historic than watching Queen Elizabeth bow her head to our Republic.

10. DAY

Kathleen Sharkey from Tory Island, off the coast of
Donegal, is one of the most impressive women I have ever
met. A daily Mass-goer and mother of six children, she
defied the Catholic Church and much local hostility to
canvass in her home county during the Marriage Equality
referendum in 2015. She campaigned from door to door
to support one of her sons, who is gay, and to honour the
memory of her brother Anton, a gay adult who took his
own life. 'They treat people differently because they are
gay here in Donegal,' she told me when I interviewed her
in her home shortly after the referendum campaign.

Kathleen and the other parents and siblings I interviewed
during that campaign are, aside from the Stardust families,
the people with whom I was most privileged to work after
I retired from RTÉ. As an RTÉ journalist I had been obliged
– for nearly forty years – to keep my personal opinions
to myself and I had avoided getting involved in any political causes since my retirement in 2012. In early 2015,
however, I was contacted out of the blue by a long-time
friend and former RTÉ Director of Communications, Bride

Rosney, who asked me if I would help a group that was being established to campaign for civil marriage equality in the referendum due to be held in May of that year.

Bride, who had helped Mary Robinson become Ireland's first woman president in the watershed 1990 Presidential election, was one of the campaign's chief strategists. Another was Noel Whelan, a prominent barrister, *Irish Times* columnist and political commentator, who was to die, aged 50, after a short illness just over four years after the referendum.

At Bride Rosney's request, I chaired the launch meeting of the 'Vote Yes' campaign in the Pillar Room of the Rotunda Hospital in Dublin on 9 March, and I hosted seven further public meetings around the country in the following weeks. The stories I heard of the stigma and shame suffered by gay and lesbian people, young and old, all over the country appalled me. 'Gay history,' as the multi-award-winning author Colm Tóibín wrote in the foreword to the book that I later wrote about the campaign, 'is a set of lonely shadows, dotted lines, stories not told, isolated suffering, silences and marginalisations.'

One of the 'stories not told' was that of Kathleen Sharkey's beloved brother, Anton, who took his own life after many years of unhappiness in Donegal. 'He definitely took his life because of his sexuality,' she told me. 'He couldn't cope anymore with his life. Growing up, Anton was a very happy boy. But I think what really got to Anton was that some of our family disowned him because he was gay. And that really hurt him. But I'm not ashamed of my brother, and I never will be ashamed of my brother. He was my pride and joy.'

I was fighting back my own tears when Kathleen told me how they had waked Anton for three days. 'I couldn't believe he had so many friends,' she said. 'They came from Dublin, from all over. We didn't know them, but they knew Anton. Some of them [were] gay and some of them straight. Everybody was so nice. They said he was one in a million.'

She said that she had no hesitation about canvassing in the referendum because of her love for Anton and because her eldest son, Noel, then aged 27, had also had a hard time when growing up because he was gay. I was amazed when she told me about knocking on doors and distributing leaflets with Noel night after night, and not being bothered about being turned away from some doors. I admired her bravery in a county where many people are afraid to admit to being gay. All she wanted was for her son to be happy and to live a normal life and to be accepted in the community, like everybody else.

Her fearlessness left an impression on me that has not faded. Hostility or indifference on the doorstep did not faze her. She said she told people: 'I will be voting Yes for my son and for, God rest him, Anton, and all the other LGBT students out there. I just want them to be happy in life because that what it is about at the end of the day.'

Kathleen's testimony and the other stories I heard broke through my journalistic impartiality and energized me. After a long career with the national broadcaster, where my hands and my tongue were tied by the imperative of pure and objective independent reporting, now I could embark on a different type of reporting and campaigning journalism. I could report and I could campaign in a way that would not have been possible when I worked for RTÉ. I was 'a newly minted civilian', as Yvonne Judge of Dublin Pride observed later.

Apart from the legitimate protests that I had led against the restrictions of Section 31 of the Broadcasting Act during the 1980s, I had never been able to support any cause in public or even verbally in the Newsroom. No matter how much some of my colleagues and I may have wanted to join public protests about the Bush/Blair invasion of Iraq, or the national tax regime, or various referendum campaigns, it would have been career-ending to do so. And any hint of bias or partisanship would have gravely damaged RTÉ's legal obligation to be fair and impartial in all of its reporting.

As the Referendum votes were being counted, Noel Whelan suggested that I should go back to many of the people I had met around the country during the campaign to interview them. For the first time in my career I had a cause that I could support in public and through my journalism. On my return visits, I recorded nearly eighty interviews with canvassers and family members. With another former RTÉ colleague, Kevin Rafter, who had helped me with my 2006 autobiography *This is Charlie Bird*, I condensed more than half of the interviews into a book called *A Day in May*, which was published in 2016 with funding from The Atlantic Philanthropies, the charity set up by the Irish-American Chuck Feeney.

'These stories collected by Charlie Bird,' wrote Colm Tóibín in the book's foreword, 'filled with bracing honesty and heart-breaking personal revelation, make clear that being gay in Ireland was perhaps a more essential aspect of Irish history and Irish reality than anyone was aware.' The stories in *A Day in May* formed the basis for the play of the same name that Colin Murphy wrote a couple of years later. His stage adaptation of the book, produced by Pat Moylan, was performed in the Olympia Theatre in Dublin in June 2018 and later in Galway, Belfast and Dún Laoghaire. The COVID-19 pandemic stymied plans to take the play on tour internationally, but I'm very hopeful that it can be staged again in Ireland and abroad.

We dedicated the play to another one of Kathleen Sharkey's sons, James. What she and I could not have known when I interviewed her for the book, or when I spoke to her on the day the book was launched, was that James too would soon take his own life because he was still being bullied about being gay, a year after the Marriage Equality referendum. He died after the book was published. He had specifically asked Kathleen not to mention him when I interviewed her for the book. I drove to Donegal for his month's mind mass.

'When you spoke to me [for the book] and I was talking about Noel and my brother, I didn't speak about James because I had to respect what he wanted,' Kathleen told me in a podcast I did for Senior*Times* in early 2021, 'but James was a very happy-go-lucky boy, a chef, and he had so, so many friends, if he only realized that there was only two or three out there who disliked him. He was being bullied. He was physically hammered, and by those people that we know, and nothing was ever done about it.'

She recalled on the podcast the harrowing and truly heartbreaking details of the night of James's death. She said he was at the local GAA club with her younger son, Michael, when the usual culprits started to bully James. 'Michael went to stand up for him,' Kathleen told me, 'and those that were bullying James broke Michael's nose, they broke his arms and they broke four of his ribs.' She said that when Michael was taken to a local GP, James went home and took his life in his own house.

Kathleen said that the family encircled James's bed and told him how much they loved him when he could not be revived by CPR or ventilation in the intensive care unit in the county hospital. She told me: 'I said an Act of Contrition into his ear and I told him how much we all loved him, but that he was going to a better place and that God would be with him, and I said even though I won't see you for a while, you'll always be by my side, and we all said our goodbyes and just like that he just stopped breathing, and that was it.'

Homophobia had cost Kathleen Sharkey a beloved brother and a son. It had also been inflicted on a second son of hers and it had caused a third son to sustain aggravated assault injuries. 'Unfortunately, it's still going on today and my plea is that it please stop. I beg to stop bullying of any kind, whether it's gay or any kind of bullying,' she said.

Kathleen said that she is still not a saint, but she's a sacristan in Dungloe Catholic church now and she does voluntary work for the St Vincent de Paul Society: 'James and Anton would not want to see me sitting here crying. That's why I help people in every way and why I do voluntary work. God is holding me up, along with my son and my brother.'

After the play had been successfully staged, one of the key 'Vote Yes' campaigners, Karl Hayden, a veteran LGBTQ+ organizer who took many of the photographs for *A Day in May*, told me that I ought to be conferred 'an honorary gay'. He was half joking, but he and his colleagues regrouped four years later, in summer 2022, to present me during Pride Week with a special book in my honour for my work during the Marriage Equality campaign. In truth, all of the people who had the courage to tell me their stories became part of my gay family of friends, even while my prominent association with the 'Yes' campaign made at least one person suggest to my future wife, Claire, that people might wrongly assume that I was gay.

Claire had joined Noel Whelan and me at the head of the Pride of Dublin parade shortly after the referendum. It was a joyful and emotional afternoon as we walked along the streets, with Noel waving a large rainbow flag. Claire was with me again in June 2022 when I was presented with the book at the Pride headquarters in central Dublin. Noel was and still is badly missed and we remembered him on that happy summer 2022 evening.

After Kathleen Sharkey, one of the many courageous women I interviewed for the book was Ursula Halligan, the Political Editor of TV3, whose public coming-out via an *Irish Times* article was deemed to have been influential in the referendum campaign. She recalled the 'absolute despair', upset and confusion of her teenage and university years when she could not even tell herself, never mind anyone else, that she was falling in love with women, not men. 'My denial was so deep,' she said, 'I needed something like a gun to be pointed to my head before I would do anything.'

She said the referendum was that gun and that she had no regrets about her *Irish Times* article. She told me: 'The Irish people were magnificent. Out of generous hearts they enabled a minority to have this crucial right, but it was much more than about marriage. It was about acceptance. It was saying, "You are OK, actually you are not second class. You are alright." That, for me, was the big thing about the Marriage Equality referendum. What a show of love, empathy, solidarity and humanity. In a way, I'm still reeling from it. I can't quite believe it.'

Another courageous campaigner that I met and interviewed for the book was Arthur Leahy, a founder of the Cork Gay Community Project and a board member of GLEN, the Gay and Lesbian Equality Network. Nearly forty years earlier, Arthur had been one of the first people in Ireland to talk on national television about being gay. He and his then partner, Laurie Steele, were interviewed for RTÉ by Áine O'Connor, who, coincidentally, had been my first girlfriend a few years earlier. 'I forget what the programme was called,' Arthur told me, 'but the reaction was very favourable. It had quite an impact . . . she was very sympathetic.'

Arthur recalled how being gay was 'kind of a taboo subject' in Ireland in the 1970s. He said his siblings were very worried that the national TV interview might cause him to be ostracized and unemployable, but his mother, presaging Kathleen Sharkey in Donegal forty years later, had stepped forward and told her family: 'Look, I think this interview is great. If he wants to do it, he should do it.'

Another Corkman, Ed O'Callaghan, brought tears to my eyes when he told me his story, after initially hesitating when some of his friends put me in contact with him. He told me that he had been married for nineteen years to his childhood sweetheart before he admitted to her, and to himself, that he was gay. 'I felt so guilty,' he said. 'She should have been really angry. Here she was, thinking she was married, had a partner and soulmate who would be with her right throughout life and into the twilight years. But that didn't happen for her. I had huge guilt about that. Three years after I came out, I actually ended up having a heart attack. And it was the stress of it all. But she has remained an extremely good friend. Even now, maybe every second or third day, we see each other.'

In Galway, Steven Sharpe, a singer-songwriter originally from Tipperary town, told me how he had stood on the ledge of his bedroom window contemplating suicide when he realized as a teenager how difficult life would be as a homosexual. 'Diversity wasn't celebrated in Tipperary town in 2004, or 2005 or 2006. I felt worthless,' he said.

I dedicated the book 'to the 1,201,607 people who voted "Yes" in the Marriage Equality referendum in Ireland on 22 May 2015'. They had been persuaded by a campaign that was 'honest, personal, true . . . personal rather than political and local rather than national', as Colm Tóibín observed in his foreword. 'The importance of this book,' he added, 'is to show how rich and interesting and utterly individual each gay voice is, and how unique and different each experience of being gay in Ireland has been.'

The campaign changed my life. Just as I had considered myself 'a postman' for the IRA during the peace process,

I was privileged to be the conduit for so many heartfelt and heart-breaking stories from people who had hitherto been silent and afraid in the hidden Ireland that had been ignored or suppressed by officialdom. Collecting their stories for the book was one of the best assignments I had ever undertaken. It's among the memories of a lifetime in journalism of which I am most proud.

The then Taoiseach, Enda Kenny, launched the book in the National Gallery of Ireland less than a year after the referendum, on 11 May 2016. 'This is a book of stories about life and love,' he said at the start of a 15-minute speech. He recalled the impact some stories of gay women and men friends of his had had on him. He said that the referendum had given people a chance to 'right a wrong' and that it had 'changed a society and changed millions of futures'. He added: 'It was the first time ever that people inside the secrecy of the ballot box decided to send out that signal of equality.'

The Taoiseach looked at me and said: 'Mr Bird, this book is a must read.' He said he hoped that it would be found in libraries, schools and homes. He said that it got 'to the heart of the subject and more importantly to the hearts of the subjects'. People in same-sex relationships no longer wanted to be able to ask their partners to join them in a civil partnership, but wanted instead to be able to say, 'Will you marry me?', the Taoiseach declared, adding that the book would 'become a social history of this time, of our time'.

I met Kathleen Sharkey again at the book launch, in the overcrowded Wintergarden Room of the National Gallery. We had a great chat. She astonished me again when she told me that it was only her second time in Dublin in her lifetime. She and the other people that I had interviewed for the book had changed my life. The book was really a co-operative effort. All the profits went to charity. I hope that it is on the shelves of every school in the country.

Colin Murphy's play was premiered in the Olympia Theatre in Dublin in summer 2018. All profits from the staging went to Pieta. In his programme note the chief executive of Pieta, Brian Higgins, said: 'We fight hard to eradicate stigma and allow people to be true to themselves. We work hard to make society aware of the truths and realities of others. This is why this play is so important to us.'

'See it this evening if you can,' wrote reviewer Brian Finnegan in *Gay Community News*, 'you're guaranteed laughter, tears and waves of that unnameable collective feeling we had on May 24, 2015, once more.' He added: 'At intervals, each activist character breaks away to become one of the people who testified about their experiences as LGB people in Ireland, before and during the referendum, for Charlie Bird's book, and it is these moments that provide the show's real heart . . . at curtain call, the audience I saw it with couldn't leap to their feet fast enough [to applaud].'

The book and the play are among the projects that I'm most proud to have been involved in during my life. I was privileged and very happy to have been involved in the Marriage Equality campaign. It was an emotional experience and it changed my life in many ways. I hope that my work all over the country during the campaign, and the book and play that I was able to fashion out of that campaign, will remain as important parts of my legacy. I have asked Karl Hayden to speak at my funeral and to make sure that a small rainbow flag is placed on my coffin.

11. ARCTIC

The *Ransom '79* podcasts that I made in early 2021 were the latest, and ultimately the last, in a series of freelance journalism ventures I undertook after I retired from RTÉ.

Wanderlust had never been a feature of my life but working for RTÉ had taken me to scores of foreign countries. Before joining the national broadcaster, I had never been abroad, or even on an aeroplane, but work assignments during my career regularly sent me overseas, even if it was usually for parachute journalism, with no time for sightseeing or sitting beside a swimming pool.

My bosses began to allow me to take time out from the Newsroom from around 2005 onwards to work on documentaries that were being made by independent production companies for broadcast on RTÉ television. A television documentary that I made in 2008 allowed me to do some leisurely filming and research, and it also showed me that I was not the first member of the Bird family whose work took them away from home. The *Who Do You Think You Are?* programme traced some of my paternal ancestors to London, Portsmouth and Bermuda before they came to Ireland.

My paternal grandfather, Timothy Collins Bird, came from London to Cork, where he helped install street lighting in the village of Macroom at the turn of the last century. Both of my parents were born and reared in Macroom. As well as my grandparents, the Macroom cemetery also holds the remains of an uncle I never knew, Charles Bird, who died young and whose first name features frequently in Bird family history and lives on in my first grandchild.

The first Bird family records were found in Portsmouth, Britain's oldest naval base, on the southern tip of England. They date back to the 1660s when Portsmouth was beginning to take shape as a base for English explorers and privateers. Some of my ancestors were sent to Bermuda to help establish a British naval base there after the American War of Independence. Some of them worked as gatekeepers at one of the island's hospitals and I found the grave of one of my ancestors, Charles Collins Bird, when I went there for the programme.

Church records in Portsmouth show that another of my ancestors, Timothy Bird, was baptised in the same church as the writer Charles Dickens and that they lived in the same area of the city, Portsea Island, at around the same time. The same register also records the baptism, only six years after that, of my great-great grandfather and of the acclaimed nineteenth-century engineer Isambard Kingdom Brunel, whose bridges, tunnels and aquaducts still stand in many parts of England.

My most distinguished ancestor was another Timothy Bird, who was captain of the HMS *Racoon* in the Battle of the Nile in 1798, when the British, led by Admiral

Nelson, defeated the French, under Napoleon Bonaparte, near the port of Alexandria. Some historians regard that battle as more important even than Nelson's famous victory at the Battle of Trafalgar.

I didn't know it at the time, but the *Who Do You Think You Are?* programme gave me a taste for travel away from the pressures of a daily news deadline. And I was lucky enough late in my career to be invited to make a number of television documentaries from some of the most exotic places on Earth.

My interest in making and presenting television documentaries had been sparked a few years earlier when John Murray of the Emmy-award-winning Crossing the Line Productions invited me to present one of the *Wild Trials* programmes he was making in remote places in Ireland. I was sent in search of red squirrels or wild mink on the shores of Lough Corrib in County Galway. It turned out to be a great bit of craic for me, even though the only thing I got to film in the end was a lovely robin in a wild setting.

John Murray's father, Gerry, was my first boss when I joined the RTÉ current affairs programme, *Seven Days*. Gerry was a soft-spoken man who always had a pipe in his mouth. John worked for RTÉ as a reporter before leaving to set up his own highly successful and award-winning documentary production company based in Greystones in County Wicklow.

The first major overseas documentary we made traced my journey along the entire length of the River Amazon in South America. The programme took me across South America from the Pacific Ocean to the Atlantic Ocean.

It warned about what climate change and global warming were doing to the vast Amazon rainforest years before these issues became as urgent as they now are. RTÉ commissioned the documentary from Crossing the Line Productions and it was produced in 2007 by Kim Bartley, one of the top documentary makers in the country, and filmed by her brother, Ross Bartley.

After my trip down the Amazon, RTÉ commissioned a two-part documentary by the same team. This time we travelled the 2,500-km length of the sacred River Ganges in India, upstream from the Bay of Bengal right up to the source of the river, high up in the Himalayas. The river is known as Mother Ganga, or Ganga Ma. For me, it was the journey of a lifetime.

The effects of climate change were also central to our next assignment. This was another two-programme RTÉ commission. It was about life in the Arctic Circle and it took me to the North Pole. John Murray brought in Doug Allan, one of the top wildlife cameramen, to film the first part of our trip. Doug had made his name working on some of the most acclaimed BBC wildlife programmes, including *Life in the Freezer*, *The Blue Planet* and *Frozen Planet*, all presented by David Attenborough.

The first part of our Arctic journey took us to Grise Fiord, an Inuit hamlet right on the tip of Ellesmere Island, one of the most northern communities in Canada. Making our way to Grise Fiord we stopped off at Resolute Bay, a larger Inuit hamlet on Cornwallis Island in Nunavut. Resolute Bay is famous for number of reasons. It has a small airport that is used by many international scientific research teams working in the Arctic and it is also a staging point for adventurers who are trying to make it to the North Pole.

The name Resolute has another big historical connection. It has given its name to the desk that stands in the Oval Office in the White House in Washington DC and is used by US presidents. The desk is made from the oak timbers of the British ship HMS *Resolute*, which was involved in the search for Sir John Franklin in 1852 when it was abandoned in the area.

My first real experience of the Arctic was to travel from Resolute Bay across the frozen ice on a skidoo to Beechey Island, to visit the graves of four sailors from the HMS *Erebus* and the HMS *Terror*, two ships which Sir John Franklin was using to try to find the Northwest Passage, in his search for a shorter route from the Atlantic to South East Asia.

We were taken there by an Inuit guide. The journey took several hours across the frozen ice. When we reached the snow-covered Beechey Island, the four graves stood out in the frozen landscape. Three of the graves were for young sailors from the lost Franklin expedition: John Torrington, William Braine and John Hartnell. The fourth grave was that of Thomas Morgan, who died a few years later while out searching to find out what had happened to the Franklin expedition. It was like stepping back in history, looking at these four graves of young sailors who were all part of the Franklin story.

As we set off from Beechey Island, en route back to Resolute, we passed some floating icebergs that had been caught up on the frozen sea. It was a weird and novel feeling, knowing that we were travelling over frozen ice that maybe in a few months' time would have thawed – a sublime and impermanent landscape.

The next day we flew from Resolute Bay to Grise Fiord, the most northerly community and one of the closest inhabited parts of Canada to the North Pole. I had been forewarned that landing in Grise Fiord would be a scary experience, and it was. It looked like our small twin-engine Otter plane was flying directly towards a snow-capped mountain until, at the last moment, it turned and landed on an ice runway.

We were arriving in this Inuit community just after they had moved out of twenty-four hours of darkness to twenty-four hours of daylight. The first night we slept there, I had to tape a black bin-liner bag across my bedroom window. Outside, in the middle of the night, I could hear the local children playing on the ice. Grise Fiord, like much of the Arctic, has six months of darkness followed by six months of daylight.

The Inuit people now number no more than 200,000. But Grise Fiord, which means pig inlet and which got its name from a Norwegian explorer in this isolated part of the Arctic, has a controversial history. In the early 1950s the Canadian government resettled these Inuit families from another Inuit settlement in Quebec and Pond Inlet on northern Baffin Island. This resettlement led to much controversy and in 2008 the Canadian government apologized for its treatment of much of the Inuit community.

During our stay there we had two remarkable guides. One was Danny Osborne, who, along with his wife Geraldine, had spent many years living in different places in the Arctic, including Grise Fiord. Originally from Dorset in England, he is a well-known artist and one of his major works is the Oscar Wilde statue in Merrion Square in Dublin. With his knowledge of this part of the Canadian Arctic, he was an invaluable source of knowledge for us.

Our second guide was Jaypetee Akeeagok, an Inuit hunter who took us out onto 'the land'. Inuit people refer to the frozen sea as the land. They go out hunting 'on land' for polar bears, musk oxen, narwhals, bowhead whales and seals. The Inuit communities have lived off the land for thousands of years, and it's only in the last couple of hundred years that they have got used to eating what they call 'shop food', which was introduced to them by adventurers travelling to the High Arctic.

Jaypetee took us out onto the land for a five-day expedition, looking to find polar bears and experience living out on the land. I travelled with Jaypetee on his sled, which was pulled by his team of twelve huskies. Each of the rest of the team, including cameraman Doug Allan and Danny Osborne, had their own skidoos. For five wonderful days and nights, all in 24-hour daylight, we went in search of polar bears.

It was eye-opening to see how the Inuit people live and survive in this Arctic region. But it was also alarming to see the signs of climate change. Jaypetee showed us glaciers whose size, he said, had reduced considerably since he first travelled to them as a young man. It was glaring evidence of how global warming was affecting even this remote part of the world.

While we were out on the land, we camped on the ice and cooked our food. But we came across another Inuit family who were also out hunting and it was amazing to see their children eating raw seal meat, just like their huskies, after they had caught a young seal for food for themselves and their dogs. Of course, Jaypetee also had to go hunting every couple of days for seals for his own team of twelve huskies.

On the fifth day of our trip out on the land, we come across our first polar bear. Jaypetee had seen the tracks on the ice and after following them for a while we finally saw the polar bear. Jaypetee had his hunting rifle hung over his shoulder, even though we were only filming this encounter with the polar bear. As an Inuit hunter, he may in other circumstances have killed the bear for food. The Inuit people are still allowed to hunt for polar bears and other animals in the Arctic, although they themselves have introduced strict guidelines as to how many they are allowed to hunt for every year. They have what they call 'a tag system' whereby the community elders will say that only a certain number of bears can be hunted for in any one hunting season. Hunters are only allowed to travel with a dog sled team and if they don't get a bear, then the 'tag' for that trip is used up.

The next phase of my Arctic adventure was to travel to the North Pole on a Russian icebreaker ship. My documentaries – my journalism's 'second wind' – were taking me further and further from Ireland. Of course, instead of trekking to the North Pole the hard way, John Murray and I travelled on a nuclear-powered icebreaker called *50 Let Pobedy*. Its name translates as '50 Years of Victory', referring to the anniversary of victory of the Soviet Union in the Second World War. We flew first to Finland and then went overland to Murmansk, in the Russian Arctic, and then the icebreaker headed towards the North Pole. A couple of days after sailing out of Murmansk we reached the sea ice. The '50 years of Victory' is one of the most powerful icebreakers in the world and it cut through frozen sea ice 8 feet thick or more with ease.

We saw many polar bears and when we finally reached the North Pole, there was a major celebration among those who had paid for this expensive trip. (These adventures are run by an American company called Quark, which organizes trips to the North Pole and the Antarctic costing many thousands of dollars.) The captain gave a countdown to the moment we were at the top of the Earth and he anchored the ship at the spot.

All the passengers were allowed off the icebreaker and some us were foolish enough to have a swim at the North Pole. The heat coming from the nuclear reactor on board the ship melted the thick ice to make room for the bracing swim. Each person going for a swim had a special strap wrapped around their waist, in case their heart stopped on entering the freezing, ice-cold water, so that they could be pulled back out immediately by members of the crew.

The first people to jump in were some of the ship's crew, who were used to swimming in Arctic waters. I had two motivations for climbing into the water: I wanted to be able to boast that I had swam at the North Pole, and John wanted me to do it for the documentary. I was brave enough, or vain enough, to take the dip for the camera, but I only did a few strokes with my arms. I lasted in the water for less than a minute before I emerged for a reviving drink of Russian vodka. To my astonishment, some of the crew stayed in the water for a few minutes. John and I were happy that my few seconds in the water of the North Pole had been captured by the camera.

I went back to Grise Fiord for another month, after I had retired from RTÉ, to do a series of articles for the *Irish Times* in 2014. I was staying with Raymond, who was not an Inuit but from a different tribe. A couple of days before I arrived, Raymond had noticed bear tracks not too far from his house in Grise Fiord. He followed the tracks, spotted a polar bear and shot it. He explained to me that the meat from this bear was shared with the community and counted for one from the quota the elders allowed to be hunted during that season. On that trip I was invited to the celebration they have every year to mark the return of 24 hours of daylight. Among the food they were serving at this celebration was seal and musk ox meat.

The audience numbers for *Charlie Bird's Arctic Journey* led RTÉ to commission Crossing the Line Productions to do another documentary with me. This time our destination was at literally the polar opposite end of the Earth, the South Pole. In *Charlie Bird on the Trail of Tom Crean,* which was shown on RTÉ in 2011, a year before I retired, I traced the life and times of Tom Crean, the great Irish Antarctic explorer who came from just outside Annascaul in County Kerry. I was thrilled to get this opportunity because sometime in the mid-1990s, I had proposed to RTÉ that we should make a television documentary about Tom Crean, whose journey to the South Pole with Robert Falcon Scott during the famous Terra Nova expedition was largely forgotten in Ireland.

Crean, who was born in 1877, took part in three major expeditions to Antarctica, including the most famous of all when he tried to reach the South Pole with Robert Falcon Scott. He was also involved in the Terra Nova and the Discovery expeditions led by Scott. And he took part in an expedition by another great Irish explorer, Athy-born Ernest Shackleton, when their ship, *Endurance*, was crushed by ice and sank in the Weddell Sea in 1915. Its well-preserved hull, with its name clearly visible on the stern, was discovered 107 years later, in March 2022, more than 3,000 m (about 3 km) below the ice.

In late 2010, again with the Quark adventure company, we sailed from Ushuaia in Argentina, right at the tip of South America, towards Antarctica. Once again we sailed on a Russian icebreaker, this time the *Kapitan Khlebnikov*. The first part of this journey took us through the Drake Passage, which is considered one of the roughest and most treacherous seas in the world. When we were sailing through it, we were warned to strap ourselves into our bunk-beds. Much of the journey in this part of the world was certainly in very rough waters, but I avoided injury and seasickness. When we reached the iceshelf on Antarctica, one of the first sights we saw were large colonies of emperor penguins.

We tried to reach Elephant Island, the barren, ice-covered island where Ernest Shackleton and his crew took refuge when they lost the *Endurance*. Tom Crean was a member of the crew of the *James Caird*, a small boat that made a journey of 800 nautical miles from Elephant Island to South Georgia to seek help for the stranded shipmates. When we failed to land on Elephant Island because the weather was too rough, we too headed towards South Georgia.

The guides on the *Kapitan Khlebnikov* brought us ashore on a very remote part of South Georgia, where John Murray and I went to film a huge colony of seals. I was walking among the seals and when I knelt down to take some pictures of them, one of the seals suddenly came up to me and lay across my body. We had been told by our guides that we must not touch the seals, but that we were to remain still if they came up to us. I followed the advice and John Murray filmed an amazing sequence of the seals surrounding me and of one of them lying across my body. This seal was extremely heavy, but I managed to keep still as John recorded this novel and very strange experience.

Most of my career had been spent interviewing politicians and other newsmakers for RTÉ news bulletins that were watched by up to 750,000 people at most. My encounter with the seals on South Georgia, one of the most remote places on Earth, garnered nearly six million hits when RTÉ put it on YouTube after it was broadcast in 2011.

Before leaving South Georgia we went to Grytviken, where Ernest Shackleton is buried. Our programmes were a homage to Tom Crean, but we paused for a memorable reflection at the grave of his remarkable Kildare-born leader.

After a break at home for Christmas 2010, we returned to the Tom Crean trail in early January, via Punta Arenas in Chile and the Union Glacier on Antarctica. John Murray had planned that we would make this last leg of our journey with a company based in the United States called Adventure Network International, one of a few companies that offered trips to the South Pole. John had also planned that we would walk the last degree to the South Pole with a Norwegian guide. Our guide Ronnie had been working in Greenland and the Antarctic for years.

On the night before we were due to fly out of Dublin, I had a very bad nosebleed, but the next morning we flew to Spain and then on to Punta Arenas where we met up with the rest of the group who were flying to the Union Glacier, which is the staging post for flights to the South Pole.

Our departure was delayed when I got another nosebleed, worse than the one I had got in Dublin. The adventure company told us that they could not risk taking me to Antarctica with such a problem. John and I feared that our entire documentary was now in jeopardy, but we eventually found a private clinic in Punta Arenas where the medical staff put me under an anaesthetic and cauterized the veins in my nose. We had come such a long way, but there would be no documentary if we had to abandon the trip without reaching the South Pole. I was petrified that the cauterization may have failed, but I was desperate to get on with the job.

A few days later I was declared fit to fly the 90-minute journey to Union Glacier and to land on a naturally occurring and maintained ice runway. We flew on an Ilyushin 76, built in Russia and used previously for moving heavy machinery to remote parts of the world. There are no luxuries on board as the plane has to carry enough fuel to make the return trip to and from Antarctica. There is no radar to guide the plane into where it is going to land on the ice runway. Somebody told me that the pilots use GPS with their phones to find the location of the unique ice runway.

The camp where we were to be based had just been erected when the daylight returned. Among those we met at the camp were six or seven climbers from many parts of the world, all of whom had made it to the top of Mount Everest. They normally go to Antarctica because Mount Vinson is the highest peak there.

All the locally based twin-engine planes that are used to fly people on to the South Pole must be flown to Antarctica from many different parts of the world, including Canada. John and I were now just one major step away from our goal but because of my nose bleed problem, which thankfully had not recurred, we had to have a meeting with the doctor at the base camp at Union Glacier. He was concerned that if I had a recurring nose-bleed at the South Pole, given the poor weather and how long it would take medical help to reach us, I could be in serious trouble. He gave our Norwegian guide a strange piece of medical equipment to insert into my nose if any bleeding occurred. He also told me that I would not be allowed to enter the Amundsen-Scott South Pole Station run by the Americans at the pole. This is because the South Pole is situated on a high plateau, almost 3,000 m above sea level, and visitors can experience altitude sickness there. Each flight to the station has a doctor on board for that reason.

The South Pole was about 600 miles from our camp at Union Glacier. In addition to the crew and the doctor, John and I were accompanied by a rich American man who was bringing his son on a day trip to see the South Pole! When we were taking off, it still hadn't been decided if we were going to be dropped off one degree from the Pole and told to walk the rest of the way. Being

unaccustomed to the extreme weather and with my nose-
bleeds a persistent worry, I wasn't at all keen on walking
the last degree. I was relieved, as we got closer to the
South Pole, when the crew told us that the weather was
not great for landing one degree away from our destination. My spirit was lifted further when the plane banked
and I could see the Amundsen-Scott station below us.
Shortly afterwards we landed on the ice runway at the
South Pole.

All my thoughts as we landed were on the Kerryman
Tom Crean, who had endured such unbelievable hardships
to try to reach this spot one hundred years earlier. Here
I was, arriving by aeroplane, after travelling first class with
two Americans on a day trip.

Once the plane landed and all our equipment was taken
off, we were allowed into the station for a short visit.
Along with the American father and son, we were given
a guided tour of this scientific station right at the bottom
of the Earth. Then we went to our tent, a short distance
away from the station. This would be our home for the
next five days or so. I had to keep pinching myself to
believe that I had actually made it to the South Pole.

Our tent was lovely and snug, but when you wanted to
go to the loo, you had to run outside into the cold and
over to another tent, which was set up as a toilet. There
is a simple rule at the South Pole: everything you take
there, you must bring back with you, including your frozen
pee and poo. At the bottom of the Earth, nothing that can
pollute can be left behind.

We spent the following days filming, including at the
scientific marker that identifies the exact spot of the bottom

of the Earth. Each year the scientists at the pole take measurements to locate the exact position. While we were there filming, I took from my inside pocket a scapular – a thin strip of cloth worn around the shoulders with a religious relic. I had brought it from Ireland, and I placed it right on the geographical point of the South Pole. The reason I had brought it was because Tom Crean always wore a set of scapulars around his neck. I felt that I was, in a way, completing his journey for him with this symbolic gesture. I then lifted up the scapular and returned it to my pocket, to be taken back to Ireland again.

My career had taken me all over the world and now it had enabled me to set foot on both the North Pole and the South Pole, an experience enjoyed by very few people and even fewer journalists. I had done it the easy way, but the extreme cold and the endless inhospitable terrain gave me a glimpse of the hardship that Tom Crean and his fellow explorers endured for hundreds of days to try to reach the bottom of the Earth.

A genuine respect for the things that are sacred to other people lay behind one of the most hitherto unimaginable, if not downright bizarre experiences of my immediate post-retirement years at home and abroad. This was when I found myself addressing a congregation of Sunday midday Mass-goers from the pulpit of the Catholic Church of St Thérèse in Mount Merrion, south Dublin, a ten-minute walk from my former workplace at RTÉ in Donnybrook.

It arose from one of the least expected but ultimately most fulfilling assignments that I undertook in the years immediately after my retirement, which was an overseas reporting journey for the Irish Catholic Church. I was not a practising Catholic and I had always kept my religious beliefs to myself while respecting the beliefs of others. I had helped to promote what was one of the first, if not the first, non-religious national schools in Ireland, the Bray Educate Together school project, in opposition to the Catholic Church's near-monopoly on primary school education in the early 1980s.

The assignment arose from an out-of-the-blue telephone call from Maurice Hogan, National Director of Mission Sunday, the annual promotion by the Irish Catholic Church of the work of Irish missionary priests and nuns overseas. Over my many years of covering stories in Africa, South America and the Far East, I had often reported on the work of Irish missionaries. Maurice reminded me that one of the first big foreign stories that I reported on for RTÉ News, and the one that many people said brought me to national prominence, was the 1985 case of the Negros Nine, when Fr Niall O'Brien from Blackrock in Dublin and another Columban missionary priest, Fr Brian Gore from Australia, were facing trumped-up murder charges for the killing of a local mayor in the Philippines.

To my surprise, Maurice agreed to my suggestion that the best way I might help him to promote Mission Sunday would be to travel to meet some missionary nuns and priests in their day-to-day work in places like the Philippines and South Korea and to make a video that could be shown in churches all over the country on Mission Sunday.

We travelled first to Seoul, the capital of South Korea. Within days I found myself at the graves of seven Columban missionary priests who had been massacred at the start of the Korean War in 1950. These seven young priests, five of whom were from Ireland, were killed in the early months of the war when they refused to abandon their parishioners close to the border of North Korea. They account for more than a quarter of the missionary martyrs of the Missionary Society of St Columban.

Their violent deaths, so far from home, had long been forgotten in Ireland. But I knew immediately that their lives and deaths deserved to be highlighted because, like scores of other Irish missionaries over the past 150 years, they had paid the ultimate price for their beliefs and self-less dedication. I knew that very few people in Ireland had heard of how these young missionary priests had given their lives to stay with the communities they had been living with and supporting. I imagined the international news coverage if this type of story happened today, and what the reaction would be in Ireland. Their lonely graves on the other side of the world moved me enormously. I did not want them to remain forgotten.

The five Irish missionaries, all aged in their thirties, were: Francis Canavan, from Headford, County Galway; Anthony Collier, from Clogherhead, County Louth; Thomas Cusack, from Ballycotton, County Clare; John O'Brien, from Donamon, County Roscommon; and Patrick Reilly, from Drumraney, County Westmeath.

In South Korea I saw how today's Columban missionary priests were continuing to do the same dangerous work as their massacred predecessors, embedding themselves with their parishioners to oppose their oppressors.

On the island of Jeju, I saw how the Columbans were openly supporting the local people who were resisting their government's approval of the construction of a giant United States naval base near the village of Gangjeong. The building of the base was highly controversial. Construction work had been halted many times by local people and by supporters who came from all over South Korea to protest about its impact on the environment and also about what they saw as a US project aimed against Korea's giant next-door neighbour, China. What I found most striking was how the local people universally respected and appreciated the outspoken support of the Columban priests.

In Manila, the capital of the Philippines, I was taken to a cemetery where I came across one of the most remarkable sights I had even seen in all my years in journalism. This graveyard, in the middle of the slums of Manila, was home to around five hundred destitute families. Some two thousand adults and children were sleeping and cooking their lives away in makeshift shelters between the tomb-stones. In the midst of these destitute families were two missionary Columban sisters, Sister Bella and Sister Julie, who had left their families in affluent South Korea to join the Columban Missionary Order and live in a cemetery in the slums of Manila.

I also visited the island of Mindanao, one of the most dangerous places in the Philippines, where tens of thousands of people had died and where almost two million others had been displaced during decades of inter-ethnic violence. Here I met Fr Paul Glynn, a Columban missionary from Mallow in County Cork, whose daily work was to try to broker some semblance of peace between the warring communities.

The exoticism of these Irish missionaries' lives in the Far East, in the original meaning of the word exotic, was perhaps best exemplified among the 'sea nomads' called the Bajau, who have lived for more than a thousand years at sea in small houseboats and who came ashore only to trade for supplies and to shelter from storms.

I recorded all of my reports on this extraordinary journey on a small video camera. When I returned to Ireland, I prepared a five-minute video that was to be shown in Catholic churches on Mission Sunday, which fell on 18 October 2015. I wanted my video to reflect that, whatever the travails and degradations of the Catholic Church in Ireland over the previous two decades, the brave and selfless work of Irish missionary priests and nuns was continuing, as it always had, in the most hostile and inhospitable locations.

I felt that the work of the missionary Irish exiles was changing and adapting to what was happening in the world around them and that they were helping their parishioners and neighbours to fight for social justice. I believed that if people in Ireland had the opportunity to see them at work, they would be immensely proud of them.

Before my sermon on Mount Merrion, the church printed tens of thousands of booklets for distribution in parishes throughout the thirty-two counties. They featured a number of photographs, including ones of me and of Pope Benedict XVI, separately, over a message that said: *World Missions Ireland is the official mission outreach charity of the Catholic Church in Ireland. It supports missionaries and mission projects throughout the world. Your continuing prayers and generosity allow us to help missionaries make a difference that transforms people's lives. By giving to us, you are giving to them. Thank you.*

The five-minute video was made available to schools as a DVD and posted on parish websites. Maurice Hogan said that it offered 'a fresh approach to the lives of our fellow Irish abroad and the difference they make to the lives of those they serve'. He added: 'Irish people do indeed have a long tradition of supporting missionaries abroad, for which we are grateful, and we believe that our DVD will show them that their support is still very much needed and valued.'

I had set out on this assignment wondering if I was doing the right thing, and if I was the right person to tell the story of the modern-day missionary priests and nuns. I came home from the Far East profoundly impressed and moved by the sights and memories of the work that they were doing on the ground. My own work had taken me all over the world, to the Far East and what might be called the Far West, as well as to the North and South Poles. I hoped that my work had not been wasted.

The Mission Sunday assignment was a fortuitous project, but its culmination on the altar of St Thérèse in Mount Merrion, Dublin, may have been the first step of a journey that took me to the top of Croagh Patrick less than seven years later.

There was a final addendum to the story of my polar travels.

At the beginning of 2022, a woman from Annascaul sent me a little stone that she had taken from the cairn on Tom Crean's grave in the village cemetery. She said that she had borrowed the stone so that it would remind me of the strength I still held in the palm of my hand, even on days when I didn't feel strong physically, mentally or emotionally – just as Tom Crean had endured so many very tough days on the Antarctic ice. She told me to keep the stone for as long as I wished, on the condition that one day it would be placed back on Tom Crean's grave, either by me or by one of my loved ones. It is a sacred promise and it will be honoured.

Tom Crean endured unbelievable hardships and faced up to the unknown in his many explorations. After the privilege of retracing his footsteps, my MND brought its own hardships and I too found myself looking into the unknown. The stone that I held in my palm and the scapular that I brought to and from the South Pole will remain in Tom Crean's Kerry after I have departed this life.

12. CLOCK

Christmas 2021 was a difficult one for Claire and me. I kept thinking that it would be my last Christmas alive, even though Professor Hardiman had told me that she thought that I would survive for longer than that. It was the first Christmas Day that Claire and I had spent alone together, away from her family and from my daughters and grandchildren. We just wanted to be on our own.

I had been wearing my emotions on my sleeve even before my diagnosis in October 2021. I had always been an emotional person, but particularly so during that terrible summer and autumn of 2021 when I lived in an unhappy limbo, waiting for a diagnosis. My frequent bouts of crying were very difficult for Claire and for my loved ones. The slightest thing set me off, no matter how much I tried to hide those episodes from Claire and my daughters. I knew the strain that they were under, and I wanted to protect them as much as possible.

I hadn't entirely dismissed the whole idea of assisted dying from my thoughts until the beginning of 2022 when I appeared on the *Late Late Show* of 7 January – the day after the Feast of the Epiphany. This felt significant to me. I had begun to realize over the New Year that I might have a real purpose in whatever time was left to me on this earth, and the response to the idea of Climb With Charlie confirmed that personal epiphany. A change had begun to come about inside me, and I suddenly knew with certainty that I was not going to travel down that road to the stony beach at Killoughter, in County Wicklow. I would not be going to Switzerland or into the cold waters of the Irish Sea. While I fully accept that other people with a terminal illness might have different views – indeed, one senior medical person told me that they understood and accepted that some people with a terminal illness might choose the option of assisted dying – it was no longer something I was going to contemplate.

The whole Climb With Charlie experience had chased away my darkest thoughts about my condition and my future. Those thoughts were miraculously replaced by some spiritual force that was pushing me and encouraging me with the preparations for my plan to climb Croagh Patrick. What had happened in the first three months of 2022 changed everything. Out of the blue, the campaign had transformed my world, and it had transformed me.

One of the strange but beautiful things that came from the Climb With Charlie campaign was that in little over three months, I had gone from being a nationally known journalist with a terminal illness to being hailed as an heroic and tireless fundraiser and disability campaigner. As a household name during my career with the national broadcaster, I was used to being stopped on the street by people who wanted to chat. This had happened frequently, even when I was working on general election or presidential election campaigns. The national newspapers regularly carried stories about me as my career progressed. The stories were sometimes critical, but at other times I was called 'a national treasure'.

Since the success of Climb With Charlie, however, the word that most often appeared on the thousands of cards sent to my home was 'inspiration'. I was blown away by the support I received from the general public. The illness had upended my life entirely, but the support and the recognition that I was getting from all over the country, and even from abroad, was what helped me to carry on. While my illness worsened, I was astonished and energised to find that, at the height of the war in Ukraine, when Irish people rightly were digging deep into their pockets to support the families fleeing that country, tens of thousands of people also contributed well over three million Euro to Climb With Charlie for two Irish charities nominated by me.

'You are a great source of inspiration,' my HSE nurse Bernie Corr told me during a house call in late May 2022. 'Everybody asks about you in every house I go into. Some people feel that they are on a journey with you. They identify with you.'

Bernie had become a frequent and treasured adviser since my diagnosis. She is one of a small number of HSE neurological nurses who specialize in care for people with motor neurone disease. Whereas an average GP might encounter a person with MND only once in twenty-five years, Bernie had twenty-five years of expertise and experience of helping sufferers like me.

'It's a dreadful disease and it's a very individualized illness,' she told me. 'It's individually driven. People always want a prognosis, but the illness moves in the individual way it moves for everyone. Our prognosis is always wrong. So far, nothing has changed for you except your voice and your [ability to] swallow.'

As well as invaluable advice on diet, exercise and the importance of keeping my other interests alive, Bernie has always been available on telephone to help Claire with queries or worries about me or my medication. 'My role is to anticipate and to have things in place,' she said. She told me that my condition would worsen gradually. She explained that she could improve my quality of life, but she could not extend my life.

'We keep people out of hospital. We keep people at home,' she said. 'You have a different conversation with people in their homes than you would have in a clinic or hospital.' She told Claire and me that we certainly should buy tickets for the Bruce Springsteen concerts scheduled for May 2023 in Dublin. 'You do not have a mobility problem. You are as fit as most of us. You are like a mountain goat,' she said.

I was enormously cheered when Bernie said this. The choking fits had increased my dread of what I was facing. I was shunning neighbours and friends again and I was thinking that I would be dead before the end of the year. Now I remembered that Daniel O'Donnell had sung a Bruce Springsteen song for me on the top of Croagh Patrick and that I had said on the *Late Late Show* in December 2021 that I wanted Bruce's 'Land of Hope and Dreams' played at my funeral.

I had been working non-stop since Christmas, but my motor neurone disease was always on my mind. 'You could not be accused of not maximizing every day. You are not defined by it,' Bernie said. 'It's about you doing what you want to do. Without blowing smoke at your feet, you are an inspiration. People feel for you. They are on a journey with you.'

I knew that I had to maintain my focus, keep working towards the goals I had set, to keep living. Bernie was inspiring me to do that.

My initial target of raising one million euros from a standing start in the second week of January 2022 seemed, and still seems, outlandish. I quickly became fixated on the figure, however, and I sought advice from two old contacts: Paul Allen, who became my voluntary Public Relations adviser; and Pat Farrell, a former Fianna Fáil general secretary who became a PR consultant to a number of banks and other financial institutions. I knew that I would need several substantial donations if I was to have any hope of nearing my target. I hesitated about approaching prominent business people, but then I also thought, 'Feck it, I'm asking for money for two great charities.'

I sent e-mails to two of Ireland's best-known businessmen, Dermot Desmond and Denis O'Brien. I had nothing to lose. I had dealt with both men during my news reporting days. Both men quickly promised to make very generous donations to the charities, via Climb With Charlie. Their prompt and generous replies were not just a big financial injection, they also gave a huge morale boost to Claire and to myself and to the team of volunteers that we had assembled.

I wanted to thank both of these hard-nosed businessmen personally because the ticking of the clock on my terminal illness had made me take a whole new approach to people in general, but especially to those I had met only briefly during my professional career. I resolved to reciprocate if anyone extended the hand of friendship to me.

I had met Dermot Desmond only twice previously: at a press conference when we chatted about our parents' Macroom roots after he had responded to a question I asked, and subsequently when he invited me to his offices in the Financial Services Centre on Dublin's Liffey Quays. I was surprised and thrilled when he invited Claire and me back to the same offices for another chat after I had sent him my shot-in-the-dark e-mail.

When I got emotional and started to cry during our meeting – a common occurrence for MND sufferers – he came round from where he was sitting and put his arms around me. He said he had been moved by how I was coping with my condition and by how I was trying to help others by raising money for the two charities. He also said not to hesitate to call him if he could do anything else to help. I jokingly asked him if he would wear a Climb With Charlie tee-shirt. On the day of the climb, two photographs of him wearing the tee-shirt popped onto my phone via WhatsApp, one of him facing the camera and the other with his back to the camera.

I also wanted to thank Denis O'Brien in person for his generous contribution. He insisted on coming to see me at my home. He came and knocked on our front door early one morning and we had a great chat in our kitchen while Claire took photographs of us. He also promised to give any further help that I might seek. Neither he nor Dermot Desmond asked to be named publicly, but I'm identifying them because they responded generously when I reached out to them. Another prominent business person also donated money on the condition they would not be named publicly.

Tea in my back garden with Denis O'Brien and an agenda-free chat with Dermot Desmond in the IFSC were events I could never have foreseen in my working days, but no one ever knows what is around the corner for them. My terminal illness had brought me to strange places, but also to one where the hand of friendship was being extended. I make no apologies to anyone. Where I am in my journey of life now, I am happy to extend the hand of friendship.

Another prominent businessman who responded with great generosity when I sought support is Pat McDonagh, owner of the Galway-based Supermac's fast-food chain and of a number of motorway plazas, including the Obama Plaza in Moneygall, on the Tipperary/Offaly border, where I reported on President Obama's visit in 2011. As my voice was almost gone by early 2022, most of our dealings with Pat were through Claire and Pat's daughter, Siobhan.

Supermac's paid for a series of radio commercials, over an almost four-week period, across many radio stations, including RTÉ, to promote the campaign. This also gave our team of volunteers a great boost, as did the Climb With Charlie posters they put up at all their outlets and forecourts throughout the country. Those posters gave a really powerful identity to the campaign. They were made from a caricature of a smiling Vicky Phelan and me on top of Croagh Patrick drawn by artist Niall O'Loughlin shortly after my January 2022 *Late Late Show* appearance. This caricature was used in most, if not all, of our advertising material and on all of the Supermac's promotions of the climb. I was on Inis Oírr when I first saw my caricature drawn by Niall O'Loughlin. I contacted him straight away and he gave me the go ahead to use the image in any way that I wanted – another very generous offer early in the campaign.

The largest single contribution to Climb With Charlie came from the customers, staff and management of Dunnes Stores. I found this strangely fitting because I had been doing our weekly shopping in the Dunnes Stores supermarket in Cornelscourt Shopping Centre for many years. Another coincidence was my discovery in meetings with the Heffernan family, who control Dunnes Stores, that we shared a Neville ancestor in Macroom, County Cork, where both my parents came from. During the summer of 2022 I developed a warm and enduring relationship with the Dunnes Stores matriarch, Margaret Heffernan. She told me that she had been watching my *Late Late Show* appearance and had told her daughter Anne afterwards that she found it very emotional and that she would love to help me in any way possible.

I had warmed to Margaret during our first meeting. This private and reputedly fearsome woman had got out of her chair and put her arms around me when I broke down and became very embarrassed and emotional while trying to speak to her with what was left of my natural voice because I didn't want to use my iPad voice app in company. It was like being comforted by a dear friend whom I had known for many years. We later joked about her forbidding reputation in business circles and about how she had refused to talk to me when I was working as a journalist.

I had contacted the Heffernans on a whim in January 2022 when I was setting up the campaign. I knew it was a long shot, but I explained that I was hoping to persuade a major nationwide retailer or business to promote the campaign. Anne Heffernan rang me back and invited me to a meeting. She and her mother and her cousin Sharon could not have been more positive or more helpful since that first face-to-face meeting at the company's headquarters in Aungier Street, Dublin. On the weekend of the climb, every Dunnes Stores outlet across Ireland had set up a system where customers could opt to donate €2 at the tills to Climb With Charlie. That alone brought in a staggering €250,000.

In the months before and after the Croagh Patrick climb my relationship with Margaret and Anne has really grown, and they have continued to offer me great support ever since. I really do regard them as very close friends now.

As we worked hard to hit our funding target, there was also the question of how the money raised would be spent by the two charities. The IMNDA confirmed Claire's announcement after the Croagh Patrick climb that it hoped to use some of the money raised to build 'The Bird House' respite centre near Beaumont Hospital in north Dublin.

It said: 'Thanks to Charlie Bird and his "Climb with Charlie" initiative, we would love to be able to provide our clients and their families with a dedicated Respite Centre as a means of providing a much-needed break for our clients and their carers in a "home from home" setting to be called "The Bird House". Nurse-led care in a pleasant, tranquil environment, away from home, provides the opportunity for some "time out" in a relaxed atmosphere to allow relationships rekindle, friendships made and renewed and simply time to reflect and re-energise. Everyone needs a break – those with Motor Neurone Disease even more so.' Alongside 'The Bird House' respite centre, the INMDA will also spend the money on further research into MND and on developing the Voice Bank App.

Claire and I were shocked and hurt when we were told that one senior medic had said that the reason that we were not putting 100 per cent of the money into research was because I didn't have a university education, and I may have undervalued research. That remark reminded me of the time, early in my RTÉ career, when my lack of a university degree ruled me out from applying for a job as a programme producer. The medic's comment was doubly galling because it came nearly a decade after University College Dublin had awarded me an honorary Doctorate of Laws, a much rarer and more prestigious parchment than any primary degree.

Pieta said it would use some of the funds raised to create what it called 'The Charlie Bird Crisis Intervention Fund' to support clients in suicidal crisis. It said: 'The creation of this intervention fund will ensure that the monies raised through the "Climb with Charlie" campaign will have a lasting legacy in communities throughout Ireland. The fund will play a vital role in preventing the heartache and devastation suicide brings.'

It said that it would also name a therapy room in its new Swords Centre in north County Dublin after me, to ensure that my name would always be associated with supporting people most in need. Pieta provides over 45,000 hours of crisis intervention therapy each year. It receives 70,000 calls and texts to its crisis helpline every year, an amazing average of over 200 every day, and it directly supports 600 households bereaved by suicide. It said it would 'always be grateful to Charlie for his extraordinary selflessness in thinking about others at his own time of crisis'.

Pieta chose Claire and me to lead its Darkness into Light walk in Bray, County Wicklow, on the morning of Saturday, 7 May 2022, exactly five weeks after our Croagh Patrick climb. We had an even earlier start than we had had in Westport on 2 April. We had to be in Bray at 3.30 a.m., so we got up at 2.30 a.m. It was a very heart-warming and emotional morning. We were joined by more than 2,000 other walkers along the beautiful coastal route just before the sun rose over our beloved Dublin Bay. We brought Tiger with us too, of course, and many of the walkers, adults as well as children, wanted to see him and to pat him.

Darkness into Light has become Pieta's biggest annual fundraising event, but it had to suspend the walk during 2020 and 2021 because of COVID-19. Claire and I wore our bright yellow Climb With Charlie tee-shirts instead of the similarly coloured Darkness into Light ones for the Bray walk. We set off on the 5 km route at 4.15 a.m. and we were back at the Bray seafront at around 5.30 a.m. to watch the beautiful sunrise.

I had to use my iPad voice App to address the walkers before we set off. I said that the walk was a powerful show of support for everyone who was in a dark place. I said that I had known a number of people who had died by suicide and that I had learned at first hand of the importance of the work done by Pieta. I recalled that one of the five candles that I had lit in the church at the top of Croagh Patrick was for people who were struggling every day, or who were in dark places with mountains of their own to climb. I urged the walkers to extend the hand of friendship whenever they could. I said that for the remainder of my life I would continue to extend the hand of friendship and kindness and that I would continue to support the work of Pieta.

The walk was organized by Bray Lions Club. Their spokesman told the *Irish Independent*: 'We were joined by the legend that is Charlie Bird. People are aware of Charlie's own difficulties with his health. He's actually lost his voice completely in the past week. He's been here with us and through the wonders of science managed to deliver a very emotional message. Of all the walks we've been involved in, today really is an exceptionally emotional morning.'

Pieta is a charity that is very close to my heart. I mentioned in a previous chapter how Kathleen Sharkey from Tory Island had told me how she had lost two family members to suicide. In June 2018 we donated the profits of the stage play *A Day in May* to Pieta.

Every time I take part in an event like Darkness into Light, or the annual Stardust tragedy commemorations, unfortunately I cannot help thinking that it will be my last time doing so, that I may not be around for the next annual gathering. I had another episode of crying in Bray and, as always, I needed Claire to support and comfort me. I have had to get used to walking away from public view and putting my head down so that people do not see me crying. I also comforted and distracted myself by taking Tiger off his lead and playing with him by throwing stones into the sea and watching him run after them as the sun rose over the bay. It was a sign of hope.

My having to leave Tiger behind for eight days when I went to New York with Claire in May 2022 was one of the most difficult and daunting anxieties I had about the trip. Family and friends had been urging us to take a holiday because Claire and I had been working non-stop, seven-days-a-week, since the beginning of January on Climb With Charlie and its related projects. We desperately needed rest and respite, but I knew my health was worsening relentlessly and I was worried about getting a bad coughing fit on a crowded aeroplane, or in a restaurant. More than six months had passed since my diagnosis was confirmed. My ability to swallow food, and even saliva, was now severely impaired. The types of food and drink that I was able to consume became more limited with every passing week. Sitting down to eat had become a nightmare.

Friends had offered us places to stay, including at one resort in Barbados, but we opted for New York, where my friend and Wicklow neighbour John Fitzpatrick had been urging us to stay in one of his two hotels. He and I had been friends for more than twenty years. His hotels are said to be the only Irish-owned and operated properties in Manhattan. Jim Fahy and I had stayed in his Lexington Avenue hotel in mid-Manhattan for a month when we were reporting on the September 9/11 atrocity.

I had also stayed there when reporting on visits to New York by President Mary Robinson and Taoisigh Albert Reynolds and Bertie Ahern.

John and I had become good friends. He had spent much of the pandemic in Wicklow and he often came to dine with Claire and me, or to go for walks with me and Tiger, who had really warmed to him. John did a brilliant podcast with me for the Senior*Times* series early in 2021, where we discussed, among other things, the obstacles he faced in opening a hotel in Manhattan and his friendship with Meghan Markle. And he flew home from New York to join us on the Croagh Patrick climb, even though he had broken his wrist in six places a short time before that and was wearing a cast.

Despite his very generous offer of accommodation and his constant urgings to travel over, I thought that a trip to New York would be very risky for me, but I knew that Claire was in need of a break after minding me night and day, and sharing my worsening MND nightmare, for more than a year.

In the days and weeks before our departure, I was still unsure about going. I was having nightmares about getting a coughing fit on the aeroplane, to my own distress and that of fellow-passengers. We got our tickets upgraded to business class, but I was still very worried that something awful would happen on the aircraft or in New York. I worried about what might happen if I took a turn for the worse while we were there. I knew that I would have to be ultra-careful about what I ate. But in spite of all my fears, I wanted to go because I wanted Claire to have some more happy memories of our remaining time together.

I had always loved working in the Big Apple, or just walking around Manhattan, but I knew that this would be my last springtime in New York. This would be a visit like no other. I wondered how I would feel walking through Central Park or through Times Square for the last time. I was determined to keep extending the hand of friendship during my visit. I planned to use my voice app to address a charity event organized by John Fitzpatrick in memory of his parents, the 28th Annual Eithne and Paddy Fitzpatrick Memorial Fund golf fundraiser, in aid of an organization called Solace, which is the US branch of Pieta, at the Sleepy Hollow Country Club. I also planned to talk about the Climb With Charlie project, and the two charities that would benefit from it.

I broke down and cried several times at Dublin Airport while Claire and I were preparing for our departure on the morning of 10 May 2022. Several people approached me to sympathise or to express admiration. One airport worker ran after me to give me rosary beads. Another one came and stood beside me to assist us while we were going through the US pre-clearance formalities.

While waiting to board the Aer Lingus aircraft *St Colmcille*, I could not help thinking that this would be my last time to fly out of Dublin Airport, from where I had departed for so many foreign assignments and holidays and from where I had often reported. Memories came flooding back to me. I vividly remembered interviewing President Mary Robinson and Taoiseach Charlie Haughey at different times in the VIP Lounge. I remembered the time that I nearly fluffed a 'doorstep' interview with Nelson Mandela when he reached out his hand to shake mine on the airport apron.

That was in July 1990, when Mandela was leader of the African National Congress but not yet the elected leader of South Africa. After his release following twenty-seven years in prison, he had been invited to Dublin to receive the Freedom of the City and to address Dáil Éireann. He was not scheduled to meet the media until after the Freedom of the City conferring at the Mansion House in the afternoon, but I persuaded Foreign Affairs Minister Gerry Collins, who was hosting the red-carpet reception at the airport, to steer Mandela towards me in the media scrum on the apron. To my surprise, Collins succeeded better than I had expected, but I was so overwhelmed when Mandela reached out his hand to shake mine that I was only able to babble a banal question instead of the one I had been hoping to ask.

I was better prepared four years later when I was in another media scrum on the day Mandela voted in South Africa's first democratic, non-racial, post-apartheid election. From my position in the huge line of international media outside the polling station on 27 April 1994 at the Ohlange High School at Inanda, in Natal province, I managed to throw two questions at Mandela. He responded to both questions and he later recalled the incident in his best-selling autobiography, *Long Walk to Freedom*. 'Before I entered the polling station,' he wrote, 'an irreverent member of the press called out, "Mr Mandela, who are you voting for?" I laughed. 'You know,' I said, 'I have been agonising over the choice all morning.'

His answer to my second question was even more newsworthy. He said: 'This is a historic day for which our people have struggled. It's the realization of our hopes and our dreams. And it's an unforgettable moment.'

Our flight to New York was my first time on an aircraft since before the COVID-19 pandemic and since the onset of the first symptoms of my illness in early 2021. Everything about the flight was weird and unprecedented for me. Claire was sitting beside me, but I could not talk to her. Neither could I respond to any greetings or remarks by the cabin crew. Even though the Wi-Fi allowed me to communicate with anyone in the world, I felt totally isolated from the people around me. The arrival of the food trolleys left me scared out of my wits that I might get a bad fit of coughing or choking.

We had checked with Bernie Corr, our specialist motor neurone nurse, about the wisdom of going on a long-haul flight and of staying away from home for more than a week. She said that it was up to ourselves. Claire pre-booked the type of food that would be easiest for me to eat on the Airbus. I did have some difficulty with the food, but we were very relieved when we got through the Atlantic crossing without any major incident.

Arriving into Manhattan and being unable to speak a single word in one of the most vibrant places in the world was very unsettling and frightening. John Fitzpatrick sent a car to pick us up from the airport and met us that evening at the hotel. He reminded me of the time Jim Fahy and I had stayed in his Lexington Avenue hotel after the 9/11 attacks. He said that the hotel was overflowing with people who were stranded in New York and he was astonished when one of his receptionists told him that Charlie Bird from RTÉ was on the phone looking for a room. He told his receptionists that it must have been an imposter as all flights into and out of the US were grounded. He could not have known that I had just walked over the Mexico/US Border at El Paso, having travelled up from Bogotá in Colombia where I had been covering the trial of the 'Colombia Three', as described earlier.

Jim Fahy and I had worked from the Fitzpatrick Hotel on Lexington Avenue for nearly a month after the Twin Towers attack. Twenty-one years later, Jim was no longer alive and my inability to speak had put me into a locked-in regime that made it impossible for me to have any kind of conversation with anyone. My iPad app did allow me to remind John that he had not just found me a room in 2001 but that he had also managed to obtain for me a mobile phone and a small cine camera that I used when working inside the 9/11 disaster site at Ground Zero, after Conor O'Clery of the *Irish Times* had introduced me to a top New York policeman from Donegal who arranged my much-sought-after accreditation.

Everybody in New York had been on edge following the Twin Towers attacks, but I was in the full of my health then. Back walking through the streets of Lower Manhattan in May 2022 was a very different matter. I was scared every hour of every day for a different reason – my fragile and deteriorating health.

When I awoke on my first morning in New York, my left arm was numb from my elbow right down to my fingers. These stark reminders of my terminal illness hit me instantly as soon as I awaken every day. I open my eyes, but when I open my mouth to try to speak to Claire, no intelligent sound emerges. It is a harsh and horrifying start to every day. Trying to eat breakfast is the next struggle. I knew that I would have my usual difficulties with eating in New York, even though John had secured the types of food that should have been easiest for me to consume.

Claire and I went for a walk in Central Park on our first morning. I'm sorry to say that I could not enjoy what should have been a beautiful, happy experience on a sunny May morning because my illness was with me every step of the way. And I was remembering my many carefree walks in the same park every time I had been in working New York over the years gone by.

I had a good sleep on my second night and I ate soft food for breakfast and had no coughing fit. I got a great boost after breakfast when I read an e-mail from Sarah Joyce of the Climb With Charlie project to say that the funds raised had passed the three million euro mark and that this total would be posted on the official website in the coming days. I find it hard to believe that we reached this stunning figure after barely four months of fundraising. I am still pinching myself at the realization that we have raised such a staggering amount of money in so short a time. It must mean that tens of thousands of people contributed to the fund. When we set a target of one million euros in January, I was genuinely worried that we might struggle to reach that figure.

Claire and I went to the top of the Empire State Building after breakfast. As I looked towards the site of the former Twin Towers and Ground Zero, I thought that if a big story happened in New York today, I would be useless to RTÉ because I had no voice. Claire has to do everything for me now. To be blunt, she is my full-time carer. Moments like that one, at the top of the Empire State Building, bring home to me the reality of my illness and what it is doing to my mental state.

We had a lighter moment as we walked along a street in midtown Manhattan. I noticed an elderly lady looking at me as we passed each other and then she turned around and caught up with us and asked us if we were Irish. When I nodded, she said that she had seen Facebook posts about people climbing a mountain in Ireland and she thought that I looked like the person leading the climb. I was amazed that the Croagh Patrick climb had been noticed by so many people in New York.

My choking scares and my inability to speak overshadowed and very nearly ruined our time in New York. Some of my crying fits were also becoming almost uncontrollable. I was so emotional about topping the three million euro mark that I was breaking down regularly and unable to stop crying. I had to stuff my fingers into my mouth and bite down on my index fingers to try to stop my crying.

An old friend from my journalism days, Niall O'Dowd, contacted me to do an interview for his IrishCentral website and he confirmed to me that the Croagh Patrick climb had attracted widespread coverage on Irish community social media. He made the interview his site's lead story and he headlined it 'A Profile in Courage' – a play on the 1955 Pulitzer Prize-winning book by future US President John F. Kennedy. He wrote that 'Ireland's most famous journalist' had become 'more popular than ever' by raising more than three million euros for charity. He said that while my motor neurone disease had stilled 'the most distinctive voice in Irish media', I had not taken the illness lying down.

Veteran Irish-American broadcaster Adrian Flannelly got in touch to invite me onto his popular Irish Radio Network USA show, which has been running for over fifty years and is broadcast all over the United States. Claire had to tell O'Dowd and Flannelly that I had no voice now and that I could only communicate via a keyboard or through my voice app – another reminder of the stark reality of my condition.

I knew that there would be no more radio chat shows for me, but I joined Claire and John Fitzpatrick in a make-shift studio in John's hotel for a 40-minute interview with Adrian Flannelly. He welcomed me as 'an icon and hero' and said that I was 'a very special guest'. I was only able to utter a deeply gutteral 'Thank you' when he welcomed me and a barely comprehensible 'Yes, it is' when he asked me if living with MND was devastating. Claire and 'Fitzie', as we now call John, did most of the talking on the show before I contributed a series of pre-recorded voice app messages about my illness and about the Croagh Patrick climb.

I had got used to not being able to contribute to conversations with family and friends at home, but my inability to speak was really affecting my spirits whenever I was in company in New York, where volubility is almost manda-tory. I was upset and uncomfortable at a dinner hosted by John on Saturday night in advance of the golf event because I could not utter even one word to contribute to the conversation.

Claire and I were among about twenty diners, including the Irish and European Ryder Cup golfer Eamonn Darcy, former Republic of Ireland soccer manager Mick McCarthy and his wife Fiona, broadcaster Ronan Collins and his wife Woody, and John's sister, Eithne, owner of the Fitzpatrick Castle Hotel in Killiney, Dublin, and her husband James. I was sitting beside John and the conversation flowed over a beautiful meal, but all I could do was to listen and nod without being able to contribute a single word.

The other diners were not ignoring me, but their efforts to try to involve me with smiles and facial expressions were futile. At one point, I was so frustrated that I got a pen from John and wrote two messages that he and Claire read out to the other guests. It was weird and uncomfortable, but it could not be helped. I know it's not politically correct to say this, but it gave me a glimpse of what it must have been like to be the village idiot in times past.

I was also petrified about trying to swallow the food, even though John had arranged a special menu for me. Once again, a near-choking fit forced me to leave the table and go outside the restaurant, followed by Claire carrying a glass of water to try to help me.

Episodes like this were now increasingly frequent. I was always embarrassed when it happened, but the stress of the choking scare was even worse than the embarrassment. I'd get so upset that I'd think that I could not go on living like this, even though I knew that this was my fate, whether I liked it or not. Every time I sat down to a meal, I did not know what was going to happen, no matter how carefully Claire had tried to find something that I would not have difficulty swallowing. I was living from one meal to the next and I felt a huge relief when I got through any meal without incident.

Ever since my diagnosis had been confirmed in October 2021, I had felt like I was skating on thin ice. By mid-May 2022, I knew that the ice was much thinner. In New York on Sunday, 15 May, what I had been fearing for months almost came to pass – I had a choking fit so terrible that my life flashed in front of me and I was sure that I was going to die.

What should have been a perfect sunny Sunday turned into a nightmare for Claire and me when I suffered two of the worst choking fits of my life. We spent the day with John and Eamonn Darcy at the upmarket Sleepy Hollow Country Club, overlooking the Hudson River, about an hour's drive from Manhattan. It was a beautiful day with the temperature in the early 80s Fahrenheit (over 28 degrees Celsius), but I had to leave the table twice when I got two bad coughing fits during lunch on the veranda overlooking the 18th green. Claire had to race after me with a glass of water each time.

Claire also had to come and help me when I was unable to ask anyone for directions to the men's toilets in the clubhouse. I could see that the staff wanted to help me when I got lost, but I was unable to speak to them. It was demeaning to have to run to her and get her to tell the staff what I wanted. Once again, I felt like a village idiot. I relaxed after sinking a few balls with Claire and Eamonn Darcy on the putting green, but worse was to follow when we got back to Manhattan.

At a barbeque at John's second hotel, near Grand Central Station, I took a mouthful of pasta and I immediately felt that something had got caught in my throat. I left the table so as not to embarrass the other guests, but I knew

I was choking. Claire realized that I was in trouble, and she asked the waiters for water. I was coughing and choking, but nobody was bringing us water. Claire recognized the loud and strange sounds coming from my throat and she saw the colour drain from my face. She shouted at one of the waiters, 'For fuck's sake will you get me some water, please? My husband is choking.'

My coughing was now so bad that I could not drink the water when it arrived. We made our way out of the hotel and onto the street, but I could still feel that something was caught in my throat. I was sure that I was going to end up in a New York hospital – one of my worst nightmares when we were wondering if we should undertake the trip. I really thought that I was going to die there and then. It took me ages trying to force myself to cough before I managed to dislodge the piece of pasta that was stuck in my throat.

I was trembling and shaking. Claire and I both knew that this was the worst episode of choking since I had learnt my diagnosis. She is the only person who can understand any of the sounds coming from my mouth. She understood that I was trying to voice the words, 'I can't live like this. I can't go on like this.' She was holding my hand and trying to comfort me. We knew that we had just survived my worst choking fit thus far.

We didn't go back to the barbeque, but on our return to our hotel room my head was spinning. My worst fear had nearly come to pass. I was more convinced than ever that I would soon choke to death because of my Bulbar MND. I felt that I knew how my nightmare was going to end. What should have been a sunny springtime Sunday in great company in New York had turned into another nightmare. I felt that I had entered a new phase in my terminal illness.

I was very weepy again the next day when we returned to the Sleepy Hollow Country Club for the Eithne and Paddy Fitzpatrick Memorial Fund tournament and meal. It was from that memorial fund that John donated $100,000 to the Climb With Charlie campaign. Mick McCarthy and Eamonn Darcy presented the trophy that they had received for winning the golf tournament to Claire and me as a souvenir. The Irish Consul General in New York, Helena Nolan, speaking on behalf of the government, told the guests that I was a hero in Ireland where I had united the whole country through my Croagh Patrick climb. She recalled in her speech how the Taoiseach, Micheál Martin, had praised me for highlighting the work of the motor neurone and suicide prevention charities.

John Fitzpatrick and I were both in tears after my speech, delivered via my voice app, which I finished by saying that none of us knows what might be facing us around the next corner and when we might need a helping hand. Mick McCarthy told me later that, despite his image of being a hard man during his career as a football player and manager, he had tears streaming down his face while listening to my speech. He also suggested that he and I should do a parachute jump later in the summer to raise more money for Climb With Charlie. 'I bleedin' mean it,' he said, in his thick Yorkshire accent, when my face betrayed some doubts.

I had serious doubts about the summer that I was facing as we packed our bags to return home. I believed that I had made my last trip abroad and I was filled with worry and concern about how my own final journey would end. The omens from New York were not good. The choking fits, far from the safety of home, told me that foreign travel was now very risky. My days of dining out in restaurants or cafés were certainly numbered.

My voice app helped me enormously when I was asked to make formal speeches, but my complete inability to speak was upsetting me more and more during and after our break in New York.

Even before mid-summer 2022 I was in a much darker place. When Claire and I were alone together there were now long silences. Where before we would have had natural discussions, now I was trying to use facial expressions or a sort of sign language with my hands to communicate with her. We had to take to conversing through my writing down messages on a notepad and then Claire answering verbally. We had to buy a bundle of notepads so that I could write down the things I wanted to say to her, even when she was sitting beside me.

Every month brought a new and more frightening deterioration in my condition. Barely eight months after I had gone public about my voice worries, I had completely lost the ability to utter any comprehensible sounds. I had a frightening and humiliating experience while shopping in our local supermarket. I pointed to the fish I wanted, but when the assistant asked me which particular pieces I wanted, I instinctively tried to respond, but no sound came from my voice. My momentary forgetfulness left me distressed and humiliated in a supermarket full of Saturday shoppers. It wasn't the shop assistant's fault – it was simply me forgetting that I no longer had a voice.

A card given to me by the HSE nurse Bernie Corr was designed specifically to avoid problems like the one I experienced in the supermarket. It carries a simple but stark message: *I have a physical problem which affects my speech, but I can hear and understand you. Your help and patience will be appreciated. Thank you.* I kept postponing having to pluck up the courage to use it, but I knew that soon I would have no choice.

Doing our weekly shopping, as I had always done, or even going into a shop on impulse, was no longer practical. My voice app was no good to me when I met people on the street. I could not face having to scribble a note on a piece of paper when I met someone outside. I was keeping my head down to avoid eye contact even with the neighbours I met while out walking with Tiger. The emotional toll of not being able to communicate with people was killing me. I had entered another new scary place.

I was even more disturbed and depressed about no longer being able to talk to my daughters and my five grandchildren. Having to get pen and paper to communicate with my own flesh and blood when I was sitting beside them was a new low. Having to send a text message from my phone or iPad to a grandchild sitting beside me filled me with helplessness and sadness. Having to sit silently with close friends and being unable to take part in the conversation except by nodding or writing a note was a new, darker phase of helplessness caused by my disease.

Losing my voice also meant that that I could no longer speak to my beloved Tiger. I could type a message into my voice app, but I just found it too hard to do that to the faithful four-legged companion of my gradual descent into voicelessness.

But by far the most awful and draining pain that I felt during the summer of 2022 was the silence that reigned between me and Claire when we were in the car or just sitting together at home. The easy chatting that had characterized our relationship was replaced by an almost unbearable silence and stillness. Yes, I could still hug her, but the possibility of saying 'Give us a hug', or whatever other words come naturally in a loving relationship, was gone forever.

I had another awful choking scare when I appeared on the *Late Late Show* for the third time in under six months at the end of May 2022. It was a special programme to mark the show's 60th anniversary. I came within a cat's whisker of having to walk off the set just before Ryan spoke to me because I took a sip of water and I could not swallow it. I was within seconds of having to stand up and walk out. I was looking to the exit and planning where I would walk. Ryan knew that I was in trouble and he said later that he thought he was going to lose me. Claire, who was sitting beside me, also saw that I was in trouble.

I still get the shivers thinking about what a frighteningly close call it was. I cannot imagine how I would have felt, and what the newspapers would have written, if I had walked off the set on the 60th anniversary show. In those 30 seconds I feared the worst. I was panicking and thinking that I would disgrace myself, and RTÉ. I put my finger into my mouth to try to stop the sound that was coming from my throat and I bit my finger hard. The gods were looking down on me and I managed to swallow the water. That's why I ended up messing with Tubs and laughing out of pure relief. It was nervous laughter after a moment of real terror. My nerves were shattered.

I had to use my voice app to contribute a few words, in which I said that the show had helped shape modern Ireland and that it was the show that most politicians and newsmakers wanted to be on. I also said that it was the *Late Late Show* and the people who were watching it on 10 December 2021 were responsible for raising over three million euros for two charities. 'The emotional centre point of the broadcast [was] an interview with Charlie Bird and his wife Claire Mould,' wrote the *Irish Times* television critic Ed Power in the newspaper the next day. Neither he nor the audience at home could have known how emotional and frightening it really was.

Claire and I went to Inis Oírr at the beginning of June to spend time with Peadar and Bríd and to sit on the chair I had specially made, overlooking the Atlantic Ocean. Bríd had to prepare special food for me, and I had to use a pen and notebook to communicate with her and Peadar, but we were thrilled to see them again. The weather was fine and it was a very welcome break for Claire and me after all the pressures of the campaign.

I also had a reunion with my WestAwake pals in Galway en route to Inis Oírr. Foremost on my mind, and on all our minds, was a huge sadness at the absence of our great colleague, Jim Fahy. It was hard to believe that he had declined and died within months of our last get-together in Galway, almost a year to the day earlier, in June 2021.

That had been our first get-together since before the COVID-19 epidemic. Truly, none of us knows what is waiting around the next corner.

Another huge difference from twelve months previously was the harsh reality that I now needed a pen and note-book to communicate with my pals because my voice was completely gone. My diction had been imperfect when we'd last met in Galway, but at least I had been able to communicate clearly with them that time. Now, as we walked along the Promenade towards the city centre, I could no longer participate in the chats and discussions. We stopped a few times so that I could write notes. Once or twice I had to turn away, so that my friends would not see the tears welling up in my eyes.

I surprised myself by not being weepy during most of our day in Galway. When two men approached me on Henry Street, it was they, not me, who welled up as they spoke to me. One of them crossed the street to shake my hand and the other one stopped his car, rolled down the window and spoke to me. I held back my tears in Taylor's Bar on Lower Dominic Street where we had a drink before we went for a meal. The most senior of the bar staff, Cormac Conway, recognized me as soon as we walked in. He immediately said: 'This round is on the house.'

13. LEGACY

I had begun to make preparations for my death, and for my funeral, even before my diagnosis was confirmed. In summer 2021, when my concerns about my health were at their height, I sent the scapular that I had placed on the magnetic South Pole in 2010, in memory of Tom Crean, to the Tom Crean Museum in Tralee, County Kerry, near where he was born and died. Immediately after my diagnosis, I told my WestAwake pals that I wanted them to carry the coffin at my funeral. I also asked Peadar and Bríd Póil to try to find a plot for my ashes and headstone on Inis Oírr. A few days after my diagnosis was confirmed, I met a close friend in Dublin and I immediately took off the overcoat that I was wearing – a lovely soft-leather Hugo Boss coat that was my favourite – and gave it to him to keep and to wear.

I was starting the process of letting go, divesting myself of belongings that had meaning and that I could share with others. Knowing that I could leave items to them that carried happy memories was a source of comfort.

In summer 2022 I added to the 'peace process' mementoes that I had donated to the National Museum in Dublin.

I knew there was a 'Troubles' archive in the University of
Galway and a journalism archive in Dublin City University,
but I thought that the National Museum of Ireland would
be the most fitting repository for items that signalled an
end to 800 years of violent conquest and militant conflict
on the island.

The National Museum intends to display the items in
a major exhibition on twentieth-century Ireland that it is
planning for 2024 in its former Collins Barracks building
on Wolfe Tone Quay in Dublin. The items comprise twelve
statements by the Irish government and the leadership of
the IRA, as well as what is probably the only extant audio
recording of the 1994 ceasefire announcement, and a DVD
of former IRA prisoner Séanna Breathnach (Walsh) reading
the July 2005 statement on the IRA's 'total cessation of
the armed campaign'. The DVD is one of only three or
four copies made by the IRA and on it Breathnach became
the first IRA member since 1972 to represent the organization without wearing a mask.

Also included are the joint statement by the then-
Taoiseach Albert Reynolds, the then-SDLP leader John
Hume and the then-Sinn Féin leader Gerry Adams when
Adams was welcomed at Government Buildings in Dublin
for the first time after the August 1994 ceasefire. It is
signed by Albert Reynolds, with the words *Thanks Charlie
for everything, 2/12/94*' over his signature.

My spiral-bound shorthand notebook, containing my
longhand handwritten copy of the 1997 IRA ceasefire
announcement on a page later signed by the then-Taoiseach
Bertie Ahern is also included, as is the internal RTÉ copy
of the IRA statement dictated by 'Brendan', using the

codename Eksund, to a Newsroom colleague in my absence announcing the end of its ceasefire one hour before the February 1996 Canary Wharf bombing that killed two men. Other items include typed off-the-record briefings on arms decommissioning given to me by the IRA for use as background but not broadcast.

The curator of the National Museum's military collection, Brenda Malone, examined all of the items with me in summer 2022 as she was preparing them for inclusion in the '20th Century History of Ireland' exhibition. They are one of my real legacies. I regard the peace process as the most important part of my reporting life. In some ways, it was my life.

By Easter 2022, I was disposing of more and more of my possessions. I despatched my largest and most expensive item to Mayo on Easter Sunday. This is my former giant garden sculpture, 'The Warrior', which now stands in the grounds of Westport House. It's a larger-than-lifesize sculpture of a medieval Irish soldier carved from a giant Lebanese cedar tree by my County Wicklow neighbour Séighean Ó Draoi, the stone and wood carver. The sculpture had pride of place in my front garden for several years. I acquired it during one of my garden renovation projects following my retirement from RTÉ, after noticing it during one of my visits to Séighean's workshop in Rathdrum.

I had gone there to see if he would carve a small stone monument for my garden, to bear the names of my daughters and grandchildren alongside the Bird family crest. I could not help but notice the magnificent carving of what I took to be a Celtic warrior in his workshop. It fascinated me more and more with each subsequent visit. Séighean told me that it was based on one of the figures in a 1521 watercolour-and-ink painting by the German artist Albrecht Dürer. I was even more intrigued when a Google search revealed a translation of Dürer's caption on the painting: *Thus go the soldiers of Ireland, beyond England/Thus go the poor (peasants) of Ireland.*

Séighean told me that he had carved the sculpture from an enormous Lebanese cedar tree trunk when he was commissioned to make a piece of art for a village in Northern Ireland, but that nobody was prepared to buy it after the 2008 economic crash. I was already smitten. Now I was tempted. Much haggling followed. I have never told anyone – not even Claire – how much I paid him when we finally struck a deal and I came to own 'The Warrior', or *An Saighdiúir*, as I sometimes called the piece.

My family and neighbours were amazed to see this most unusual piece of garden sculpture in front of my house. It's over 10 ft (3 m) high. It weighs about a tonne and it is carved from the hardest of Lebanese cedar hardwood. Séighean said that it would survive for hundreds of years, like so many Indian totem poles do in the United States, if properly maintained. I often thought that I might give the sculpture away, so that it could be displayed in a more fitting location where the public could enjoy such a lovely piece of art. I can think of no place more suitable than Westport, County Mayo, where people embraced me so generously and so selflessly before, during and after the Croagh Patrick climb of April 2022.

It was on the day of the climb that I decided that 'The Warrior' would be an ideal and enduring symbol of my thanks to the people of Westport. When I told Fr Charlie McDonnell about my idea, and about the size of the sculpture, he suggested that the grounds of Westport House might be the best location. It was a brilliant suggestion because over the months leading up to the climb, the first people to come on board to sponsor tee-shirts for Climb With Charlie and to offer accommodation for my family and close friends were the Hughes family, the owners of Hotel Westport and recent purchasers of historic Westport House.

Harry Hughes, of the Portwest clothing company, was one of the first and most enthusiastic supporters of Climb With Charlie. He had sent me a present of a lovely outdoor rain jacket made by this company and a couple of woolly hats as soon as he heard that I was thinking of climbing the Reek. Claire and I met Harry and his daughter Orla on our first visit to Westport in January and they immediately agreed to print tee-shirts for us. This was the start of a great relationship with Harry and his wife Deirdre and Orla. On our next visit to Westport, we stayed at Harry's Hotel Westport. And even though it is not strictly a dog-friendly hotel, they welcomed Tiger with open arms.

Hotel Westport became our base for the whole Climb With Charlie campaign. Almost all of our families and friends stayed at the hotel on the weekend of the climb and they also accommodated the *Late Late Show* crew when the show went 'live' from there on the Friday night before the climb. Harry has written a number of books about Croagh Patrick and he gave us lots of advice and introduced us to more people in the Westport area. He and his brother Cathal did much of the planning for the climb with Claire and me in the snug of Matt Molloy's pub.

I was delighted when Harry agreed to give 'The Warrior' a new home in the grounds of Westport House. This historic house, centrepiece of the 400-acre estate that skirts the town of Westport, is the ideal location for the sculpture. The estate was owned for centuries by the Browne family, direct descendants of one of the greatest warriors ever to emerge from Connacht, the famous sixteenth-century Mayo woman Grace O'Malley, or Gráinne Mhaol, the so-called 'Pirate Queen', who also owned the Clare Island castle that can be seen from the summit of Croagh Patrick. When the Hughes family purchased the house and the estate in 2017, they opened the grounds to the people of Westport and to visitors. I could not be happier than I am to know that 'The Warrior' now stands at the Quay Entrance to the grounds of historic Westport House, where it will be seen every day by the people of Westport and other visitors long after I have gone from this Earth.

I have also handed over two other works of art for the people of Westport and Murrisk. Hanging in the Community Centre in Murrisk and in the Town Hall in Westport are beautiful paintings that I commissioned specifically for them from the artist Tim Goulding, who lives near Allihies in West Cork and whose mother, Lady Valerie Goulding, set up the Central Remedial Clinic in Dublin in 1951.

In the weeks after the Croagh Patrick climb, I also decided to add a memento of the occasion to my grave plot on Inis Oírr. I have chosen a beautiful spot on the island as my final resting place. I asked Séighean to sculpt an image of Croagh Patrick with a path leading to the top onto a stone plaque, to be placed beside the headstone over my ashes. On it he has carved simply: *climbwith-charlie April 2, 2022*.

The plaque will stand in testament to another Mayo miracle – the friendship I developed with Fr Charlie McDonnell and the consequences of that friendship. Although I am not a practising Catholic, I began to draw great comfort from the blessings that Fr Charlie gave to Claire and me every time we walked him to his home beside St Mary's Church on the South Mall in Westport. He changed my attitude to religion, and he will be my friend and my priest for as long as I am alive. I hope to have him by my side when I am passing from this world.

I have always respected other people's views about religion and now my own view has changed, undoubtedly due to my illness and to Fr Charlie, but also because of the hundreds of Mass cards that people have sent to me and the loving spirit in which they have sent them. I have asked myself if this makes me a hypocrite. Throughout my life I have always believed in the goodness of people and that is still my philosophy. I will not reject anyone's good wishes or prayers if they come from the heart. My illness has changed my perspective, but I have known nothing but goodness and kindness from friends and strangers since my diagnosis. I try to see the positive side in everyone, and I try to extend the hand of friendship whenever I can. When you live like this, it opens you up to meeting and appreciating more people. Would I have forged such a friendship with Fr Charlie in times gone by? I can't be sure, but I don't think I would have been as open to it. So I'm grateful for the shift in perspective that allows me to see the good in everyone and respond to it in kind.

There are other legacies that I am very happy I can leave behind. Planning the climb had occupied Claire and myself fully every day between January and April. We devoted every day of the rest of April to selecting photographs for a coffee-table book on the climb. We selected over three hundred photographs from the 640 that had been sent to us by professional and amateur photographers who had taken part in the climb. This book will live on as a testament to our campaign and that special day.

In June 2022, I was given a special honour by Dublin Pride for my work during and after the Marriage Equality referendum in 2015. It is a limited edition, bespoke book titled *Climb Every Mountain: Charlie Bird's Marriage Equality Journey*.

'We wanted to celebrate Charlie Bird's unique contribution to that 2015 referendum win, one that changed Ireland,' said Yvonne Judge, one of the co-editors, at the launch in the Dublin Pride Hub on 9 June. 'We are here for Charlie Bird because he was there for us in 2015. He is a national leader. We decided to publish this book, collating contributions and photographs from many people who worked with Charlie on that momentous campaign.'

LGBTQ+ campaigner Brian Sheehan said that I had shown great courage during the campaign, and that I had started a national conversation. He said that I had persuaded people to speak for the first time about their sexuality. 'That was where the magic and the fairydust of the campaign began,' he added.

The book contains thirty-four essays recalling the campaign and my role in it. Proceeds will go to the Irish Motor Neurone Disease Association and to the charity belongto.org, the national organisation that supports LGBTQ+ young people across the country. My role in the campaign is one of the memories that I am most proud of and it is an honour to have it recorded in this way.

In late-July 2022 I presented two cheques totalling €3,376,000 in value to the Irish Motor Neurone Disease Association and Pieta, the two charities that are so close to my heart. I handed the cheques, for €1,688,000 each, to Lillian McGovern, chief executive of the IMNDA, and to Stephanie Manahan of Pieta. I said that the huge sum collected was an amazing gesture of support for me and my family. I am still truly humbled and inspired that so many thousands of people took part in Climb With Charlie events throughout Ireland and across the world on 2 April, 2022.

It is a source of comfort to be able to choose legacies like this, to leave behind me, but there are other things that I must leave behind that are a source of great sorrow. Aside from Claire and my daughters, my dog Tiger has been the closest and most comforting companion on my illness journey and it is painful to think of going on without him. He sleeps on our bed and he comforts me on our couch every time I break down and cry. Claire has promised me that he will be at my funeral. He's always with me in newspaper photographs or Twitter videos and he has become one of the most famous dogs in Ireland, perhaps almost as famous as Brod and Misneach, Michael D Higgins' beloved dogs whom we met during our visit to Aras an Uachtaráin in June 2022. Tiger was with us and had a great time sharing treats with Brod and Misneach and generally being spoiled by the staff.

Tiger came into our lives in 2016 after a long campaign by Claire. She loves dogs, but I had rejected every one of her frequent entreaties, even after she had inveigled the ashes of her deceased pet, Garby, into our house and under our bed after she moved in with me. I had had no friendly dealings with dogs since my early childhood. My life would have continued like that had I not met Claire.

I was afraid of dogs for most of my life. I was bitten by one when I was working as a delivery boy. Many years later I had the living daylights scared out of me when I was chased by a pack of dogs while running on a beach early one morning during a holiday in France. We had a Boxer puppy at home in Goatstown when I was very young, but my mother never took to him and he was gone one day when I came home from school. I think that my father had brought him home. My only other friendly contact with dogs as a child was with a neighbour's black Poodle puppy that I would sometime cuddle when it came into our house.

It was a cuddly puppy that finally broke my resolve. We were walking up Glendalough one Sunday when Claire drew my attention to a little puppy that was running around in front of us. She again begged me to consider getting one like it for her. We sought advice and we did extensive research before purchasing, but we were duped into buying a Cockapoo puppy that had been born on a puppy farm, a story I later told on the *Late Late Show*, despite legal threats from the vendor. I still don't know whether Ryan Tubridy was more frightened by the legal letter that arrived before we went on air or by the prospect of Tiger jumping from my lap and onto his during the show.

Claire picked the puppy, which we soon named Tiger, because he had run up to her when we were viewing a litter of newborns. I should have been more suspicious when the lady who was selling the pups became evasive after I asked if I could see the litter's father. We settled on the name Tiger after Claire rejected my first choice, Fangio, after a famous racing-car driver I had admired in the 1970s.

We were horrified to discover shortly after we brought Tiger home that that he had come from a puppy farm that had been raided by the Irish Society for the Prevention of Cruelty to Animals. We tried in vain to get the puppy farm shut down. I went on the *Late Late Show* with Tiger at the end of 2016 to try to alert people to beware of puppy farms if they were planning to buy a dog as a Christmas present.

I wish I didn't know now what I didn't know then – that Tiger would again be on my lap on the *Late Late Show* five years later, comforting me while I talked about my diagnosis and my hopes of climbing Croagh Patrick. We had become almost inseparable in the intervening years. I became so smitten that I found it very hard to leave him even for a weekend if Claire and I wanted to go away. We used to crumble when he saw us packing and he would start to whine and look at us with pleading, mournful eyes. We brought him to Inis Oírr when we flew there before Christmas 2021, even though I knew that Peadar Póil hated dogs. We also brought him to Belfast with us when I went to launch the book *Reporting the Troubles* in March 2022.

Tiger and I walked with each other for miles and miles every day during the COVID-19 pandemic while Claire was working from home. He was with me every time I was photographed for a newspaper or magazine article. And in the six or so months of 2021 when I was going through the horror of not knowing what was wrong with me, I would often sit on my couch crying and holding Tiger so tight.

I'm convinced that Tiger sensed that there was something strange happening to me during those awful months of summer and autumn 2021. Every day while I was waiting for the latest medical test results, Tiger and I walked the Murrough, which ran from Wicklow town to Killoughter. As we walked along during this daily ritual, all sorts of strange and frightening thoughts ran through my mind. I feared what I was facing, even before I got my official diagnosis, but the companionship of Tiger helped me enormously to cope with what was going through my mind.

Tiger was walking with me on that bleak October morning when I got the phone call that told me that the latest tests were indicating that I had motor neurone disease and that an appointment was being made for me with Professor Orla Hardiman. He was due to be with Claire and me during the second part of our *Late Late Show* appearance on 10 December 2021, but he became so upset during our absence on the set for the first part of the interview that the young researcher who had volunteered to mind him had to take him for a walk around the RTÉ campus in the dark, in case his crying and whining became audible to us.

He was on my lap again for the January 2022 *Late Late Show* appearance that became the formal launch of the Croagh Patrick campaign. He became the mascot of the campaign. I was sorry that I could not bring him up the Reek with us on 2 April, but the climb was hard enough without having to mind him, too.

I find it nearly impossible to put into words the comfort that he has given me during my many low days and nights. Each night my routine when I head to bed early is to ask Claire to bring Tiger up to me. The feeling of joy that I have when he jumps onto the bed and cuddles down beside me is indescribable. Often, too, when I wake up in the middle of the night fearing the worst, I reach my hand out to search for him. Even when he is fast asleep his very presence is hugely comforting for me.

Every schoolchild we met during our visits to Mayo and elsewhere took an instant shine to Tiger. He was the star of the show at every school and he was prominent in practically every drawing that the schoolchildren sent me after our visits. He became the centre of attention during our visits to Westport, even whenever we went into Matt Molloy's pub. Even pubs and coffee shops that normally refused to admit dogs made an exception to their rule when they saw Tiger with me and Claire.

Tiger had been a priceless comforter to Claire and to me during all the difficult days and nights of my deteriorating health. As someone who since childhood had never liked dogs and never wanted to be near one, I find myself getting very emotional and at a loss for the right words when talking or writing about Tiger and the role he has played during the most difficult times of my terminal illness.

* * *

Approaching my 73rd birthday in late summer 2022, I thought how crazy it was that I had contracted a terminal illness even though I had never spent a night in hospital in my life. I kept recalling how happy and healthy and carefree I had been when I celebrated my 70th birthday over a meal with my Kehoe's Gang friends and my former boss, Ed Mulhall, at an outdoor restaurant in Dublin.

On that sunny afternoon in September 2019, the day after I had completed the 'three score years and ten' that my father had often spoken about and that the Bible allots to all men, one of the books that one of my friends gave me as a birthday present was Derek Mahon's final collection of poems, *Against the Clock*.

I have found that the last nine lines of the collection's title poem have steeled me and guided me through the months since my diagnosis and especially in the writing of this book.

> *You're here for one purpose and one only,*
> *to give us of your best even if your best*
> *is rubbish and your personal testimony*
> *of little general interest.*
>
> *You thought you'd done, the uneven output*
> *finished at last, but that wasn't the end,*
> *Was it, since we're obliged to stick it out*
> *Until the pen falls from the trembling hand;*
> *So just get on with it.'*

I was preparing to die, but I was still getting on with living.

14. ARAN

Inis Oírr is baked into my heart.

I have been going there for so long, I'm not sure exactly when I went there for the first time. It was in the summer of 1968 or 1969. I had been camping with friends in Connemara while my eldest brother, Colin, who was an actor in the first RTÉ soap, *Tolka Row,* was on holiday on Inis Oírr, the smallest and most south-easterly of the three Aran Islands at the mouth of Galway Bay. I decided to go out there to visit him. My first image of the island is still etched on my mind more than fifty years later.

The night before I went out to Inis Oírr, I stayed in the Castle Hotel in Galway city. It was on Lower Abbeygate Street, which led down to the docks where the Aran fishing trawlers tie up. It was frequented by Aran islanders who stayed there, or in one of the other three-storey houses on that street, when they spent a night in Galway.

My friend from Inis Mór, Breandán Ó hEithir, who helped me to get my first media job in the *Irish Times* library, used to stay there. It was also the hotel in which he set part of his award-winning 1976 novel *Lig Sinn i gCathú*

(Lead us into Temptation), which chronicles a wild weekend in Galway just twenty years before my first overnight stay there.

The hotel was opposite Galway's Pro-Cathedral, which had recently been deconsecrated when Galway got its new Catholic cathedral, the last stone cathedral to be built in Europe, the locals said. The old Pro-Cathedral's new secular status may have given the hotel a renewed licence for late-night craic because the Castle was a magical place on my first night there. It was full of islanders speaking Irish and dressed in their traditional tweeds. Adding to the atmosphere might have been a few actors and regular patrons from the Irish language theatre An Taibhdhearc on nearby Middle Street.

Over the years I got to know many of the people who frequented the Castle Hotel. I still remember Bartley Beattie, who was the purser on the *Naomh Éanna*, the Córas Iompair Éireann-owner passenger and freight ship that plied between Galway and the Aran Islands two or three times a week. It was decommissioned in the late 1980s and can be seen rusting away in Dublin's Grand Canal Docks. Bartley was a great character, as were all of the ship's crew.

The *Naomh Éanna* usually sailed first to Inis Mór, docking at Cill Rónáin, before moving on towards Inis Meáin or Inis Oírr. The harbour on Inis Oírr was too small to accommodate any big ship, so in those days the *Naomh Éanna* used to drop anchor twice a week a couple of hundred yards offshore from the island's amazing, lovely white sandy beach, one of the most beautiful in the West of Ireland.

I'll never forget the sight of that beach on my first visit. It was crowded with islanders and *cuairteoirí* (visitors) watching the men launching the currachs that would ferry the passengers and cargo between the ship and the shore. As the currachs raced towards us, there was frantic hustle and bustle below deck while the crew prepared the cargo to be brought ashore, mainly barrels of porter and boxes containing food and newspapers.

I thought that I was taking my life into my hands when I was ushered below deck and told to jump into one of the currachs that was bobbing up and down in the swell. Nobody was wearing a lifejacket as the currachs rushed off towards the beach, where one or two of the oarsmen helped me onto the dry sand.

My first impression of the island was that it was like landing on a remote desert island. All of the islanders were speaking Irish and most of them were dressed in traditional garb. I think that it cost half-a-crown to be brought ashore, onto this magical wonderland.

When all the toing and froing was done, a few sudden blasts of sound came from the ship's funnel and the beach immediately emptied as everyone seemed to head for the island's two pubs, where the barrels of porter and other cargo were deposited.

I quickly learned that many islanders were known by a descriptive nickname because so many of them shared the same surname and first name. There seemed to be only five or six names that everyone shared. One of the first people I got to know was 'Paddy CIÉ', a really lovely character. He was known as 'Paddy CIÉ' to distinguish him from the other Paddys on the island. He was a CIÉ employee and his job was to oversee the safe transfer of people and goods and animals between the *Naomh Éanna* and the Inis Oírr shore.

As a raw twenty-year-old Dubliner who had never previously been west of the River Shannon, I was fascinated to be meeting and chatting to men who had lived and worked on this beautiful rugged rock 30 miles out onto the Atlantic Ocean. Their lives and their lifestyles enthralled me. I drank in their stories as thirstily as I swallowed the newly arrived Guinness.

I also got to know 'Thomás BA' and I would regularly have a few pints with him. He was known by that name because he was the only Thomas on the island who had graduated from university with a BA degree and the name stuck to him for the rest of his life. I also struck up a relationship over a few pints with Murrucha Posta, another man with a tell-tale nickname. The island's two pubs were known to all as Tomás an Siopa's and Seán an Siopa's.

My second trip to Inis Oírr was also unforgettable. I had noticed two very attractive young women on the *Naomh Éanna* as we sailed from Galway. I was very shy, but I was introduced to them in Seán an Siopa's pub that evening. They both worked in RTÉ in Dublin. One had distinctive long blonde hair. Her name was Áine O'Connor. I thought that she was very glamorous. I was smitten and we dated on the island and for about six months after we returned to Dublin. She was not the first girl I ever kissed, but I didn't have many girlfriends in my teenage years, partly because I was working regularly in The Goat bar and other places. I had been working since I was eight years old, having started with a daily newspaper delivery round for a shop near my home.

Áine and I remained friends and we bumped into each other from time to time, but we were not really close after our summer of 1969. She became a well-known presenter and later a ground-breaking producer at RTÉ. She was a presenter on programmes including *Tangents, P.M.* and *Last House*. In 1979 she broadcast Ireland's first interview with a gay couple, Arthur Leary and Laurie Steele from Cork. She married one of the researchers that I later worked with in my early RTÉ days, Larry Masterson, and she had a twelve-year relationship in Dublin and London with the actor Gabriel Byrne, whose early career she managed. She died tragically young in 1998 after being diagnosed with cancer. I met her on Grafton Street shortly before she became ill and we had a chat. Áine was my first real girl-friend, and it was on Inis Oírr that I met and courted her.

My best friends on the island were and still are Bríd and Peadar Póil. Peadar can trace his ancestors on the island back over 350 years. He and I became best pals and he used to come to Dublin to meet me before he got married. On one occasion he arrived outside my house in Goatstown after a night out in Dublin and threw stones at my bedroom window to waken me. I was glad that my mother was fast asleep in the next room while I sneaked him into the house and bunked him down in the spare room. Over the years I always tried to get him a ticket for the All-Ireland final in Croke Park when the Galway hurlers or footballers were playing there.

Some of Peadar's relations have long-established and strong commercial footholds in Galway city too, on the

Aran Islands enclave of Abbeygate Street. A first cousin of his father owned the Castle Hotel, where I stayed on the night before I first set foot on Inis Oírr. Another of his cousins owns the landmark Powells Four Corners music shop a few doors from where the Castle Hotel stood. Also known as Na Ceithre Coirnéil, this shop has been in business since 1908. It stands at the corner of Abbeygate Street and William Street. The building has some sixteenth-century features and it is named the Four Corners because it was the location of one of the first two crossroads in medieval Galway.

Peadar used to drive me to and from the two Inis Oírr pubs in what we used to call his 'Yellow Rolls Royce'. It was a battered old building-site dumper that he had bought in Oranmore and brought to the island on a small cargo ship. It was the only mechanically propelled vehicle on the island. It had no safety features and no road tax disc. The roads were primitive and the island is barely 3 sq. km in length and breadth. When he swapped the 'Yellow Rolls Royce' for a tractor, he continued to ferry me to and from the pubs. One night before either of us was married, we carried six young ladies back to their Bed & Breakfast abode in Castle Village in the tractor – eight young adults ensconced in the tractor cab with no tax disc and no health and safety warnings.

Bríd is from Feakle, across the bay in County Clare, between the Burren and the Slieve Aughty mountains. She and Peadar have been running a guesthouse on Inis Oírr for decades and it became my home-from-home there. The house is called Radharc an Chláir and it commands spectacular views across to the Cliffs of Moher at the edge of

Bríd's native county. Peadar has had his finger in many pies, but his main work has been building houses for his fellow islanders. He built all the houses, including his own, with walls 2 ft thick, from stones quarried on the island. In quieter times he set up a deer farm on the island and he also tried his hand at growing daffodils for the markets around the country. At another time, he and his friend Peadar Beag Seoighe used to go diving for sea urchins that they collected and exported to Japan.

Peadar was the first person to raise the alarm when the cargo ship M.V. *Plassy* ran aground on the island during a violent storm in March 1960. The ship was grounded on the Finnis Rock, off Trá Caorach. The crew had abandoned ship, but then clambered back on board from their lifeboat because the waves were so mountainous and violent. The storm also made it impossible to try to swim ashore or to get a lifeboat or currach close to the stricken vessel, which was being pushed further onto the rock by the pounding waves. All of the crew were rescued, miraculously, after daylight by the use of a breeches buoy, which two people in every village on the island had recently been trained to use.

The grounded and rusting hulk of the *Plassy* has become one of the island's tourist attractions over the past sixty years and it can be seen during the opening credits of the popular TV series *Father Ted*.

During my first visits to the island, I spent many great days and nights with a Danish man named Orla Knudson, or 'Orla the Dane' as he was fondly known by the islanders. When he first arrived on the island, after the Second World War, he used to sleep under a currach, but eventually the islanders took him in and he had a house down near the beautiful, white strand beach. He was a great weaver. His hand-woven ties and *croiseanna* were much sought after by visitors.

I think it was during my third visit to the island, in 1970, that Orla allowed me to put my blue tent up in his attic and to stay with him for a few weeks. This was just before Breandán Ó hEithir helped me get my real first job in the media as a library assistant for the *Irish Times*. Breandán was one of a group of journalists and friends who used to frequent The Goat bar and grill in Goatstown, where I worked as a lounge boy while attending Sandymount High School. I often ended the night in Breandán's house on Taney Road. At that time he was working for RTÉ and the *Irish Times*, whose News Editor, Donal Foley, was another member of The Goat gang. Prompted by Breandán, Donal invited me to work as a library assistant in the *Irish Times* after I lost my first job as a trainee journalist on a start-up newspaper in Carrick-on-Shannon.

The Goat bar, now owned by Charlie Chawke, was also where I first met the great showband singer and saxophonist Paddy Cole. Whenever we met over the years, we used to laugh about the night I tripped and spilled a tray of drinks over him and his wife in The Goat. He had very gallantly laughed about it when it happened too, and he even gave me a tip that night. I helped another regular customer from The Goat, Eoghan Harris, in the *Irish Times* library one day and he invited me to join RTÉ as a researcher on the current affairs programme *Seven Days*, another life-changing foot-in-the door for me.

It was in Orla's Knudson's house on Inis Oírr that I first met Peadar Póil. He used to go out in the currachs to the *Naomh Éanna* and try to sell some of Orla's *croiseanna* to passengers who were not disembarking. He told me that he thought I was a hippy when he first saw me, although I thought that my demeanour and my lifestyle were far from hippy-like.

Orla and I used often walk to the lighthouse at the back of the island, because the lighthouse-keepers were the only people on the island at the time to have a black-and-white TV. One of the lighthouse-keepers was from Goatstown. He used to allow me to climb to the top of the lighthouse and wind the machine that kept the big light turning around to warn seafarers of the danger out in the South Sound between the island and the Cliffs of Moher, where the M.V. *Plassy* had gone astray in poor visibility in the March 1960 storm.

Most evenings Orla and I would end up in Tomás an Siopa's for a Guinness or two. We always had mad fun there. If you needed to go to the toilet after a few pints, Tomás or one of the islanders would ask: '*An bhfuil an asal amuigh ór istigh?*' This was their way of asking if it was raining, so that you could be directed either to the small indoor toilet or to the uncovered outdoor latrine.

Tomás was a lovely man. He told me that he became a great friend of Brendan Behan and he used to allow him to run up a tab in his pub when Behan was living in a house near the pier for about six months while writing *Borstal Boy* and *The Quare Fellow* during the 1950s. He told me that Behan, a *fíor Gaeilgeóir*, always cleared his tab when he received a cheque for his newspaper articles.

Whenever there was a session during my nights in the pub, the islanders used to call on me to sing 'The Auld Triangle'. It was my perennial party-piece and it came, by coincidence, from Behan's play *The Quare Fellow*. My rendition always got a rousing reception. 'Jingle Jangle' was the name some of the islanders put on the song.

Tomás died only a couple of years ago at the ripe old age of nearly one hundred. A cousin of Peadar, named Paraic Ó Conghaile, now owns and runs the pub as Tig Ned. During the mid-1990s, two Gardaí disguised as backpackers raided a pub on the island. When the case came before the courts a defendant told the District Judge: 'Every Tom, Dick and Harry knows there is no Garda on the island and they [customers] just laugh when I try to get them out.'

I cannot deny that we had some late-night sessions in the 1970s, but my friend 'Orla the Dane' Knudson was very protective of the Islanders, especially when drink was being consumed. He told me about the time the well-known American magazine *National Geographic* did a major feature on the Aran Islands in the mid-1960s. When the reporter and her photographer arrived on Inis Oírr they went directly to the two pubs on the island and splashed out lots of money, buying the islanders drink. Orla was very upset at this because he knew that the islanders were always quite shy about talking to strangers and he felt they were pouring drink into the lads in the pub to make them talk.

The reporter and photographer called to Orla's house a few days later to see his weaving and because he was regarded as one of the colourful characters on the island. Shortly after they arrived at Orla's house and had taken pictures of him at his loom, the reporter asked if she could use his 'restroom'. Orla told me that he decided to vent his anger at her for buying the islanders drink to try and loosen their tongues. He went to the corner of the room and got a shovel and placed a toilet roll on top of it and told the reporter to go out into the sand outside his house and do her business there.

'Orla the Dane' died in December 1970. My first wife, Mary, and I named our first daughter Orla after him. I met Mary when I was working in the *Irish Times* library. She became my first 'steady' girlfriend. People used to get married at a young age in Ireland in the 1970s; I was 24 years old when I married Mary. We had a number of family holidays on Inis Oírr when Orla and her sister Neasa were young. Because I always left home before 7.00 a.m. each day and because I was sometimes working abroad for weeks on end, I tried to have quality time with my daughters on the island whenever we could as they got older. We used to fly from Carnmore Airport, outside Galway city, and stay with Peadar and Bríd in their guesthouse. We used to walk the length and breadth of the island or sunbathe and read our books near the lighthouse. Those times brought me closer to my daughters and to the island. Only foreign assignments or other work commitments have prevented me going to Inis Oírr nearly every summer since 1970.

It was Peadar Póil who first brought me to a remote place on the back of the island that became my favourite spot there. He told me a story of what had happened to him one morning when, as a young man, he used to go there to comb the foreshore, looking for driftwood or other flotsam from passing ships, a centuries-old island tradition.

He told me that one summer he was out at the back of the island between five and six o'clock in the morning when suddenly he saw in the far distance, out on the ocean beyond Inis Meáin, a strange vision of a city that came up out of the sea. He said he could see the city's streetlights and moving cars. I often joked with Peadar that he must have been on the beer the night before, but he told me that it was the truth and that he knew from stories that had been handed down that there was a mystical land known as Hy-Brasil (also known as Hy-Brazil), a phantom island said to lie in the Atlantic Ocean west of Ireland. He said that he had sat down and gazed at the scene for about fifteen minutes and to this day he believes that on that morning he saw Hy-Brasil.

Many other older islanders also believe that they have seen Hy-Brasil. Some believe it might be some kind of reflection coming up into the clouds from Newfoundland on the Atlantic seaboard of eastern Canada. Others think it's the lost island of Atlantis, or a kind of Tír na nÓg where islanders will go when they die.

I had a healthy mainlander's scepticism of the Hy-Brasil story, or myth, but I always used to look westward in the distance across the Atlantic when I visited Inis Oírr after Peadar's story had fascinated me. I'm still not convinced about it, even though I know that my own time in this world that I now inhabit is ebbing away. But I must have been thinking about Peadar and Hy-Brasil when, out of the blue in early 2020, during the first COVID-19 lock-down and a full year before I noticed the first symptoms of what became MND, I suddenly became fixated on the idea of leaving a small token on my favourite spot on Inis Oírr. This most westerly place on the island is called Béal an Chalaidh, the mouth of the harbour. Peadar told me that it's the safe harbour that islanders head towards if the weather turns bad when they are out fishing near the Cliffs of Moher or at the back of the island. I have always loved to linger there, especially when the sun is sinking below the western horizon.

I resolved to get a carved stone plaque attached to the island's limestone rocks and to dedicate it to my friendship of over half a century with Peadar. I wanted it placed where Peadar said he had seen Hy-Brasil all those years ago. I wanted to prompt others to see if they could glimpse the same vision from that spot.

I rang one of my Galway friends and told him that I was developing a mad notion. I didn't give him any details, but I swore him to secrecy before I asked him if he had ever heard of Hy-Brasil. He told me that in his youth, every Galway child was told all about Hy-Brasil by their parents or grandparents. He said that it was an island far out on the western horizon of the Atlantic Ocean that you could see sometimes from Inis Oírr at sunrise or sunset. It was a paradise, a mixture of Eden and Tír na nÓg, and it was where Aran islanders and some Galwegians went after they died. It appeared on some early sixteenth-century maps and it was the subject of a Jack B. Yeats oil painting in 1937.

'The Isle of the Blest far, far away' was how the Limerick-born writer and poet Gerald Griffin described Hy-Brasil in a poem he published in 1854. He wrote:

On the ocean that hollows the rocks where ye dwell,
A shadowy land has appeared, as they tell;
Men thought it a region of sunshine and rest,
And they called it O'Brazil, the Isle of the Blest.
From year unto year on the ocean's blue rim,
The beautiful spectre showed lovely and dim;
The golden clouds curtained the deep where it lay,
And it looked like an Eden, away, far away!

Oh, who at the proffer of safety would spurn
When all that he asks is the will to return;
To follow a phantom, from day unto day,
And die in the tempest, away, far away.

My friend told me that some Galway people say that it was the quest for the fabled land of Hy-Brasil that prompted the first European explorers to sail westward across the Atlantic on their voyages of discovery. Some Galwegians even claim that the biggest country in South America was named Brazil because the first crewman to sight landfall there on Pedro Álvares Cabral's voyage of discovery from Portugal in the year 1500 was a Galwayman and that, instead of shouting 'Terra', he had shouted 'Hy-Brasil'. There is no evidence for this theory, but that does not lessen its allure to Aran islanders and to Galway people, many of whom have named their homes Hy-Brasil.

The person I got to make the plaque for the chair is my friend and neighbour in Wicklow, the stonemason Séighean Ó Draoi, a cousin of the late Ronnie Drew of The Dubliners folk group. He told me that his inscription of the words chosen by me will last between four hundred and five hundred years.

The ongoing restrictions caused by COVID-19, including a ban on inter-county travel, prevented me from moving my stone from Wicklow to Inis Oírr throughout 2020. But the very brief lifting of the ban on inter-county travel in the week before Christmas 2020 allowed me to transport the stone as far as Galway city. I was going to delay my journey until after Christmas, but on Friday, 19 December I was awake early, as usual, and I set off from Wicklow for the Galway docks at 5.00 a.m. with the stone plaque in my car. It was a strange journey because I had not been outside the county of Wicklow since the big lockdown began in the middle of March. I was like a six-year-old, full of excitement at being allowed to travel down the country heading west.

It was a mad drive, but I found the warehouse at Galway docks where goods bound for the Aran Islands are stored. The gods had been smiling down on me when I made that early-morning dash across the country, because all inter-county travel was banned again two or three days later. There must have been some spirit on my shoulder urging me to undertake that drive on that morning, because if I had waited until after Christmas, as I had originally planned, the plaque would not have arrived for another six or nine months because of the renewed ban on inter-county travel. Instead, I was delighted to be able to tell my friends that 'the eagle' had made the first part of the journey.

By a remarkable coincidence, while I was packing the stone for the journey west, which was some three months before I first noticed any ominous symptoms and a full ten months before my diagnosis, my Galway friend sent me a strange photograph of another stone that somebody else had erected in Galway nearly 240 years earlier.

His photograph amused me more than it shocked me, but in retrospect it was undoubtedly uncanny. In an old history book that he was reading on that very morning, my friend had found the wording of an inscription on an eighteenth-century gravestone in the cemetery of the Franciscan friary that had been established in Galway in the year 1296 and that contained, in the words of the historian, 'the burial places of some of the most considerable families in the province'. Under a carved cross the inscription said:

> As I was once like thee
> So thou shalt surely be
> A skel'ton like me;
> Then haste and snatch the present hour,
> Implore the mercy seat,
> Lest death should rob thee of thy power,
> And doom thy eternal fate.
>
> God be merciful to the Soul of Charles Bird,
> who died ye 18th Feb.1781.

I'll never know what mysterious forces made my Galway friend stumble upon the amazing wording of this particular gravestone on that particular day, or what motivated him to send it to me as soon as he saw it, but it now seems eerie, if not supernatural, that it should arrive into my smartphone when the as-yet-undetected markers of MND were awakening in my body and when I was preparing to transport my own stone plaque to Inis Oírr.

My stone lay in a storehouse at Galway docks until the following Monday, when it was shipped to Inis Oírr. By the middle of May, Peadar, *mo chara*, and his cousin Paraic Ó Conghaile, better known as Ned, had found a large limestone boulder and expertly cemented my plaque onto it at my chosen spot. It took them a few days to make a road to move the rock to a place where the sea would not wash it away in even the stormiest weather. They also fashioned a stone chair in front of the rock for people to sit on. Peadar sent me a photo of himself putting the finishing touches to the installation. I sent the photograph to close friends to get their opinions, but I asked them to keep the news of the stone under their hats for the moment.

'Charlie, it's magnificent. People will be looking at that when you are long planted,' Joe O'Brien said. I told him that the chair would last hundreds of years. I said that I particularly loved the link to Hy-Brasil, the mystical country so many of the islanders believe they have seen. I said that we may all be going there eventually.

My diagnosis was still nearly four months away at this point, but I was desperately worried about my worsening symptoms. I was in turmoil. On impulse, I drove to Doolin on my own and sailed to Inis Oírr on Bill O'Brien's tourist ferry. I had never previously felt so strange and bothered arriving on the island. I went for a swim on the beach before going up to Peadar and Bríd's house. Chatting over tea and a scone, I could see that they had noticed a change in my voice. I told Bríd about the twitching in my arms and legs and I said that Google kept linking those symptoms to Parkinson's disease or motor neuron disease. She told me that her mother and died from MND, but she did not think that I had it.

After our tea and scone, Peadar and I set off for the back of the island. I could not believe my eyes when I saw the massive limestone rock with my inlaid plaque and the stone seat. I got very emotional. I broke down and hugged Peadar. I was blown away by the sight of the stone, overlooking the Atlantic Ocean, with the Cliffs of Moher to the left and the island lighthouse nearby. I could not have been happier that my mad idea of a year earlier was now a reality. I read the bilingual inscription that I had toiled to compose over twelve months previously:

> *Suigh síos agus lig do scíth*
> *and behold the beauty of Inis Oírr*
> *perhaps see Hy-Brazil.*
> *Buíochas le Peadar Póil*
> *as a chairdeas le 50 blian.*
> *Charlie Bird, Iriseoir 2021.*

A little later I walked around the island and I had a couple of celebratory pints in Tigh Ned's, but I was very troubled by my worsening voice and my twitching limbs. I had arranged to stay with Peadar and Bríd that night before catching the ferry back to Doolin in the morning. After dinner I went on my own again to the back of the island, to sit on the stone chair and watch the setting sun.

I sat on the chair for about half an hour, but I could not stop thinking about what was happening to my body.

I took dozens of photographs. Then I walked back to Bríd and Peadar's house on the Doolin side of the island, passing the 150-year-old lighthouse where I spent so many happy evenings during my early visits. I kept telling myself that I had accomplished something, but I knew in my heart and soul that something weird was happening to me. I had brought two bottles of champagne with me, but we decided to leave them with Bríd for the official unveiling, which we planned for the middle of August.

Frequent medical appointments and gruelling tests in June and July meant that Claire and I didn't travel to Inis Oírr to see the stone until late August. In the meantime, my health continued to deteriorate. I kept telling Claire and my family that I believed I was dying. I had begun to use that word. They all told me that I was not dying, but I was increasingly convinced that I had motor neurone disease.

Claire and Tiger and I took Bill O'Brien's ferry from Doolin to Inis Oírr on a lovely August Sunday morning. The three of us went for a walk along the beautiful horseshoe-shaped beach when we disembarked. Before heading up to Peadar and Bríd's house, I went for a swim, just as I had done on my previous, panicky solo visit.

After the usual tea and scones with Bríd and Peadar, we headed to the back of the island where the chair and plaque are located. Some islanders were already there, including Peadar and Brid's son Eoghan with his wife Caroline and their three children, Keely, Niamh and Luke. Paddy Crowe, who was married to an islander and who was the manager of the island Co-op for many years, brought his camera to record the unveiling.

The unveiling was a quiet, private affair. It was a subdued occasion because I could not stop thinking that I was struggling badly with my health. There was no ceremony, but we opened the two bottles of champagne and a few people raised a glass. Peadar and I sat on the chair and had our photo taken. Tiger joined in the celebration as well. Bríd's three grandchildren loved Tiger and they jumped at Claire's suggestion that they should get a dog of their own. It was just a lovely moment – a group of people at the back of this beautiful island marking a very simple occasion.

Even on this beautiful day that I had been looking forward to for over a year, my sickness was not far from my thoughts and at one point I asked Bríd to walk a short distance away with me. I told her that I was secretly putting my affairs in order and that I regarded Inis Oírr as my real home. I knew that I wanted it to be my final resting place. I said that if I ended up dying with MND, I wanted my ashes to be scattered on the island. Bríd looked at me with a tear in her eye and she said: 'Are you sure, Charlie? Maybe you don't have it.' But my inner soul told me that she was wrong.

Paddy Crowe and I took lots of photographs of the chair and the plaque. My mad idea was a beautiful reality at last. Afterwards, Claire and Tiger and I walked around the rest of the island and we ended up back in Tig Ned's with Peadar and his cousin, Paraic, who had helped build the chair. We had a few celebratory pints before catching the ferry back to Doolin.

I kept in regular touch with Bríd and Peadar and my next visit to them was for a new purpose. My connection with Inis Oírr is so unbroken and so enduring that when I got my dreadful diagnosis in late October 2021, I was fully resolved that my remains would rest in the island's beautiful cemetery, the graveyard that dominates the skyline when you arrive by sea or by air.

I said nothing to Claire or to my daughters, Orla and Neasa, about my decision, but I secretly started to plan my funeral and I asked Peadar and Bríd to make enquiries about a final resting place. Claire and I do not keep secrets from one another, but I kept putting off telling her my plan through fear of upsetting her. I asked my pal Séighean Ó Draoi to get a new stone and I asked Bríd if my ashes could be laid to rest in the beautiful island graveyard. After consulting the priest and the Co-op manager, she told me that there would be no issue, and that Peadar would find a spot for me. Séighan and Peadar and Bríd now knew of my furtive planning, even before Claire or my daughters did.

Peadar, *mo chara*, is over eighty years of age now. All his ancestors are buried in the Inis Oírr cemetery, beside Teampall Chaomháin, the church named after the island's patron saint, who is said to be buried there. The ruins of the old church in the graveyard go back to the tenth century and are connected to St Kevin's Church in Glendalough, a 15-minute drive from my home in Ashford, County Wicklow. Naomh Chaomháin of Inis Oírr was said to have been a brother of St Kevin of Glendalough. Peadar had picked a spot for my ashes near Leaba Chaomháin, which lay close to his own family plot.

In a strange way, it has been a comforting decision for me. I had devoted one of the *A Living Word* broadcasts that I did on RTÉ radio in the late 1990s to Inis Oírr. I had said in that short broadcast that I had never met anyone who had not come away from the island filled with a sense of spirituality. I had now made the arrangements for my epitaph. Peadar and his cousin Paraic found a lovely stone from the *oileán* to be used as a headstone, and Séighean Ó Draoi, who had become a pal of mine, made a new engraved plaque that will be inserted onto it. On it is written: *The Ashes of Charlie Bird are laid in this beautiful spot. 1949 to 202X.* Below the dates of my lifetime the inscription has the words I remember my father saying so often: *Time and Tide wait for no man.*

The shock and upset of my MND confirmation convinced me that my life would be over within a few months. My daughters did not even know about my secret planning for my funeral until they read about it in the *Irish Times* on the weekend after I went public about my diagnosis. I had been planning my funeral in secret from August to the end of October. I could not wait to see the spot that Peadar had chosen for my ashes.

Claire and Tiger and I went back to Inis Oírr in late November 2021. We stayed overnight in Galway, where I met one of my WestAwake pals, Michael Lally, who was in his own wars, battling cancer in his neck. Just days earlier he had got the dreadful news that his cancer had returned. We talked as we walked along the Prom together, both of us carrying our own crosses. It was the same walk that we had done with our other WestAwake pals in June, before either of us had been given the worst possible news.

Next morning, Claire and I flew to Inis Oírr with Aer Arann. It was Tiger's first time on an aeroplane, but we all landed safely shortly after 10.00 a.m. It was a beautiful, clear and sunny November morning. Over tea and scones Bríd was comforting and consoling, saying that someone was looking out for us to give us such a beautiful morning.

Peadar and I went down to the graveyard in his tractor, with Claire and Tiger following behind. Claire started to film us on my mobile phone. We walked into the graveyard and went first to where my old pal 'Orla the Dane' was buried. Then Peadar showed me where his parents were buried. Then he pointed to the spot that he had picked out for me. We both had tears in our eyes.

There was one light moment when Peadar said that he was going to be buried just a stone's throw from me. He joked that he hoped we wouldn't have a row or kick one another by mistake when we are reunited underground, like the buried characters in *Cré na Cille*, a novel by Brendan Behan's friend Máirtín Ó Cadhain, which is set across the bay in a Connemara graveyard. We looked across to Connemara in one direction and to the Burren, Doolin and Black Head in the other from our lovely spot in the graveyard. It is a magical location.

I felt so happy that I was going to be laid to rest in this most beautiful and wonderful place, a graveyard that has a history of over one thousand years. Peadar and I hugged again before I set off with Claire and Tiger to our chair at the back of the island.

Claire and I sat on our chair for nearly two hours and, yes, on that beautiful, sunny November morning we both imagined that we saw a glimpse of Hy-Brasil. We walked the rest of the island and we stopped in Tigh Ned's where we were joined by Peadar and his cousin, Paraic. With everything arranged, Peadar started to drive us back to his house to say goodbye to Bríd, but out of the blue he suggested we should pop in on the owner of the other pub on the island, Seán an Siopa's.

I have known Seán too for almost fifty years. He's now in his eighties and he has retired from running the business. He lives in a cottage at the back of the pub. Seán and his wife were at home and they were delighted to see me, but all the conversation was about my illness and how sorry they were for me. Seán tried to press a hot brandy into my hand and another one into Peadar's, but I told him that I could no longer drink spirits because of my illness and also that I would be driving when I got back to the mainland.

After about half an hour chatting, Peadar drove us home to his house. The 'Yellow Rolls Royce' and tractor were long gone, and his latest banger now had valid road tax. It was a memorable journey at the end of a memorable day – the day that my pal for more than fifty years had shown me my final resting spot on the *oileán*. A short time later we all hugged and cried with Bríd and Peadar as Claire and Tiger and I left for home. Claire told me that she had been upset when she thought that my ashes would rest on their own in the island cemetery, but she was happier when Peadar and Bríd had assured her that her own ashes, in time, could lie beside mine.

The last joke on that day was about Tiger. Peadar had never allowed anyone with a dog into the guesthouse, never mind allowing a dog to stay overnight there, but he made an exception for Tiger. Claire reminded Peadar that the first time we brought Tiger, he had called him 'that bastard of a dog', but now, given all that had happened to me, Peadar said that we could come again as often as we wanted and 'you can . . . bring that bastard of a dog Tiger with you'.

A couple of weeks later we were back on Inis Oírr again, this time with a TV documentary team who wanted to film me with my friends on the island that I love and at the place where I will finally be laid to rest. Peadar smiled again and said that of course Tiger was always welcome here. As we were getting on the plane with Tiger, someone who had once worked with Bríd and Peadar in the guest-house remarked: 'I can't believe that Peadar has allowed Tiger to stay over.' I jokingly replied that I had paid a high price for the concession. With true friendship, anything is possible.

The documentary on my life and times had been commissioned by RTÉ after my diagnosis. The producer, John Kelleher, director Colm Quinn and cameraman Kevin Minogue flew from Inverin to the island with Claire and me and Tiger. It was the Saturday before Christmas 2021 and it was meant to be a flying visit to see Peadar and Bríd and to do some filming in the cemetery and at the chair I have dedicated to Peadar.

We went to the cemetery after our usual tea and scones. Peadar and I shed more tears at the spot where my ashes will lie. Séighean had refused to accept any payment for his work on my epitaph. He said it was a Christmas present and that he hoped that I would see many more Christmasses. When I was being interviewed in the cemetery for the documentary, I said that I was not certain that I would be alive to see another Christmas. Claire, holding Tiger, said: 'Bird, don't keep saying that.'

We spent more than an hour in the cemetery and then we went to the back of the island to film Peadar and me at the chair. Even though it was late December, the weather was fine. Peadar and I sat on the chair and Peadar talked about the time he had seen Hy-Brasil from that spot when he was a young man.

Over soup and sandwiches in Bríd and Peadar's house a little later, I had a dreadful coughing fit, one of my regular reminders of my disease. It silenced everyone at the table and it showed what I now faced every time I sat down for a meal. Bríd broke the silence by telling us that her nine-year-old granddaughter Keely had, on her own initiative, asked for my home address in Wicklow and had sent me a Christmas card because she had heard of my illness and because she loved Tiger. I found Keely's card when I got home and it made me cry – a lovely card with a beautiful message handwritten off her own bat by the nine-year-old grandchild of two of my oldest friends.

Inis Oírr is my home-from-home, and now it always will be. I cherish the memories of every day and every night I have spent on the island. I recall the awe and wonder I felt on my first arrival. I ask myself if I will be able to set foot again on its beautiful beaches and roads.

It may be an odd and even a strange thing to say, but I have drawn great comfort from knowing that if it's my fate never to set foot on Inis Oírr again, then the beautiful cemetery beside Teampall Chaomháin will be my final resting place when I pass away. My final journey will be when the ashes that are my last mortal remains are carried to the cemetery by my family and my loved ones.

The stones of Aran have stood on the three islands for several millennia. I hope that my headstone and my chair and plaque will survive on Inis Oírr for a fraction of that time after I have vanished from this Earth. I hope to stand at my stone one more time before I make my eventual journey westward to Hy-Brasil.

In the meantime, I think every day of the final words of John Millington Synge's classic Aran Islands play, *Riders to the Sea*: 'No man at all can be living for ever, and we must be satisfied.'

I think too of my father's words, engraved on the headstone that will stand over my ashes on Inis Oírr, my heavenly haven for more than two-thirds of my lifetime: Time and Tide wait for no man.

ACKNOWLEDGEMENTS

I want to thank my beautiful wife, Claire, for her constant love, care and support; my two lovely daughters, Orla and Neasa; my five grandchildren, Charlie Jnr, Hugo, Harriet, Abigail, and Edward; as well as my sons-in-law, Rob and Aidan.

I also want to thank my former RTÉ colleagues, who gave me such amazing support, especially Ryan Tubridy, Joe Duffy, and the entire Late Late Show team.

A special word of thanks should also go to my great colleagues in the Kehoes Gang, Dympna Moroney, Joe O'Brien and Ray Burke. Thanks also to my pals in the West Awake group, Tommie Gorman, Michael Lally and Sean O'Rourke, as well as my great former colleague the late Jim Fahy.

My thanks are due to the great team who worked with Climb With Charlie: Paul Allen and Rory Sweeney, Lillian McGovern, from the Irish Motor Neurone Disease Association, and Denise Cronin from Pieta. Also: Claire Corbett, Kerry Fitzgerald, Sarah Joyce and Gemma Watts.

Special thanks are also due to Fr. Charlie McDonnell and Garda Inspector Denis Harrington for all their work and support, and to Harry Hughes of Westport House and Portwest for his help and advice.

I owe undying gratitude to Peadar and Bríd Póil on Inis Oírr for hospitality and friendship and to John Fitzpatrick for his kindness and support in New York and Wicklow.

Mayor James Byrne welcomed me to Drogheda on Tuesday 15 February 2022. I was delighted to collect two cheques totalling €2,500 from St Nicholas Gaelic Football Club and Drogheda Dolls.

Claire and I went back to Westport, where I joined the Scoil Phádraig children for another lively rendition of Ar Aghaid Le Chéile. On Saturday, 5 March 2022, exactly four weeks before the climb, Claire and I trekked half-way up Croagh Patrick. It was a beautiful, clear, if cold, early-spring day and the sight of Clew Bay as we descended was magical. At the base of the Reek shopowner Damien Gibbons pledged to give half of his takings on 2 April 2022 to the two charities. And the pupils of Murrisk National School raised €700 in a cake sale. The pupils of St Finian's National School in Waterville also sent me a lovely bundle of letters and cards to support me.

The hairdressing chain Grafton Barbers very generously pledged that all of the takings in their 51 salons in 11 counties on Sunday 3 April 2022 would go to Climb With Charlie. 'Cuts for Charlie' was how they advertised their fundraising.

The singers of Westlife in early March collectively urged people to join the climb. Then an amazing song, Shine A Light, was written.

A beautiful poster was created by the people who attend Henley House in Ballinlough, Co. Roscommon.

Two students from St Colman's Community School in Midleton, Co. Cork, sent me a video they made demonstrating the importance of reaching out the hand of friendship. Students in Ratoath College in Co. Meath organised fundraising in their area.

Adrian McGing of the Westport-based McGing Taxi & Minibus company offered to carry any of my family and friends who needed a lift from Westport to the Reek.

My friend Tim Goulding, the artist and Aosdána member, who is based near Allihies on the Beara Peninsula in West Cork, created two beautiful drawings featuring Croagh Patrick and my face. I'm donating them to the people of Westport and the people of Murrisk.

I want to thank all my colleagues in RTÉ who I worked with down through the years, especially John Kelleher and two great Newsroom bosses, Ed Mulhall and Joe Mulholland.

I also want to thank Ian, David and Richie in Kehoe's Bar on South Anne Street, Dublin, for their hospitality and for always reserving their Select Snug for Claire, me and the Kehoe's Gang.

Special thanks are due to Ray Burke, who took on the task of writing this book for me, and to his wife, Marian.

Finally, I want to thank HarperCollins Ireland for taking on this project and especially Publisher Conor Nagle, Commissioning Editor Catherine Gough, Assistant Editors Stephen Reid and Kerri Ward.